DEATH
AND THE FAMILY

About the Author

Lily Pincus is a social worker who lives and practices in England. She is a founder of The Institute for Marital Studies at the Tavistock Institute for Human Relations in London. Among the books she has coauthored are *Marriage: Studies in Emotional Conflict and Growth, Social Casework in Marital Problems,* and *Shared Phantasy in Marital Problems.*

DEATH
AND THE FAMILY

The Importance of Mourning

by LILY PINCUS

FABER & FABER
3 QUEEN SQUARE
LONDON

First published in England 1976
by Faber and Faber Limited
3 Queen Square London WC1
Printed in Great Britain by
Whitstable Litho Limited Whitstable

ISBN 0 571 10875 X

Grateful acknowledgment is made to the following for permission to reprint previously published material:

Harcourt Brace Jovanovich, Inc., and Faber & Faber Ltd: For three lines from "Sweeney Agonistes" from *Collected Poems 1909–1962* by T.S. Eliot, copyright 1936, by Harcourt Brace Jovanovich, Inc.; copyright © 1963, 1964 by T.S. Eliot.

Insel Verlag: For three lines from *"Stundenbuch"* by Rainer Rilke.

The Viking Press, Inc., and The Society of Authors as the literary representative for the Estate of James Joyce: For "Ecce Puer" from *Collected Poems* by James Joyce. Copyright 1927 by James Joyce.

CONTENTS

Preface

When I started to write this book I was seventy-five years old, had been widowed for ten years, been at the deathbed of many friends, and had shared the pain of bereavement with their families. I was also on the point of retiring from long years of work with marriage and family problems, leaving a close-knit group of colleagues, which in itself constituted a loss.

While the wish to write this book stemmed from my personal and professional experiences, it also seemed to me that there was an urgent need to participate in the recent attempts to lift the taboo from death, dying, and bereavement by promoting discussion of these fundamental themes.

Death and the Family, which contains many personal memories and some theory, is about people whom I have come to know in the course of my work as a social worker, psychotherapist, and teacher. In dealing with marital and family problems it has been of fundamental importance to develop skills based not only on understanding the individual, but beyond this on understanding the relationships and interactions within the family.

In my accounts of these people I explore whether their various responses to bereavement might best be understood or even predicted by focusing on the particular relationships which made for unique family patterns. The different ways in which I describe these families will indicate the conditions of our encounter, and I hope will also convey something of the many different ways in which people react to bereavement.

Interwoven with these stories are accounts of my personal bereavements, which will inevitably be colored by my emotional involvement, most especially the account of my husband's death. In this personal situation, in contrast to the accounts arising from my work, I am not concerned with analyzing the link between responses to bereavement and the preceding marriage relationship, which, like everybody else's, had its conflicts and problems. My own response to the loss of my husband was confused and uncertain; as the reader will see later, I had to fracture my foot before I could allow myself to feel the depression which is an inevitable part of the mourning process. But what was of immeasurable importance about this experience was my sharing with my husband the full knowledge of his long fatal illness, and my being with him in his death.

I have continued to live with my own experiences and am aware of my changing responses to them as time goes on. On the other hand, I entered into the lives of most of the people I am describing in a situation of crisis, and only know of their reactions to their bereavement at that point. This is one reason why many of my stories are open-ended.

Although this book is not based on systematic research and makes no claim to be representative of patterns of grief and mourning, I try to focus on some of the elements of bereavement which have been identified in other studies, and which will be useful for the bereaved and those who care for them to understand.

I am deeply grateful to all those who have given me permission to retell their stories, and in the process of doing so have relived them with much pain. I like to think that they share my hope that their experiences will help others who are bereaved, and help us all to approach grief and mourning in a way which gives support and encouragement when death and bereavement have to be faced. Beyond this there is the hope that our society may relearn that death is an essential part of life, and that free discussion of the processes of grief, mourning, and bereavement may contribute to a changed, more accepting attitude in the community.

Acknowledgments

The foundations for this book were laid in my work at the Institute for Marital Studies (Tavistock Institute of Human Relations) in London. I can never repay my debt to past and present colleagues for the interest and stimulation throughout the time I was writing and for their generous approval of my use of concepts and formulations which we have shared in our work.

I would like to thank individually Dr. Geoffrey Thompson, Mr. Herbert Philipson, Mrs. Elspeth Morley, and Mrs. Kathleen Bannister for many helpful criticisms and suggestions, and my friend Miss Brenda Snook for her unfailing support and her patient battles with my poor grammar.

My special gratitude must go to Juliet Mitchell, whose editorial expertise was of immeasurable help to me, and who, in addition, shared with me the pains which the theme of the book involved and the emotional pressure to get it written.

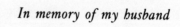

In memory of my husband

I.

Personal Memories

My husband Fritz died in May 1963 after eleven years of suffering and several operations for cancer. We both knew the diagnosis from the moment it was made, and while Fritz was a very good patient, cooperating fully in all that was medically required, he and I never forgot that his illness was not curable and would lead to his death. Yet except for periods immediately after major operations when he was desperately ill, the long years of shared knowledge of impending death were rich and happy ones, especially the last eighteen months when Fritz was suffering from cancer of the lungs. He had been bothered for some time by a persistent cough and consulted a specialist who made light of it, until he returned from the darkroom with the X-ray. Immediately noticing his changed expression, Fritz walked toward him and said, "I am so sorry, Doctor, this is very difficult for you!"

Because the doctors accepted and respected Fritz's wish to have no further surgical intervention or drastic treatment, he was able to stay at home. In spite of inevitable moments of anxiety and strain, most of the time he

was relaxed and happy. He knew that he had no more
fighting to do. One of his favorite sayings during that
time was: "There is no arguing with life, there is only
acceptance." This felt right at the time, and only later
did I begin to wonder what it meant, coming from a man
who had always actively argued with life in the hope of
bringing about social change. Did it express a reversed
development from that of the Buddha, for whom enlight-
enment had meant the end of striving, but whose last
words to his disciples were: "Work out your salvation
through diligence"?

Only much later, through Teilhard de Chardin, did I
understand better what Fritz might have meant:

> There is a time of growth, and a time for diminish-
> ment in the lives of each one of us. At one moment the
> dominant note is one of constructive human effort,
> and at another mystical annihilation. . . . I can only
> unite myself to the will of God (as endured passively)
> when all my strength is spent, at the point where my
> activity toward betterment (understood in ordinary
> human terms) finds itself continually counter-
> weighted by forces, tending to halt me or overwhelm
> me. Unless I do everything I can to advance or resist,
> I shall not find myself at the required point.[1]

Whatever it was that Fritz wanted to express, he felt
that during these last months of his life, he had acquired
a new intensity of perception, of enjoyment, of being in
touch with what was beautiful, and I could share, on our
gentle walks, his sheer delight in small children, birds,
flowers, trees, clouds. We were probably closer during
that time, more united in mutual trust, than at any other
time in our long marriage. Friends, attracted by the spe-

1. *Le Milieu Divin* (London: William Collins Sons & Co., 1960), pp. 73–74.

cial quality of relaxed acceptance in our home, loved to come by. They enjoyed Fritz's affectionate concern and asked for his advice, literally to his last day. His sense of humor and fun, the smile, the twinkle in his eyes, hardly ever left him, and he never lost his keen interest in what was going on in the world, or in my work, to which he gave much thought and support. I had the overwhelming experience of life being enhanced by the acceptance of death.

When Fritz's last night came, he made sure that I shared with him the full awareness of it, and when I could give him this assurance, he said with a smile, "Then all is well." He died a few hours later in complete peace. The night nurse, who had kept watch with me, had mercifully left the room to make her breakfast, so that I was alone with Fritz in his last, peaceful hour, for which I shall be eternally grateful.

This "perfect death" was the culmination of a life striving for perfection—not so much in terms of achievement, to which Fritz never seemed to attach very much importance, but perfection of himself in human terms. This is borne out by the following passage from *Midrash*[2] which he wrote out for use at his funeral service.

And Isaac asked the Eternal . . . "King of the World, when Thou didst make the light, Thou didst say in Thy Torah that the light was good; when Thou didst make the extent of the firmament and the extent of the earth, Thou didst say in Thy Torah that they were good; and every herb Thou hast made, and every beast, Thou hast said that they were good; but when Thou hadst made man in Thine image, Thou didst not say

2. *Midrash* is the interpretation of some of the Hebrew Scriptures in which allegory and legendary illustrations are freely used, which was compiled by Jewish rabbis from about A.D. 200.

in Thy Torah that man was good. Wherefore, Lord?"
And God answered him: "Because man I have not
perfected, and because through the Torah man is to
perfect himself, and to perfect the World."

Fritz's attitudes toward life and death were in complete harmony, as I had always believed they must be.
Yet his mother also had died a perfect death—and her life
had been full of fears and anxieties. She was the type of
Victorian lady that hardly exists any more: polite, kind,
charming, without malice, a faithful friend, but completely divorced from the realities of life. All practical
things were mysteries to her. For everything, even boiling water, she was dependent on others, and therefore
life was full of hazards and dangers. Bodies, physical
processes, did not seem to exist for her. I always wondered how she had managed to conceive and produce her
three children. She was frightened of everything, fell
sick before each social engagement, even before dress
fittings. Her family had always kept "unpleasantnesses"
away from her. They were scared of how she would take
them, and she certainly did her utmost to avoid knowing
anything that might be distasteful or troublesome.

The last three years of her life, when both her daughters were abroad, she lived in the house Fritz and I
shared with some friends. In spite of her utterly different
outlook on life, which in theory we despised, we all loved
her. She in turn, in a puzzled way, admired our mode of
living and tried to fit in as best she could. For the last two
years she suffered from cancer of the esophagus, and had
a complete loss of sphincter control. But even in the most
undignified situations she remained "the perfect lady,"
and I often had the impression that she refused to notice
what was going on. When it became clear that she was
dying, Fritz got ill with terror about how his mother,
who had never been able to face any difficulty in life,

would face death. On the day before her seventieth birthday she had a stroke and was unconscious for a few
hours. When she awoke, she asked to be sat up in bed,
and then with the most lovely smile and shining eyes
demanded to see all the different people in the house. She
said good-bye to each individually as if she were going
on a long journey, with thank-you messages for friends
and relatives and all who had cared for her. She remembered especially all the children who had given her pleasure. When after nearly an hour of this "reception" her
strength left her, Fritz and I stayed on with her alone
until she bade us farewell most lovingly and said, "Now
let me sleep."

Half an hour later her doctor stopped by, and inquired
how she was. When I replied, "She is dying," he became
beside himself with fury, accused me of defeatism,
threatened to remove her to the hospital, and immediately prepared an injection to resuscitate her. I tried
desperately to stop him, pleading that he respect her
wish to be allowed to sleep now that she had said her
final good-byes. Angrily he shook me and my argument
off, and with the injection needle in his hand bent search-
ingly over his patient. She had apparently been unconscious, but at this moment she opened her eyes and with
the same brilliant smile with which she had said good-
bye to us, put her thin arms around his neck and whispered, "Thank you, Professor." Tears sprang to the doctor's eyes, and there was no further mention of an
injection. He left us as a friend and ally, and his patient
continued the peaceful sleep from which she did not
awake.

The experience of this death raises many questions
about dying which this book, specifically about bereavement and the problems of the bereaved, cannot explore
but which will always be in our minds. What hidden
strengths in this delicate, frightened woman, who

throughout her life had avoided facing anything difficult and who had never been able to make a decision, had enabled her not only to die in this way, but to ensure that her final sleep remained undisturbed? What had happened to her during the hours of unconsciousness to so transform her? It was as if this had been a preparation for her physical death and a final break with her past life. Can we hope ever to understand how a person who was never in control of anything could be so strikingly in control of her dying? How can we learn what an apparently unconscious person is taking in? What in the treatment of terminal illness, in the atmosphere around a dying person, in the attitude of those close to the patient, can support the sort of internal work which may be a feature of approaching death and may help toward a good and dignified end?

Recently I had the opportunity to discuss some of these questions with a young Roman Catholic priest who works with dying patients and the staff in the terminal ward of a teaching hospital. He has frequently experienced inexplicable changes in dying patients who regain temporary consciousness, changes which made him feel that they have come back from another world with new and enriching experiences and have learned something about themselves they never knew or were able to express before. "I cannot understand why and how this happens," he said, "and frankly I am reluctant to look for explanations. All I know is that this phenomenon places a great responsibility on the people around the dying patient, not to interfere through drugs, thoughtlessness, or impatience with what may well be his most important experience, and may give meaning to his dying."

Later, the young priest talked about bereavement and mourning: "In my concern for the dying, I have so far paid too little attention to the bereaved. Yet the two should not be looked at separately. For a relative to witness the almost miraculous changes which may occur in the dying patient not only must be of tremendous importance to the outcome of the mourning process, but may well change the attitude of the bereaved toward his own death. We, the hospital staff, must make sure not to deprive the relatives of this experience."

Certainly for all of us who were privileged to witness it, the death of Fritz's mother was an unforgettable experience. How closely was the life and death of Fritz, this woman's son, linked with that experience? Did it help him to face his own death in the way he did? He too showed an almost miraculous mixture of acceptance and control up to his last breath, and beyond, by keeping us all so closely in touch with him through the choice of the *Midrash* passage for his cremation service. There may never be an answer to these questions, never perhaps any theories to lead to a better understanding.

There is and always will be much that we do not know, or that we cannot allow ourselves to know. We all have the absolutely certain knowledge that we must die, but how many of us can enable ourselves to "know" it, as Fritz did, so that we can build it as an accepted fact into our lives? If we could, we might then be able to live more fully, less burdened by fears and anxieties, and thus improve the quality of our lives and of our deaths. Mysterious transformations such as that of Fritz's mother are exceptional—conscious acceptance of death should be an essential part of life, for "death belongs to life as birth does, the walk is in the raising of the foot and in the laying it down."[3]

When our doctor, who had been of the greatest support to Fritz and me throughout the long years of illness,

3. Rabindranath Tagore, *Stray Birds* (Mystic, Conn.: Lawrence Verry, 1971), CCLXVII.

came to sign the death certificate, all he could say to me was: "And now you have to be very busy." I recently reminded him of this, and he was silent for a while before he said, "Yes, that was before I had my coronary." He seems now to have come to feel that only by facing our anxieties about our own deaths can we become able to give support and encouragement to those who have to suffer bereavement. Only then can we help them with their process of mourning without becoming too disturbed by their depression and their apparently unreasonable behavior.

For a few days before Fritz's cremation I stayed in my brother's house where I was supported and cared for with all tenderness. This was a great comfort, but I was restless and longing to be in my home—our home. Yet when I put the key into the apartment door I had a moment of panic and stood hesitatingly on the doorstep, until I felt clearly a "Welcome home" emanating from inside. The sun was shining and a neighbor, who had heard me come in, called out to offer a cup of tea. In spite of the emptiness and the sense of desolation, it was a homecoming and the beginning of a new life.

Throughout the first days and weeks, my family, friends, neighbors, and colleagues showed me love and sympathy. They left me alone, and yet were there whenever and for whatever I wanted them. A young male colleague with my husband's build came with suitcases within the first week and emptied wardrobes and drawers. For many years I enjoyed encounters with Fritz's clothes on him, and even now, ten years later, I still recognize sometimes with a pang of pleasure a familiar tie.

But in spite of all the affection and care, I was often depressed and lonely, however much I tried to apply to the situation of bereavement what I had learned from Fritz's dying. I knew that here too the full acceptance of the finality of loss, and all the pain that goes with it, need not diminish life but could give it a new quality of fulfillment. I also knew that this could not be achieved without going through the agonies of grief and mourning. I had had eleven years of expecting this loss, which should have given me the opportunity for anticipatory mourning—and I had deceived myself into believing that I had used this opportunity in spite of my conscious chief concern, which had been to support Fritz in his dying. I had often been puzzled by statements in studies about bereavement that the severity of grief may not be lessened by years of anticipating loss, but quite the contrary, may even be more severe than in the case of sudden death. Now, thinking about my own experience, I am beginning to understand that if so much of one's life for many years has been absorbed by the joint task of facing death, sharing it with the dying person by complete involvement, then one's own feelings may have to be almost completely obliterated in order not to deprive both partners of the possibilities still remaining in the relationship. In these circumstances the healthy partner has to remove himself so much from living experience that it may be difficult to be sufficiently in touch with himself to experience his own feelings of anticipatory mourning. In this sense, the shock of an unexpected death can be easier to cope with than a long-prepared-for loss.

An additional strain, connected with Fritz's long illness, and one others in my situation have shared, was my inability for two or three years to recall him as he was before he got ill. I remember lying awake at night, struggling in vain to recapture his image. All my visual memories were of the emaciated, suffering Fritz, a beautiful image but not that of the man with whom I had spent and enjoyed such a large part of my life. How much I suffered through this blockage I only realized fully through the ecstasy of joy and relief when finally

I could again recall the younger, healthy Fritz.

After the first few days of exhaustion and numbness, of a degree of confusion which made living a virtually insurmountable task (I lost and mislaid everything and got myself into the most painful situations), I went back to work. My job was to help people with their problems, mostly marital, and although I understood the roots of their lack of mutual tolerance and their often childish, unrealistic demands on each other, I found that the work with them was a great strain at the moment when my own marriage had just so sadly ended.

It began to dawn on me that now, as before, I was using my concern for others to avoid facing my own pain and loss. I had even gone to the Clinic on the evening after Fritz's death to see a man who had been particularly distressed at our previous meeting and who I felt could not stand the strain of a missed session.

This "good deed" and my growing physical exhaustion helped to convince me that I needed to get away from my commitments, to give up being in the helping role, to have time for myself and my grief. I was therefore glad to accept an invitation to go to Israel for three months and give lectures and seminars on "Marital Interaction as a Focus for Casework" at the Hebrew University and various other institutions.

On my way there I planned to stay for a week in Zurich with a dear friend of Fritz's and mine, a beautiful woman, full of energy, health, and vitality, who had shared much of our lives. Within an hour of receiving a letter from her with plans for our time together, a telegram arrived with the news that she had electrocuted herself through a faulty appliance in the bathroom. This news completely overwhelmed me; it was as if my carefully maintained defenses against breaking down could not withstand the shock. I collapsed helplessly and then did all the crying, expressed all the grief which really belonged to the loss of my husband. After a few days I did what I was expected to do, "I pulled myself together." This did not seem to be the time for mourning. I was on the eve of departure to a new land, exciting new impressions, pressing new demands. That I managed to fracture my ankle within ten days of my arrival in Israel and was forced to rest, may indicate, however, that I had learned something from my previous attempts at avoiding grief. When I asked the orthopedic surgeon who treated me whether people often fracture bones after bereavement, he said, without even looking up from my injured foot, "Naturally, people lose their sense of balance," and perhaps some have to fracture limbs or hurt some other part of themselves before they can acknowledge what has happened to them. Is it possible to enable them to do so in a less self-destructive way, by encouraging and supporting them in their mourning process?

In our society people are full of admiration for the bereaved who keep "a stiff upper lip" and behave "maturely." Even if this is not put into words, the implicit demand on people is not to let themselves go. This may well collude with the mourner's own defenses and increase his denial of a need to grieve.

For me, the essence of the experiences I have tried to describe in these memories is the certainty that life is not conducted alone, nor for that matter is death, even though death has to be achieved by each individual. Rilke said in his *Stundenbuch:*

> *To each, Oh Lord, give his own death;*
> *A dying issued from the very life*
> *In which he knew of meaning, love and pain.*[4]

When we think about bereavement, we are thinking of those who have given "meaning, love and pain" to the

4. Rainer Maria Rilke, *Stundenbuch* (Leipzig: Insel Verlag, 1928), p. 86.

dead member of the family, and whose lives have been shaped by the "meaning, love and pain" they have experienced. To understand their responses to bereavement we, therefore, have to understand not only something of their relationship with the deceased, but also something of their life history, and especially of their earlier attachments and losses, which inevitably affect their attitude toward the present loss.

These were the thoughts and questions in my mind when I arrived in Israel six months after my husband's death. Martin Buber, who lived in Jerusalem, had heard about my work and invited me to come and talk with him about it. Buber, an important Jewish philosopher, had expressed in many of his writings a concern with relationships, human encounters, life as a meeting, I and Thou. It was a great challenge for me to discuss an approach to relationship problems with him. My visit happened to be one day before his eighty-sixth birthday and a week before his admission to the hospital for an eye operation. This was his first and rightly dreaded hospital stay—he died soon after. That our meeting turned out to be such a special one may have been due to the particular factors in both our lives at that time.

The ostensible purpose of my visit was to tell Buber something about my work with marital interaction, which up to this point had been the focus for all my clinical—and teaching—experiences. And until quite recently my own personal life had had a marital relationship at its center.

Nothing was further from my thoughts than discussing bereavement. Yet we both had death very much on our minds, and the ostensibly accidental selection of case material revealed an unconscious communication about that preoccupation.

Buber was very critical of the theoretical basis for my

work, and hoping that concrete case material would be more convincing, I told him the story of Mr. and Mrs. Brandt, as a particularly clear example of the process of projective interaction.

Mrs. Brandt had suffered a mental breakdown on a family vacation in Italy, and was admitted to a mental hospital there. The family had been sharing a house with their closest friends, a very happy, mature, and supportive family, who, just like the Brandts, had three children. It is likely that their easy, relaxed relationship highlighted for Mrs. Brandt the tension between her and her very bossy and demanding husband. This led first to increasing depression and later to violent outbursts of aggression and a physical attack on her husband, which was so out of keeping with her usually helpful and pleasant behavior that it was seen as a symptom of mental illness and confirmed as such by the local psychiatrist. The husband coped most competently with all the arising difficulties, and returned with the children to England. The Italian psychiatrist felt that he could not discharge his patient unless an English colleague would arrange for her admission to a hospital there. He contacted Dr. Jones, who promised to meet Mrs. Brandt on arrival and make the necessary arrangements, but insisted on seeing her husband before taking any further steps.

At this meeting Mr. Brandt, a successful businessman, aggressive and very masculine in appearance and manner, gave only the most factual information about himself and his family and resisted discussing possible causes for his wife's illness. While expressing sympathy and concern for her suffering, he seemed to have an investment in seeing her as the patient who needed to be hospitalized so as not to upset the children or himself. His defensive attitude made Dr. Jones question whether the wife should be accepted for treatment as an individual patient. These doubts were confirmed at his first meeting with Mrs. Brandt who, while readily talking about her symptoms, wanted it to be understood that she always felt under stress when on vacation with her husband. "At home he is so busy, and I see little of him. But on vacation he is always at me, orders me about, makes me feel I have to live on his terms. He drives me crazy, and this time I just cracked." She seemed to be aware that the presence of her supportive friends enabled her "to crack." But like her friends and her husband, she was bewildered about her outbursts of fury and her violent attacks on him. It was this totally uncharacteristic violence which made her readily accept the verdict that she was a mental patient and must be locked up.

After this meeting, Dr. Jones told her husband, "Your wife is ill but her illness is not just inside her alone and cannot be treated individually. It has something to do with your marriage relationship, with your attitudes toward each other, and I cannot help your wife unless you too have treatment." Mr. Brandt was at first very upset, but seemed to begin to understand what Dr. Jones had in mind and agreed to see a psychiatrist who was used to working closely with Dr. Jones and was experienced in focusing on relationships. This psychiatrist soon understood why Mr. Brandt was so frightened of being affected by his wife's illness. His father had always been on the verge of mental breakdown, and a slightly younger brother of his was in and out of mental hospitals. In talking about his brother, Mr. Brandt used much the same language as in talking about his wife. The brother had been accepted as the patient in his parental family, and his wife was the patient in his present family. He described her as overemotional, hysterical, and disorganized, while he was motivated only by logic and reason, keeping emotion under strictest control. He acknowledged, however, that his wife could show unexpected strength in emergencies, had devotedly nursed him during a recent illness, and had been of great help to him sexually, as he had had occasional bouts of impotence.

In talking about his family, he described his mother as dominant and bossy and his father as weak, helpless, and completely at her mercy. Mrs. Brandt also had had a very strong, controlling, and dominant mother, and an always sick and dependent father. It seemed that Mr. and Mrs. Brandt had an unconscious agreement that in their marriage they must assert the opposite: the husband must be the strong and dominant one and the wife weak and submissive, whatever the cost.

After a short spell of treatment, this picture changed dramatically. Mrs. Brandt, for whom Dr. Jones had arranged a stay at a rest home and who had daily sessions with him, improved considerably. Mr. Brandt gave up his defensive attitude surprisingly quickly. The crisis of his wife's breakdown seemed to prepare the way for understanding his share in her illness and for thinking back over their married life. He began to feel very guilty about what he had done to her, keeping himself well at her expense. He felt that he had exploited her and driven her into the illness. He was most remorseful and became rapidly very depressed, agitated, and unable to work. These were important indications that for the first time he could let himself go and at the same time relinquish his need to victimize his wife. He could risk this because he had gained the confidence that his therapist would support him in his weakness. Meanwhile the wife had sufficiently recovered to rejoin him; and the friends with whom they had stayed in Italy invited the Brandts and their children to visit with them in their country house. Mr. Brandt cried most of the drive there, begging his wife's forgiveness for what he had done to her. He felt that he could not face these friends who had helped him to define his wife as the sick one and to lock her up. Now he was the patient, and his present changed personality was all the more dramatic because it involved his loss of social meaning and power. All he wanted was to die.

By the time they arrived at the country house, he was in a state of collapse. His wife was terrified when he refused to get out of the car where he was having a weeping fit. She feared that if she left, he would drive away and commit suicide, which he had threatened to do. In the end she and the friends succeeded in persuading him to come into the house. He then went straight to bed where he stayed for several weeks. The friends arranged what amounted to a hospital situation for him. He must have dreaded that he would be taken to a mental hospital as his wife had been when she had her breakdown. But his wife nursed him herself and there was no mention of sending him away.

In the past she had submitted to his demands to support his aggressive, rigid personality which she knew was not altogether real. She had also helped to guard his secret weakness, very much at her own expense, until on the vacation she was so exposed to his incessant pressure that her rebellious fantasies, hitherto repressed, took over. Now that his weakness was recognized, she could nurse and support him in a way that was true to herself and to him. She said that she had come to life in a way she never could before: "Now I am able to look after him as a real woman, mothering him, taking care of him, rather than as somebody who is supporting something in him which had been drained out of myself."

This reverse picture, in which he was the patient and she his caring nurse, saved the situation for the time being and gave them both a breathing space in which to recover, supported by their friends. But this was as misleading as the previous picture, for the husband also was not just an individual patient. It was impossible to understand the situation in terms of illness and patient. The problem was two people in relationship; their marriage with its destructive and self-destructive interaction was "the illness." The focus for therapy, therefore, was neither Mrs. Brandt's nor Mr. Brandt's pathology but their marriage relationship.

Buber had listened attentively but strenuously rejected my interpretation and proceeded to counter it with an experience of a friend of his. Harold, a very gifted Dutch scientist, suffered a schizophrenic breakdown at the height of his career. His wife, who had always been his closest friend, felt that she could help him only if she shared his illness. Whenever he went into catatonic withdrawals, she would make the same movements, speak in the same tone of voice. Repeatedly, while telling me this story, Buber stressed that this was a completely conscious decision on the wife's part. After several such emphatic statements, I could not refrain from mumbling more or less to myself, "I wonder why she had to do this?"

At this Buber stopped, as if struck by lightning. After a long silence he began to review what he had been trying to tell me. He recalled that several years later, when he had visited this friend again, he was back at work and apparently all right, but his wife had had a breakdown and was in a mental hospital. "And you know," Buber went on, "this man had an equally gifted brother, Peter, who had married a woman who for many years was in and out of mental hospitals. He was devoted to her, nursed and cherished her; we all admired him for his patience and compassion. Soon after her death he had a mental breakdown and never recovered.

"Why, why? What happened to these couples? Could they have gotten help, if they had asked for it? And why were their doctors not able to offer it? What in them was so different from your Mr. and Mrs. Brandt?"

Buber and I then tried together to understand the collusive patterns of interaction in the three marriages about which we had talked. Buber's two couples seemed to be in many ways alike. Both had a strong need to identify with their partners, and share and interchange their mental illness. In each case the actual patient was cherished and supported by the other one. There was awareness that the illness belonged to them both, like a baby it was passed from one to the other. But it was only one baby, they could not both hold it at the same time. When the "appointed" patient was no longer prepared or able to carry the burden of illness, the other one collapsed. When Harold got well, his wife got ill; when Peter's wife died, he himself became a mental patient.

In marriages like those of Buber's friends, in which there was a strong need to identify, to be as alike as possible to the partner, the autonomy of each individual seemed not to be strong enough to find an independent solution to a crisis—such as mental illness or death.

In marriages based on the mechanism of mutual projection, as was that of Mr. and Mrs. Brandt, there is always the hope that an emotional crisis may enable a withdrawal of projections and make a redistribution of forces possible. The Brandts did not want to be alike or to identify with each other. Nor did they want to identify with their parental families, which had both presented a similar picture: weak, damaged men and strong, dominant women. This constellation was equally threatening to Mr. and Mrs. Brandt—he frightened to be destroyed, she frightened to turn into the destroyer. To escape this, they were determined to develop the extreme opposite of the parental images: he must be strong, masculine, and successful, she weak, dependent, and submissive. On one level, however, they knew that these images did not match the reality of their personalities. They were both aware that Mrs. Brandt could have considerable strength which they had colluded in using only to support her husband's fundamentally precarious masculine identity. Mr. Brandt's need to use his wife in this way expressed his fear of his inherent vulnerability, of which he saw his insecure potency as a warning. When his wife became ill and turned on him in fury, she threatened the entire structure of their relationship and with it his personality. In his terror he completely disowned her and his illness, wanting her to carry it all alone, as far away from him as possible. At the suggestion of his own need for help, however, which the previous relationship with his wife had masked, the denial could no longer be maintained. He acknowledged his share in the illness—and collapsed. This was more than he could bear; he feared that he could not survive with this shattered self-image, and wanted to die.

His wife was terrified that he would kill himself, and that then the fantasies which had made her physically attack him in Italy, and which had been avoided by locking her up, would come true. Although she now understood that she was not really helping him by accepting the projections of his own weakness, she was still frightened of the consequences of refusing them. She was contributing to the death of his old personality, but was as yet uncertain whether her own liberation and change were strong enough to bring into being a modified pattern of relationship in which they both could survive.

If Mr. Brandt had committed suicide, however, as he had threatened to do, and his wife had been left alone at a point when the change in roles had led to extreme opposites (with her strong and him destroyed) she might have had to face a severe bereavement crisis, and great difficulties in establishing a new identity.

Buber seemed to be very moved by this discussion. He wanted to clarify several points about processes of interaction in families and then asked the question that this book asks: "What happens when these interactions are interrupted by death?" He then added, "What happened to us?"

He had moved close to me, took my hand, and began to talk to me about his wife, who had died five years earlier. "She was so tall," he said, "so strong." He clearly had a great need for her just now before going into the hospital. We sat together for a long while, talking about bereavement in a very personal way.

Since this meeting ten years have passed, and although I did not realize it at the time, I now know that my conversation with Martin Buber marked a bringing together for me of my concern with marriages and a new concern with bereavement and, thus, the genesis of this book.

2

Patterns of Interaction in Marriage

During most of my working life I have been concerned with marriage and family problems, and have learned something of the way people relate and interact, use and misuse each other in small urban Western families. Although my knowledge has been derived mainly from those who seek help with their difficulties, it has become increasingly clear that outside the realm of the imagination there exists no family totally free of problems and conflicts. It is from those who seek help that we can learn about the so-called normal and healthy, and realize how slender is the dividing line between them.

Most of the stories about bereavement which follow have come to my knowledge either because the bereaved asked for help or because he or a family member developed symptoms which revealed a problem. But the responses to the loss of an emotionally important, loved person which emerge from these stories seem to be fundamentally the same as those we have come to understand as normal processes of mourning and grief. Any differences are only in degree. Studies of patients in mental hospitals also indicate "that the bereaved psychiatric patient had experienced more or less the same grief symptoms as the widows in the normal sample studied."[1] Prolonged or delayed mourning, two types of "patholog-ical" reaction which were more frequently observed in the hospitalized patients, could in most cases be at-tributed to excessive guilt and/or pronounced ambiva-lence in the relationship to the deceased.

There are many factors which influence responses to bereavement, such as mode of death, timeliness, previous warning, and preparation for bereavement, but the key factor seems to be the relationships, the interactions that existed between the surviving and the dead.

In studies of child and personality development it is now widely accepted that from the moment of birth people should be seen less as isolated entities than in their interactions with others, and especially in their close emotional relationships. As D.W. Winnicott put it: "There is no such thing as a baby," implying that there is always the nursing couple, the mother and the baby.[2] The fundamental importance of close relationships con-tinues from the cradle to the grave—and beyond. There is rarely just the dying person, there are those he leaves behind; there is never just the bereaved but the dead person too. Between them they create the psychological situation which makes for the responses to bereavement. These will bear the weight of the relationship that has been formed by the personalities of the people con-cerned, by their life experiences, and by the attachments and losses they have experienced in the past, especially during their early formative years. The emotions and ties of infancy and childhood remain the most important

1. Colin Murray Parkes, *Bereavement: Studies of Grief in Adult Life* (London: Tavistock Publications, 1972), Chapter 8, p. 117.

2. *Collected Papers: Through Pediatrics to Psychoanalysis* (London: Tavistock Publications, 1958), p. 99.

and binding in everyone's life, even though they are mostly lost to memory, buried in the unconscious. The interrelationships and interactions between husbands and wives, parents and children, which are largely expressions of these buried memories or half-conscious experiences, can serve as an important guideline to understanding the personalities whose responses to bereavement we are studying.

These interactions can be observed most clearly in marriage, a relationship of two adults of, one hopes, more or less the same degree of maturity, normally entered into with an intention of lasting commitment, affecting all spheres of both partners' lives and all aspects of their personalities. In marriage these interactions are highlighted by each person's choice of the other, which most likely has been motivated by the need for a pattern of interrelating in which both can cooperate.

I like to think of this complex process as the weaving of a carpet of many colors in complicated patterns, wondering how the many different strands of wool are ever going to fit. Of course the pattern in the carpet, once designed, remains static, while in the marriage, unless the established pattern is defensively maintained in compulsive repetition, it changes constantly with life situations, though keeping basically its same elements.

To try to study such interactions in a bereavement situation is particularly complicated because one of the interacting partners has been removed from the dynamic process, leaving behind on the pattern the imprint of his contributions. We cannot hope to view these objectively, for the survivor who tells the tale will put his own lights and shadows on the pattern, which will change with the various phases of bereavement. Nevertheless, in spite of all the distortions, the idealization of the deceased, the delusions caused by guilt and the pain of grief, what will come across is a still continuing pattern of interaction in the now disrupted marriage, which may help us to understand and thus assist the bereaved.

The patterns of interaction I have most frequently observed in the marriages and families with whom I have been working are best described as projection and identification. Identification is the process by which a person either extends his identity *into* someone else, borrows his identity *from* someone else, or fuses his identity *with* someone else. Projection is the process by which a person imagines specific impulses, wishes, aspects of the self, or internal objects to be located in some person or object external to himself.

There is a third psychodynamic process, projective identification, the definition of which is very controversial. Among those familiar with psychoanalytic theory, from which these concepts are derived, it is being asked how far the three mechanisms are separate or distinct. Rosemary Gordon comments: "How does the process of projective identification differ from either of its components, that is, identification on the one hand and projection on the other?"[3]

Melanie Klein describes how "the Ego takes possession by projection of an external object—first of all the mother—and makes it into an extension of the self. The object becomes to some extent a representation of the Ego, and these processes are in my view the basis for identification by projection—or projective identification."[4]

In her introduction to Klein's work, Hanna Segal explains further:

In projective identification part of the self and internal objects are split off and projected into the external

---

3. *The Concept of Projective Identification* (unpublished paper, given by courtesy of the author).

4. *The Emotional Life of the Infant, in Developments in Psycho-analysis* (London: Hogarth Press, 1952), p. 207.

object, which then becomes possessed by, controlled and identified with the projected parts.

Projective identification has manifold aims: it may be directed towards the ideal object to avoid separation, or it may be directed towards the bad object to gain control of the source of danger.

Projective identification, too, has its valuable aspects. To begin with, it is the earliest form of empathy, and it is on projective as well as introjective identification that is based the capacity "to put oneself into another person's shoes." Projective identification also provides the basis of the earliest form of symbol-formation. By projecting parts of itself into the object, and identifying parts of the object with parts of the self, the ego forms its first most primitive symbols.[5]

In view of the controversy about this definition, and since we are not primarily concerned here with the scientific exploration of these processes, I will confine the discussion to identification and projection, and use the latter term to include what may be called projective identification.

Clearly these patterns of interaction are very complicated, especially since aspects of the three operations may be prominent at different times, and though they may take place at different levels of consciousness, in varying degrees they go on all the time and in all of us.

Rosemary Gordon writes: "There seems to be in general a growing awareness among psycho-analysts that what were originally considered neurotic or primitive or infantile mechanisms must finally be assessed in terms of the extent to which they serve or obstruct the development of the person."[6]

5. *Introduction to the Work of Melanie Klein* (London: Heinemann, 1964), p. 73.
6. *Concept of Projective Identification.*

In looking at these mechanisms of interaction in the marriage relationship, we are also primarily concerned with how they help or hinder growth and development in the people concerned, whether they promote a degree of trust and security in the relationship which makes it possible to tolerate the inevitable stress and frustration, and—in the context of our theme—how far they foster sufficient individual autonomy within the marriage to enable each partner to accept, endure, and survive the finality of separation through death.

Because of the difficulty of distinguishing these mechanisms clearly by definition, it might seem impossible to recognize them in patterns of interaction in marriage— and family—relationships. Yet, when we look at relationships without trying to theorize, we often see couples who cling together like Siamese twins, having an intense fear of being separate individuals, and finding it difficult to tolerate differences in their partners. They need to identify closely with each other. John and Eve, in Chapter 5, are an example of this constellation. In Chapter 4, however, are three couples who express through their partners different, often contradictory, aspects of their personalities. Their interaction is based on mutual projection.

The processes involved in the distribution of feelings between a couple, whether by identification or projection, must always be mutual. One partner is never simply the victim of the other (except in cases of severe mental illness); the needs of both must always be met on some level. In either pattern of marital interaction there is probably always the conscious or unconscious aim of reworking experiences of previous close relationships, in which secure autonomy and mutuality were damaged or not sufficiently achieved. What, then, do these processes of identification and projection mean to husbands and wives and their children and in what way can they affect their responses to bereavement?

The need to identify and the task of differentiation are central to every marriage. Let us look first at the process of identification, with its often contradictory features. It can make for a conflict-free but limited relationship, or for extreme intensity in passionate involvement.

One example of passion in an identified relationship is the story of Michael and Vivian. They were a young couple who not only looked like brother and sister, both being very tall and blonde, but were also mentally and emotionally similar types and had very similar backgrounds. Both had lost their fathers, with whom they identified and whom they resembled in appearance, at an early age, and both had experienced close exclusive relationships with their mothers, intelligent, dynamic women, for whom they replaced the lost husbands by developing responsible, caring roles. This fitted their almost compulsive need for independence, which in turn was a defense against the symbiotic closeness inherent in their relationships with their mothers.

Already so alike when they met, they trapped each other into claustrophobic identification. The fulfillment of physical intimacy stirred up their mutual repressed and denied symbiotic needs, which terrified them. Both sought individual therapeutic help in which it became clear that each partner's terror was based on fear of loss of his identity in symbiotic closeness (a repetition of the relationships with their mothers) and on fear of loss of each other through death, which became insurmountable even in minor separations and was connected with the loss of their fathers. When Michael spoke about his premonition that he, like his father, would die young, Vivian said that she would have to die with him. Their fear of losing each other, and their selves, was so overwhelming that from the beginning of their marriage they built in withdrawal clauses. Almost immediately both accepted jobs which took them away from each other. This first attempt at separation created mental and physical agonies for both and made them realize that any normal separation would only result in increased dependence—every attempt to loosen the tie would in fact tighten it. With great pain, these two young people decided to part rather than lose their autonomy and finally die together.

This story is an extreme example of symbiotic identification in marriage. But other people, who cannot easily exist as individuals and have an intense fear of separateness, choose partners equally unsure of themselves and in every respect as alike as possible, with whom they can therefore identify. These couples are trying to gain strength from each other for aspects of their personalities of which they are and want to be aware and which have formed their self-image. They aim to fortify this self-image by an image of the other one which fits their own. The unity of the two provides a living context in which they can have an identity. They are one person rather than two.

Unlike Michael and Vivian, couples who identify in this way do not seem to come from families where there has been an intense symbiotic relationship with *one* parent, but rather from those where differences and deviations from accepted and expected patterns were not encouraged, where conflicts were avoided and dreaded, and where children had little opportunity to experiment with and test out their own individual and perhaps deviating needs and drives.

Such marriages can be, and often are, happy and conflict-free but they are also limited and limiting. They rarely have an overt marriage problem but may become known to helping agencies through mental or physical illness, or more frequently through the problems of their children. In such families the children may have to carry the projections of aspects of their parents' personalities which do not fit their mutually strengthened self-images and which they have found too anxiety producing to develop in themselves.

The Millers, a family of this kind, had a daughter named Polly, who, at ten, was a delightful creature, pretty, lively, charming, but excessively adventurous. She climbed the highest trees, jumped from the steepest banks, and was in constant danger. She was an adored only child, and her parents, who were understandably anxious, asked for help at a child guidance clinic. But although Polly attended regularly and happily and was liked by everyone, there was no change in her overdaring behavior. After two years, her therapist began to feel that this child's acting out could only be modified if her parents were drawn into the therapeutic situation. They had presented an ideal, loving, united couple and were puzzled when they were advised to consult the Institute of Marital Studies, an agency for marriage problems which they felt was the last thing they could possibly need. But because they were very anxious to do anything which might help their daughter, they agreed.

At the Institute, the husband and wife usually each have their own therapists so that always four people are working on a case: the married pair and the therapeutic pair. In this case, I worked with the husband while a colleague of mine saw the wife. Mr. Miller was a most pleasant young man, eager to do anything for his daughter, whose risk-taking he saw as the one flaw in an otherwise perfect family. He was well-educated and intelligent but held a job which seemed far below his potential. When I commented on this, he explained that it was the first job he had taken when he finished his studies. Later, as a family man, he could not "afford to take risks," and therefore it had never occurred to him to change jobs. This phrase, that "one cannot afford to take risks," recurred constantly in our discussions. He had met his wife, who was slightly older, while still a student. Because he would not consider getting married until his income allowed him to offer her a good enough home, they were engaged for twelve years. She conceived soon after their marriage, and had a difficult pregnancy and confinement with Polly. The doctors advised against another conception, and since the Millers believed that no contraceptives were foolproof, they just could not take the risk and stopped sexual intercourse. And so on! My colleague described Mrs. Miller as a very attractive, imaginative woman. She was rather delicate, and spent much of her time in bed, where she wrote science-fiction stories, which satisfied her need for adventure without any real risk. All the risk-taking and the excitement of adventure which these parents had denied themselves were projected onto their only child, who, as we saw, acted it out.

This is a story with a happy ending, for as soon as Mr. and Mrs. Miller understood some of what was going on, and felt understood and supported in their therapy, they were able to risk a little more, and Polly no longer had to do it all for them. We may wonder, however, about what would have happened to these parents if Polly had suffered a fatal accident in taking their risks for them.

The fundamental risk this nice couple so strenuously avoided taking was to become more separate, to face the conflict which inevitably arises from differentiation, perhaps even to quarrel about "taking risks." The acceptance of separateness is often essential for survival, yet for this couple, separateness was associated with danger and loss.

Another patient of mine, who was aware of the necessity for separateness, pleaded, "Please help us to separate, so that we can stay together!" She was saying, "Help us to become whole enough, better integrated people, so that we may become able to develop our own separate identities." She might equally well have

pleaded, "Please help us to separate, so that we can survive if one of us loses the other through bereavement."

At the time that I met her and her husband they
seemed unable to survive any separation. They were
both highly intelligent people with considerable academic attainments, but neither had been able to hold a
job for it would have meant their being apart. They both
worked at home, writing books, constantly together; neither could do anything without the other. When at one
point the husband had a mental breakdown and had to
be admitted to a hospital, his wife broke down within
weeks, was admitted to the same hospital, and was furious that she was not seen by the same doctor. Soon after
this episode she became pregnant—it was her first pregnancy. This was during the war. Her husband was a
passionate conscientious objector. He had refused all
compromises, and was given a nine-month prison sen-
tence with the option of suspension until after his wife's
confinement. She had a baby boy, and in a book in which
she described this birth, she wrote: "At the moment of
my son's birth, I knew what it meant to be potent." Her
husband, while in prison, also wrote a book, which he
presented to everybody as "my baby."

This example raises a crucial issue which will help us
to understand better the inability of some married couples to be more separate. This couple's underlying anxiety about life was based on severe sexual envy. The wife
envied the husband's potency, the husband his wife's
power to create babies. As long as they were closely
identified they could contain the sexual conflict and cope
with the contradictions about the bisexual drives within
themselves.

In varying degrees everyone has the needs and desires
of the opposite sex. These may raise great anxieties, particularly in people who are very insecure about their
appropriate sexuality. If the anxieties are not resolved

before the death of a partner, the integration of the normal bisexual needs of the survivor may not be accomplished. Either he will not be able to survive the loss of
the other half of himself or he will return to a repudiation of heterosexuality.

Some of the stories which follow show that it is couples with such a strong need to identify who are most in
danger of finding the loss of a partner unbearable; they
cannot survive the separation, die soon, or collapse into
paralyzing illness. Or they may find another object of
identification, a son or a daughter, a close friend or a
good cause. Divorced from their own personal identity,
they borrow an identity in the eternal hope of forming
an attachment which will make them feel good enough,
safe enough, to risk depending on their own autonomy
and thus strengthening it. Unless they achieve this, perhaps with the help of a therapeutic relationship, they
will remain unable to break the vicious circle of lack of
identity leading to a degree of dependency, which makes
loss and bereavement an insurmountable task. As we
have seen in the story of Michael and Vivian, some couples are so overidentified and so terrified of the prospect
of loss that they precipitate it by building loss of each
other into their marriages.

In marriages in which the couple establish a complementary relationship, differences are not avoided but
sought, so that each can express for the other feelings
and ideas the partner finds difficult to own or to express.
A husband can be grumpy at a party because he knows
that his wife will be friendly for them both; another
husband, who is always pleasant and never makes a fuss,
knows that his more aggressive wife will see to it that the
family gets what it needs. As R. D. Laing put it: "Each
partner strives to find in the other, or induces the other
to become, the very embodiment of the other whose
co-operation is required as 'complement' of the particu-

lar identity he feels compelled to sustain."[7]

For relatively well-integrated personalities, who can react most of the time realistically to each other and are flexible enough to adjust to changing situations, such processes of "projection" can make for good and productive partnerships. They may constitute a therapeutic drive, an attempt on the part of each partner to remain in contact, through a loved person, with those aspects of his personality which he could not hold onto inside himself, and had disowned or neglected to develop. The process of increased self-integration which is thus set in motion may well, not be destroyed if such a marriage is terminated through the death of one partner. Indeed, the self-integration may be continued by the survivor with increased urgency, for now he has to find the "complement" inside himself and further develop it. The therapeutic drive may become renewed, and with some luck and support in his life situation, the growing ability to integrate may lead to a richer and more fulfilled life for the survivor.

The mechanism of projection, through which feelings and ideas from inside a person are attributed to people and objects outside, is in itself a normal part of all relationships. It can, however, be carried to extremes. The more at war with himself an individual is, the more of himself he may want to get rid of by projecting it onto the other, thus impoverishing his own personality and invading the other's. In marriage, the resulting conflicts then increase the pressure of anxiety to maintain the situation. The chances for a withdrawal or modification of projections diminish as both partners become too rigid to be able to change.

The relationship with the partner who is thus invaded

7. *The Self and Others* (London: Penguin, 1971), p. 101.

partly becomes a relationship with the self, and the partner ceases to exist as an individual in his own right. Where the pattern of defenses is excessively fragile or too rigid, each partner may cling to a false image of himself and the other, and reality-testing, which makes for growth and development, becomes impossible. The more this happens, the greater will be the pressure to maintain a situation in which the rejected parts are completely split off from the rest of the personality.

The hard-working wife, who keeps herself, her home, and her children meticulously clean and runs from one authority to another to complain about her dirty, drunken husband, may well be worried about her own bad and dirty aspects, perhaps what she perceives as her bad sexuality. It may be this anxiety about herself which makes it so important for her to keep all the "bad" things firmly fixed on her husband. One such woman made it clear to me how complete the split was when she said, "While my little Charlotte was distributing flowers in a white dress at the local hospital, the swine of her father was lying drunk in the gutter." (Young children in such cases are seen as the extension of their mothers but usually start creating anxieties when they reach adolescence and begin to be interested in sex.)

On one level, this woman's frantic demands for help expressed her great need for reassurance that she was good and he was bad, and on another level, she unconsciously craved for recognition and acceptance of her own bad and dirty side by somebody she respected, a parent figure. This alone would relieve her of the guilt which she was all the time increasing intolerably by her destructiveness toward her husband.

How much greater still is the guilt likely to be in cases where the partner who has been the recipient of the other one's split-off bad, rejected feelings dies, and the projected bits can then never be withdrawn and the guilt relieved. We shall see from some of the stories which follow that these situations often lead to long and excessive mourning and grief, a grief which the bereaved cannot give up because it is his only hope for restitution.

But it is not always the "bad bits" that are projected onto the partner—or onto a child. People whose self-confidence has been severely undermined, perhaps from earliest childhood, find it difficult to believe in, and hold onto, anything good in themselves, such as beauty, talent, kindness, or love. There may be many reasons for such a denial. They may be afraid of the too great demands on a loving, giving person, which can be avoided by not being loving or giving. They may feel that they will never be able to fulfill the expectations "good people" should fulfill. They may be frightened of disappointment, because the real attainable "goodness" can never come up to the perfect fantasied "goodness" which is the only one worth having. Such people may choose partners whom they can idealize and adorn with all desirable characteristics, with everything that is good and beautiful, hoping that they can put them in touch with what might be good inside themselves. When such a partner dies, he takes all the goodness away with him and leaves the survivor emptied of all that makes life worth living. The bereaved may feel so impoverished that he becomes deeply depressed and cannot continue to live. He may not even want to live, for only the dead have value. Mothers or fathers who have lost idealized partners may so instill in their children the feeling that everything worth having belongs to the dead that they burden them with constant self-doubts. This living with death is the very opposite from accepting death.

We must remember that these extreme responses to bereavement are only an exaggeration of the very common one, encouraged by most societies, of idealizing the deceased, which reinforces the denial of real feeling and the memory of a real relationship. A recognition of the universality of the need to idealize may help the mourner who shows exaggerated responses to feel accepted. If he then can be helped to see the lost partner with all the loved and admired aspects of his personality but also with the irritating and feared ones, the exaggerated mourning and idealization may become modified, and the bereaved may become able to see himself—and the deceased—more realistically.

3

Interaction as a Concept for Understanding Bereavement

At this point it may be appropriate to try to see how we might apply some of the concepts and understanding used in marital therapy to a discussion of responses to bereavement. In this chapter, therefore, as in the previous one, I have drawn freely on publications of the Institute of Marital Studies, using both my own contributions and those of my colleagues.

When the Institute of Marital Studies (formerly the Family Discussion Bureau) started its service for men and women seeking help with marriage problems, we tried to understand our clients as individuals. We asked ourselves: What are these two people like? Why did they choose each other? What has gone wrong in their conscious and unconscious expectations?

The couples who came in were often in a great deal of confusion as to which of them was at fault. Gradually we began to see that these marriage partners were not simply two individuals, that the boundaries between them were blurred and confused, and that the perceptions each had of the other were often remarkably distorted. We began to realize that these distorted perceptions were a sort of mirror, reflecting each partner's inner world and revealing his own problems and internal conflicts.

In dynamic psychology the traditional tendency has been to think in terms of the relationship of a subject to its objects. Concepts are centered on a "person" or "subject" and one thinks primarily in terms of the existence and function of that person. This is essentially a "one-person psychology," each person being thought of as the center of a world consisting of himself and his objects, to whom he relates by complicated processes and manipulations.

When dealing with marriages, however, both the individuals and the relationship between them must be studied. We have to be aware that each is both subject and object. Each is a subject in his own right but has taken the other, in some measure, as his object and is also the object of the other's attachment. There is a complicated interaction going on between the two in which the adaptive and defensive processes of each are geared in with those of the other and have to function in relation to the other. As long as the partners are sufficiently flexible and mature, these mechanisms make for a mutually gratifying relationship.

We have seen earlier how problematic too great a fusion of personalities can be. Where stress leads a couple to seek help, the broad aim of marital therapy is always to strengthen the psychological boundaries between them, enabling each to be a more separate person with a more clearly defined identity, and to increase the area of reality, so that each partner can see himself and the other one more objectively.

These same therapeutic aims are applicable, indeed essential, in helping the bereaved to cope with the loss of a partner, or in preparation for such a loss. The methods must be adapted to this situation, and since there is only the surviving partner to work with, the dangers are even greater of developing a "one-person psychology" with its falsifying perspective.

Any change in life situation has the potential of mobilizing growth and maturity, and simultaneously of reactivating regressive elements. This dual process is particularly striking in marriage, for the regressive elements seem so blatantly to contradict the achievement of a mature status, which the marriage publicly announces and celebrates. These celebrations, especially in rural areas with their often noisy enjoyment, teasing of the young couple, and playing tricks, do express a recognition, however, that what is being celebrated is not only a step toward maturity but also an event through which every adult's favorite dream may come true—to re-enter the lost world of infancy where he enjoyed physical gratification from another's body, commanded a paramount loyalty, and was in fact the center of that other person's life. Therefore, the young couple's childish behavior— holding hands, using baby-talk, and so on—stirs up feelings of nostalgic amusement or the sort of "regressive" feelings connected with sensuous pleasures, which are welcome and enjoyable to the observer.

Less public are anxieties of husbands and wives about their own or the other's "bad" infantile behavior: childish rivalries, envy of the cherished baby, temper tantrums—all so reminiscent of the nursery. Such anxieties may lead to requests for help, and all who work with marriage problems are familiar with them. The acceptance of these "regressions" and the ability to link them with the more mature aspects of the couple's personalities can do much to alleviate stress.

Loss through bereavement, above all the loss of a marriage partner, constitutes another major change in adult life with the same dual potential for maturity and regression. Here, however, the powerful regressive element is ignored in our culture, and its expression in grief and mourning is not only not encouraged but actively discouraged. The expectation is that the bereaved will be brave, behave in a dignified way, and will not embarrass others with his grief. For unlike the pleasant feelings stirred up by lovers, the loss of a loved one reactivates everybody's most painful nightmares, the most primary infantile fears and panic, the anguish of abandonment and the terror of being left alone, having lost love. The baby experiences the loss of his mother as a threat to his existence, and it is this primordial fear that is reactivated at the loss of the closest person. Every significant death may bring in some sense a repetition of this anxiety.

In addition to the existential fear of abandonment the infant has anxieties that it was his naughtiness that drove the mother away. If he does not have more separation than he can bear and repeatedly receives the reassurance of his mother's return, his developing memory and sense of time will enable him to hold her inwardly when she is away from him.

At the loss of a loved person through death, the adult mourner, too, has to cope with the anguish of abandonment and of guilt about much that he has or has not done or felt in relation to the deceased. He also has to learn to hold the lost person inwardly during the mourning process until he feels sufficiently separate to accept, endure, and survive the reality of the loss.

Nobody wants feelings of panic and despair recalled; hence they reject them in the mourner, which in turn confirms his worst fears, that he is isolated, without love and comfort. In our culture such comfort can be sought only in strictest privacy. A friend of mine told me that in one of the moments of greatest despair after her husband's death, when she just did not know what to do or where to turn, she wrapped herself, head to foot, in a soaking hot bathtowel and curled up in her favorite chair, as in her mother's womb.

People who are less able to accept their infantile needs might be frightened that they would get lost in such explicit regression but this was a woman who was able to read one of the lessons at her husband's memorial service in a clear and ringing voice, a lesson which had had a special meaning for the two of them and which she felt only she could read.

Not only do the people around us frown on regressive behavior, but also our own inhibitions often make it impossible. A woman of about forty told me that a year ago her husband was killed in a motorcycle accident, in which she herself injured one leg. She was laid up for two weeks, and her mother-in-law treated her like a baby, doing everything for her, even bathing her. "My injury was a blessing in disguise," the woman told me. "Without it, I would never have been able to let go, or allowed myself to be babied in this way, nor allowed my mother-in-law to do this for me. Yet it was the greatest help to us both. For her, to have a child to care for in memory of her lost son, and for me, to be receptive to her caring and give in to my grief. I really don't know which of us gained most through this."

In cultures in which people are more used to living with death, and where more childish expressions of joy and sorrow are encouraged, the bereaved can feel more supported in his needs for regression. In the Jewish tradition relatives and friends gather in the mourner's home for the first week after the death. They provide relief from all work and duties, and not only cook and provide the food but may even feed the chief mourner like a baby, thus showing their acceptance of his infantile needs at this time. Their presence can help the mourner to feel that he is not isolated in his loss, and their talking about the deceased may be a great relief. We all know the hushed voices and embarrassment when the name of a person who has recently died is spoken. But for the bereaved, it is important to name the lost person, as it can help to restore his identity as someone to whom he must now relate in a different way. Unfortunately, however, much of the healing potential in this Jewish tradition is now often prevented by doctors, who give the bereaved so many sedatives that grief and regression are slept away.

A highly cultured intellectual Westerner who went to Israel for the funeral of his only child, killed in an accident, was consciously disgusted by the barbaric tradition of giving noisy vent to feelings, and was astonished and ashamed to find himself participating in it. Unprepared for the tradition of burying the body without a coffin, he had to be gently restrained from physically attacking the men who performed this duty, and then felt that he had behaved like a savage. After the funeral, when his conscious wish was to hide himself with his grief and shame, he succumbed against his will to the compassion and understanding acceptance shown to him. Finally he felt tremendously supported by the affection expressed by all around him for his lost child: "It was such a relief to talk about him." On his return to England, he said that this experience had thrust him against his conscious will into a process of mourning, painful and healing, which might otherwise have remained barred to him.

Earlier in this chapter we discussed the contradicting drives toward maturity and regression which are inherent in any change in life situation—marriage, the birth of a baby, death, bereavement. Such major changes constitute crises—turning-points which may lead to increased health or to deterioration, and which are part of the life of every family. Erikson speaks of such a "turning-point" as "a crucial period of increased vulnerability and heightened potential."[1] How, then, can we learn to

1. Erik Erikson, *Identity: Youth and Crisis* (London: Faber and Faber, 1968), p. 96.

help the bereaved, who is experiencing the most extreme loss, to use his crisis as a growing point?

A crisis is a new condition through which the previous equilibrium is upset. All the usual responses are completely out of tune and inadequate to meet it. One's own behavior becomes unpredictable, a real loss of self occurs. It is not just losing a state in which one had found one's balance, but rather as if one has lost one's balanced self. In attempting to regain it, one may try out some new ways of coping, giving up certain wishes, defining a new task.

"At each stage of these developments, previous experience moulds what occurs, but does not completely determine it. Every crisis represents a novel situation in which novel forces, both internal and external, are involved."[2] This is a quotation from Gerald Caplan, who has given us some awareness, provided us, as outsiders, with some tools to use for intervention toward a healthy outcome of an emotional crisis. To achieve this, the first command is to not succumb to involvement with the crisis but to try to understand what in the personalities of the people who are involved is being highlighted. A crisis is not an abstract imposition from without but a high point in the life of the person concerned. To use the concepts in this book, we might say that a crisis is a dynamic interaction between a person and an extreme event, and it would be as fatal to look at each part individually as it is to look at the two partners of a marriage crisis individually.

We must now try to understand in what way loss through bereavement is distinct from other crisis-losses, for example, from the loss of a partner through divorce or separation. In some aspects a divorced person goes

2. Gerald Caplan, *An Approach to Community Health* (Tavistock Publications, 1961).

through feelings of mourning very similar to those of the bereaved—inability to accept the reality, anger, searching, despair, an overwhelming sense of loss.

The fundamental difference in bereavement, of course, is the absolute finality of the loss. Divorced people can go on believing that their marriage may come right again at some time, or that they may be able to make a different sort of relationship with the previous partner. They are sharing the experience of the separation, to which each will respond in his own way to achieve his or her own separation, which, unlike the separation through death, can be worked out in its own time. If there are children or parents or property, they will remain shared concerns. In dealing with them, the lost partner may be helpful or frustrating, the contact with him may be welcome or dreaded. I have heard separated people say, "It would all be so much easier if he (she) were dead, then I would know where I am." If she or he were dead, however, it would be much more difficult to acknowledge or express the hate and anger, the recriminations and self-justification which in divorce or separation can serve as a vent to let out the bad air.

Without an ongoing interaction with the partner there also is no one to challenge the idealization which often makes up so much of the initial grief, nor to assuage the guilt. The whole painful and complicated process of separation has to be worked out entirely by the survivor alone. The difficult dual task for the bereaved is to acknowledge and strengthen those aspects of the lost person which he has internalized, taken into himself, and yet to accept the loss of the living reality of the deceased. This inevitably slow mourning process can help the bereaved to find a new life, which will be truly free only if it contains the memory of the lost person.

The number of families affected by divorce and separation is rapidly growing in our society. Neither the children nor the spouse of a broken home need to feel isolated. On the other hand, more and more people, particularly women, live to a ripe age, and as an untimely death becomes increasingly unusual, the untimely widow does feel singled out. Separated or divorced women may have to face all sorts of suspicion and gossip, but their experience may make them interesting and seductive people. Widows are no longer burned on their husbands' funeral pyres but they are often shirked as if they carry a touch of death, especially in social life. This touch-of-death attitude does not apply to widowers, however, and we shall discuss this when looking at rituals connected with death.

Important echoes from previous unresolved losses, uncompleted mourning processes, may hinder the bereaved person's capacity to conclude the work of mourning, but the general climate of denial in our society adds to the difficulty. Recent attention to the problem has aimed to modify this climate by making it possible to speak about death and mourning, and to try to understand the reasons for the reluctance to do so. Until a few years ago the major taboo in our society was sex, now death has taken over the role. Both sex and death involve intensely private yet universal feelings, and thus stir up in all of us our earliest fears and fantasies, as well as the defenses against them.

Just as services for marriage problems began to be effective when those who were seeking help as well as the helpers became able to look at and talk freely about sexual anxieties and the primary feelings they reactivate, it is essential that not only services for the bereaved and members of the helping professions but ordinary men and women be more honestly in touch with the emotional needs of the bereaved and the regressive as well as the angry, violent elements which are stirred up in bereavement. It was recognition of this that prompted

Geoffrey Gorer to write "The Pornography of Death," in which he states that death and mourning are still treated with the same prudery, which makes for the isolation of the bereaved and sees the proper action of a friend or well-wisher as distracting the mourner from his grief.[3]

Even professional helpers—doctors, clergymen, social workers—often defend themselves so thoroughly against the savage pain and anguish of loss through bereavement that they avoid facing it, and thus are unable to support the necessary work of mourning. But even if they are aware of their task to acknowledge and encourage grief and mourning, their own unresolved anxieties about death and loss may stand in the way, and they will feel helpless in the face of suffering of this kind. If sensitive enough, they will remain silent rather than say something that sounds false, which would only increase the anguish or arouse violent anger in the mourner.

An increasing number of social services for the bereaved are being set up, and are beginning to be staffed by better trained people. Growing publicity through writings, radio, and television about dying, death, and bereavement should help to diminish inhibitions, increase understanding, and develop skills. These are important developments, but we must never forget that however necessary it is to understand patterns of grief and mourning, in the last instance it is the bereaved person himself, with his own feelings, pattern of interaction, and experiences of life, who has to bear the loss. He must be enabled to cope with it in his own way without feeling rejected and isolated because of the paramount need to be himself at this moment of greatest stress. Here as elsewhere there is a certain danger in constructing

3. In *Death, Grief and Mourning in Contemporary Britain* (London: Cresset Press, 1965).

theories which have to look for models, as they might underestimate these vital individual needs. As Mary Stott says in her recent autobiography, "In grief we do as we must."[4] It is true that there is always a general situation but there is also always a specific person experiencing it. H. A. Williams has said:

> One of the reasons why we can be aware only of our own suffering is that suffering takes place not abstractly in a void, but in terms of a particular life-history with its infinite many-sidedness. Without knowing this infinite many-sidedness from the inside, we cannot tell how the suffering concerned articulates itself with regard to a particular person.[5]

Having underlined the importance of recognizing the needs of each individual, I want now to stress the fact that there are certain constants within a bereavement situation which will manifest themselves in varying degrees. The interplay between these constants at the time of bereavement and the individual needs of the bereaved will become apparent in the detailed case studies which follow.

4. *Forgetting's No Excuse* (London: Faber and Faber, 1973), p. 184.
5. *True Resurrection* (London: Mitchell Beazley, 1972), p. 143.

Bereavement in Marriages Based on Projection: Are There Possibilities for Growth?

This chapter is about three couples whose marriages appear to have been based on a complementary relationship in which the partners developed distinctly divided roles. Through Martin Buber's two cases we are already familiar with the process of shared and interchanged mental illness in marriage. In the very complex case which follows this same process can be seen at work in physical illness, resulting in the death of the apparently stronger partner and some gain in strength in the survivor.

MARION AND TONY

Marion was a speech therapist whom I sometimes consulted in the course of my work. At the time I met her, she had been married to Tony for ten years and had two children, a girl and a boy aged seven and nine. The marriage was under considerable strain, and the otherwise very reserved Marion had a great need to talk about it in the hope of clarifying her own mind.

To tell the story from the beginning: Marion was the older of two girls. All her life she had suffered from congenital asthma. She was intelligent and strong-willed, very different from her charming, easygoing younger sister Olive, though the two girls were very close. Their mother was a beautiful and rather spoiled woman of Hungarian origin, worshipped by her considerably older husband. He himself was a most attractive person, amusing and imaginative, but very unrealistic. He was generous to a fault—nobody could entertain as lavishly as he did, choose such beautiful flowers for his wife or presents for her and the girls. In his business he was always full of bright ideas, which sometimes came off but often did not. The family's fortunes changed accordingly, often quite dramatically, from considerable wealth to near poverty, resulting in all sorts of crises.

During one of these, when the girls were ten and eleven, the father had a heart attack and died, leaving his family unprovided for. In this situation, their mother showed considerable and unexpected strength. She had always been artistic; now she got a well-paid job as a furniture designer and kept the family going. A year after her husband's death she remarried an old family friend who had long been one of her admirers. He was wealthy and reliable, in many ways the opposite of her first husband, and, having been widowed after a childless marriage, was delighted to act as a father to the two girls. Olive soon became his darling, as she was her mother's. Marion had always been the more difficult, and now her rebellious attitude toward her mother increased, as if she blamed her for her father's death, despised her for her readiness to replace him, and herself refused to do so.

Olive had boyfriends from an early age and loved fun and the pleasures of life, while Marion had always had a strong social conscience, worked hard at school and later at her studies, and was not interested in boys, though she was trusted and admired by her girlfriends. She was delighted when Olive married young, shared in her happiness, and became a loved aunt to the children. It seemed that her own future lay in her career, and everybody was very surprised when she started an affair with Tony and a few months later announced that she was going to marry him.

Tony was about the same age as Marion. He was born and brought up in South Africa. His mother died while he was a baby, and his father soon afterwards married an attractive stepmother, whom he loved. Tony was only ten when his father died, but he did not feel that he missed him, for he now had his stepmother all to himself. She died when he was in his twenties and he was desolate. Unable to stay in South Africa without her, he came to England, where he got a job as a public relations man in an American firm and met Marion. He detested his job, and constantly threatened to quit and become a freelance writer. But he always let himself be persuaded to stay on by Marion, who dreaded the insecurity of a jobless husband. Tony reminded her in many ways of her father. He too was charming, imaginative, generous, and a spendthrift—in spite of their double income they were always in money trouble. Both were popular, with a large circle of friends who appreciated their exceptional gift for hospitality. Tony did the cooking; he enjoyed making exotic dishes and imaginative decorations. Marion did the befriending; people loved to confide in her.

Her family however, was very critical of Tony and his "bohemian" irresponsibility, and Marion had some difficulty defending him. She could point out how good and patient he was with the children, how helpful in the house, and what a perfect nurse whenever she was ill, which happened quite often. But neither in her family's mind nor really in her own did this compensate for his lack of interest in his work. Often he simply stayed at home, leaving all the responsibilities to Marion, including the paying of most bills. It seemed that as she became more and more successful in her work, rose to more important positions, he became less and less effective in his. It was as if she were getting stronger at his expense. They had many fights and both were very unhappy.

After ten years of marriage, when the youngest child, a girl, was seven years old, Marion fell in love with a colleague of hers, who in many ways was much like herself and the opposite of Tony. They had been good friends for many years and had many interests in common. He had never been interested in another woman, and had for long been a source of strength for Marion. But only now, when she expressed doubts as to whether she could sustain the conflicts in her marriage any longer, did they consider the possibility of a life together. After much heart-searching they decided against it, feeling too guilty about upsetting the children's lives and giving so much pain to Tony.

At this point, Marion accepted a year's fellowship to a California university, which had been offered to her under very advantageous conditions. Not only would it improve her career prospects and get her away from the marriage for a year, but the climate was likely to improve her health and that of her son, now aged nine, who also suffered from asthma. The little girl would stay with her sister's family and see a lot of her father, to whom she was very close. Tony had reluctantly agreed to this plan and everything was arranged in minutest detail when a week before Marion's departure Tony had very alarming asthma attacks. As he had never shown the slightest symptom of this illness before, the doctors were startled. Marion postponed her departure and intensive medical investigations began. After some weeks, it was diagnosed that an old, unrecognized T.B. had flared up. Tony's condition got steadily worse and there was no longer any possibility of Marion's taking her fellowship and leaving her desperately ill husband. He had to be admitted to the hospital for an operation, and was on the danger list. Marion stayed with him day and night. She seemed to feel responsible for his illness, as if she had given it to him or brought it about by her threat to leave.

When, after a few weeks, Tony was well enough to be discharged, Marion was completely exhausted. They went together to a convalescent home where Tony recovered but Marion got worse. She had very bad asthma attacks which she felt were quite different from what she was used to. They were much more like those she had observed in Tony. Could she possibly now have his illness, just as he seemed to have had hers? She was advised to go into the hospital, the same one where Tony had been. Although at this point she was considered to be much less gravely ill than Tony had been, she died, alone, quite unexpectedly, during the third night after her admission.

Tony went to pieces after Marion's death. He had a serious relapse, was readmitted to the hospital, and was again on the danger list. After his discharge six weeks later, he was completely apathetic, and had only one wish—to get away from everything and everybody. When Marion's family financed a stay in a T.B. sanatorium in Switzerland, he was unable to do any of the necessary preparations, and let himself be packed off like a parcel. After a few weeks there, he recovered surprisingly quickly and showed an unusual degree of initiative. He rented his suburban house in London for a year, managed to find a cheap mountain cottage for himself and his children, resigned from his job, and settled down to write his novel, as he had always wanted to do.

He was father and mother to his children, for whom

this change of life was a great help. They had been bewildered by the rapidly succeeding crises and separations in their family. Now at last they were united with their father and could mourn the loss of their mother together. When they all returned to London after a year in the mountains Tony's health was improved and so was that of his son.

A year later, Tony remarried. His second wife was a successful lawyer who had recently dissolved a conflict-ridden, childless marriage. She was happy to have a family and a husband who let her get on with her career and was content to do the housekeeping, even if she had to find most of the money for it. In her intellect, her devotion to her work, and many other ways, this second wife is similar to Marion, though stronger and tougher. Tony does not have to be afraid of destroying her, or of feeling that her femininity is threatened by his preference for those aspects of life which are usually considered to belong to a woman. He also need not fear that she will force him into a more masculine role. He still has choking attacks but they are much less frequent and severe, and he can keep them under control without getting, or making others, anxious. He is more relaxed and has finished his novel. It may be that through all the pain in his first marriage, and through his mourning for Marion, he has become a more secure, better integrated person.

Even though in many ways Marion and Tony were a good complementary match, both were too insecure in their appropriate sexual roles to work out a gratifying relationship. Neither of them had resolved the childhood conflicts which had motivated their choice of each other. After his father's death, Tony had had a very exclusive relationship with his stepmother. To keep her love, he could not become a "proper boy" and remained gentle, receptive, and passive. He developed a pattern of relat-

ing to women in which they took the lead and made the
decisions. This may have made him choose the intelligent and competent Marion. Marion, however, was too
unsure of herself as a woman to fill Tony's need to be
loved and cherished in spite of, or precisely for, the more
feminine aspects of his personality. She had chosen him
freely. Nobody in her family and few of her friends had
even known of him before she announced that she was
going to marry him. Yet we know how strongly this
apparently free choice was motivated by her unresolved
tie to her father, a tie she might have hoped to resolve in
this marriage.

Not only the choice of a marriage partner but the
development of Marion's very distinct personality was
motivated by her early experiences. Her asthma must
always have been the cause for much anger and resentment (or was unexpressed anger and resentment the
cause of the asthma?). Perhaps she became so good, so
concerned for the underprivileged, so driven to repara-
tion because the angry, aggressive part of her could be
expressed only in the asthma. What is certain is that she
could never compete or identify with either the feminine
mother or the charming, life-loving sister, and therefore
developed values and qualities of quite the opposite kind.
They brought her much gratification, but her life was
always burdened and difficult.

During her last year she was offered two opportunities
to change this: the man whom she loved and who was the
opposite of her husband and her father wanted to make
his life with her, which must have boosted her sense of
femininity; and in an exceptional acknowledgment of
her work, new doors opened for her career, a tremendous affirmation of her intellectual and professional
achievement. She declined these promises of future happiness, as if she felt that they were not her right. In her
anxieties about her conflicting drives she had to close the

door on both. Her husband's sudden illness tied her to him afresh.

We may well wonder with what degree of ambivalence Marion kept her night watches at Tony's bed to keep him alive, when at times she must have wanted him to die so that she might be free to live. These half-conscious wishes were unacceptable to her; she turned her destructive fantasies inward and died herself.

YVONNE AND DAVID

I got to know Yvonne through a colleague of mine for whom she works as a cleaning woman, and was most surprised that this elegant, well-spoken, aristocratic-looking woman had to do this sort of work, especially since she did not seem to be short of money. My interest in her was roused further when I heard that she was seventy-eight (she looks more like fifty-eight), and that she was widowed for twelve years and had never stopped mourning and lamenting her unbearable loss, but alternated this with expressions of feeling liberated. When Yvonne heard that I was writing a book about bereavement, she offered to contribute her story, although she repeatedly assured me that it was really very ordinary and could not possibly be of interest to me.

Yvonne's memories of her childhood are only unhappy ones, nothing but frustration and deprivation. Even now, her anger at this was strikingly expressed in outrageous fury, as if she had suffered a grave injustice. Her mother's background was veiled in mystery. Yvonne and her slightly younger sister knew only that she had come from France and had broken away from her middle-class family (or was disowned by them) when she eloped with, and later married, their father, who was twenty-one years her senior. She must have been very young at that time. Their father, who had been married before, had children by this first marriage the same age as their mother.

Their mother never spoke of her childhood or her family but she did occasionally teach her daughters a few words of French and she laid great stress on good table manners, which seemed incongruous in the sordid tenement in which they lived. Altogether, in spite of the poverty, there was an air of refinement about the mother which made her daughters feel that she was used to a very different sort of life. Yvonne seemed to have no compassion for this woman who had had such a difficult life and had lost so much; she felt only anger that she had so little to give to her daughters.

Their father was a musician who played the violin in an orchestra which worked mainly on cruise ships. He must have had an exciting life, and was a mysterious figure, hardly ever at home. Again Yvonne seemed to feel only fury, that her father kept all the excitement to himself, as if both parents had secret riches which they would not share with her nor even let her see.

It was never clear whether her father was away working—or for other reasons. But even when he was at home, he does not seem to have supported the family. It was the mother who had to be the breadwinner, and as she worked hard and very long hours in a packing factory, the children were left alone with keys around their necks. The family despised their surroundings and did not mix with their neighbors, so that Yvonne and her sister were left entirely on their own. Nor were the two girls close to each other: "We were too different," says Yvonne, the sister apparently being much more ordinary. Yvonne's own feeling of being "special" was already very strong—although at that time it brought her only isolation and misery.

When the father was at home, the family dreaded his violent temper, which was quite unpredictable. Even now sometimes Yvonne has nightmares about her father's violence, and still finds herself cringing in the street at the sight of a strange man who reminds her of him. Later, this dreaded, violent father turned stone-deaf and became a pathetic figure.

While the mother died in her fifties after a long and painful illness, the father lived into his eighties. The only interest he had ever taken in his daughters was in their musical education. He had tried to stimulate their interest by practicing with them, but he had been so exacting and demanding, expecting them to be geniuses, that his music lessons always ended in disaster, with him in a furious temper and the girls in tears.

After leaving school at fourteen, Yvonne managed to get herself apprenticed to a tailor, and after a year of this she left home and went to live with a girlfriend. The two girls worked in the West End of London, and went mad with the glamour of it. Yvonne was thrilled to find that men liked her. She became aware of her sexual powers, let herself be taken out and spoiled by boyfriends, and was seductive but withholding. When she talked about this time, I sensed something of Yvonne's special quality of rousing feelings of adoration in others, giving and getting pleasure, and yet withholding so much of herself in the narcissistic way which later became so powerful a factor in forming her life.

It was important to Yvonne that her boyfriends not only have money but be well educated and well spoken, and she made great efforts to learn from them. She was determined to forget her sordid past and become a lady. During this time she completely neglected her mother and now feels guilty about this. "I could think of nothing but pleasure, pleasure, pleasure, and went a bit rackety, hankering after fleshpots."

When Yvonne was about eighteen, and looking for a job, she was given a long list of addresses from the Labour Exchange. There was one in Southampton Row that attracted her. As she told me about this, she got lost in her memories and started to sing "Southampton Row, Southampton Row" with a radiant face, and I got a glimpse in this seventy-eight-year-old woman of the enchanting girl she must have been at eighteen. Her premonition was right—it was at Southampton Row that she found her husband, David.

David was the oldest son of an Orthodox Jewish East End family. His father was a tailor who wanted his son to come into the business. But David was stubborn and hot-tempered and father and son could not work together. David left to set up a business of his own, in Southampton Row, where Yvonne worked with him for five years. Then, when he was called up into the Army, they got engaged, and got married five years later when he was discharged. By that time he had decided to give up tailoring and go into business, and rapidly became a very successful businessman.

David's family was naturally very opposed to their oldest son's marrying a gentile, but David was determined and Yvonne tried her best to pacify them. She converted to Judaism, learned some Hebrew, tried to understand Jewish traditions and dietary laws, and seriously practiced Jewish cooking. Once they were married and living on their own, David did not want any of this. He had been attracted to Yvonne precisely because she was so different from all the women he knew. They had all been fat and very emotional—Yvonne was "as thin as a stick and very cool." David was fond of his family, and grateful to Yvonne for trying to please them, but he wanted to break away from his background and East End restrictions. He wanted their life to be as different as possible from all he had been used to in his youth.

And different it became. With growing success and wealth, they had better and better homes and increasing social engagements. Yvonne was house-proud and liked to polish and clean, in spite of sufficient help. David resented this. When I asked her whether cleaning then —and now—gave her pleasure, she said vehemently, "I hate it. But it is the only thing I can do well, and only if I do something really well do I feel satisfied." For David, the house was a symbol of his success, a background to their social life. He had social ambitions, and wanted to entertain and have an admired house and hostess. David had attended school only to the age of thirteen and later was too busy to educate himself, but he was very intelligent, a brilliant chess player, a good conversationalist, and highly respected. He loved to show off Yvonne, bought her expensive clothes, and supervised her appearance. He made her feel like royalty, worshipping the ground she trod. On their annual cruise vacations, and on social occasions, she had to be the most beautiful, the most admired. When at a Mason's party the local mayor asked David's permission to have Yvonne as "His Lady," David was delighted. But along with his pleasure at having such a desirable wife, there was often some anxiety: Would he be able to hold her? Did she really love him? There were doubts and uncertainties.

In this apparently so loving relationship there were whole areas of both their lives hidden from each other. This applied particularly to the area of sex, any discussion of which was taboo. Neither of them had had sexual experience before marriage or knew anything about contraceptives. They practiced coitus interruptus throughout their marriage. Yvonne was frigid and often rejecting, calling David a beast and oversexed. On several occasions she left him after he had had violent outbursts of temper which, she says, were caused by trivialities but may well have been connected with his sexual frustration. One time Yvonne left him for a few weeks but then responded to his plea to return. In later years they had separate bedrooms—"because of different sleeping habits," according to Yvonne, but perhaps because David continued to be frustrated, and on those occasions he reminded Yvonne of her father.

In 1961 Yvonne got ill with some kidney trouble and had to be admitted to the hospital. While there, resting and being cared for, she was full of good resolutions for their future life: she would be a better wife to David, try to please him more and do what he wanted. He was so good and loving: he was always the first visitor on the ward and brought the most beautiful flowers. Everyone commented on how lucky she was to have such a marvelous husband.

On the day Yvonne was to be discharged, she waited with excitement for David's visit, longing to have him take her home. Instead, the head nurse came and took her to a private room, where her younger son and his wife were waiting for her in tears: David had died of a heart attack that morning. There seem to have been some warnings, such as high blood pressure, but David didn't want to make a fuss and Yvonne shut her eyes to danger signals.

After David's death, Yvonne was inconsolable. She cried and sobbed for days, unable to accept her loss. Her sons and daughters-in-law tried to comfort her, and their old nanny came to live with her and look after her. But Yvonne felt that "nobody helped, no one understood." She felt "bloody-mad" when people tried to console or distract her. Her wild anger and fury were reminiscent of when she had talked about her early childhood deprivations. Now, as then, they expressed her hurt that life had been so unfair to her. She wished that she had never married David, the forty-five years of happiness with him were not worth the pain she was now suffering. "You must think I am mad," she said to me. She alternated between not being able to eat and losing too much weight and stuffing herself with food for comfort. She leaned heavily on neighbors, yet felt utterly let down by everybody.

This state of despair and anger went on for about two years. Then the wounds began to heal and the feelings of hurt became less painful. In the later stages of her despair she felt that she must replace David. She longed for someone to take her away, abroad, as David had done. She went to extraordinary lengths in her frantic search for a replacement, even trying Marriage Bureaus ("One loses one's judgment").

Finally she accepted the futility of this attempt, sold her house, moved into an apartment built for her in her younger son's house, and tried to regain some interest in life. But the move created further difficulties. She knew nobody in the new neighborhood and was firmly kept in her place by the young couple. In order to get out of the apartment and meet people, she began to look for cleaning jobs, "only with very nice, educated people who treat me as an equal." Indeed, this seventy-eight-year-old regal-looking woman must be quite a sensation in the households she honors with her scrubbing and cleaning. But she takes pride in her work, and her employers say that they have never had such a thorough cleaning woman. The cleaning is also a great help to her, not only because she has the satisfaction of doing it so outstandingly well and it takes her out of the apartment, but also because through it she is special, a sensation.

In the evenings she goes to classes in French—her mother's native tongue—and in music, where she plays her father's instrument, the violin. Both these activities give her tremendous pleasure, and seem to provide a positive link with the otherwise so negative picture of the past and her parents.

Although she still has crying fits—"I shall never stop

grieving for David"—she also says that in some odd way she feels much better: "I feel more myself, liberated. With David I was always tense, now I can relax." She readily accepted my comment that with David she was always trying to play a role, which one part of her wanted to play, but it was a great strain and she was never sure whether it would come off. When I asked, "What about David, did you also want him to play a role which he found difficult?" she did not know. I did not dare to make it clear that I was wondering how he felt about having always to be the successful, adoring husband, without acknowledgment of his sexual potency. Both Yvonne and David had wanted so very much to be different, to be better than anything they had known in their parental homes, that they both were likely to lose touch with their own identities, with what was right for each of them, for their own personalities. While Yvonne was trying so hard to understand what it was that David had put into her, which she felt was not altogether what she wanted, I could not help wondering which of her aspirations she had put into David which in turn had made him need a wife who was like "royalty" and accept her frigidity. Through his adoration of her she had been the special person she so much wanted to be; after his death she achieved being "special" through her cleaning jobs—and this, apparently, with more ease and less guilt. She had always felt that she had not quite kept her bargain with David, that she had been cheating him through her sexual rejection.

Yvonne did not want to make herself out to me to be better than she was, and so she came across as a rather selfish, narcissistic person who could give love only on her terms and could be cruelly rejecting of her mother and later of David. Yet she also seemed to be a fundamentally faithful person, for now her greatest satisfaction is in the return to her parents' interests, in her living memory of her husband, and in the now permitted enjoyment of polishing and cleaning, which makes her feel good and special without any guilt.

In our long afternoon's meeting, she showed the greatest interest when I pointed out to her the link between her rage about her childhood frustrations and her childish fury after the loss of David—fury at having been so badly hurt. This made sense to her, as did my acknowledging her great drive to change, to better herself, and yet fundamentally to remain the same, faithful to what she felt was truly herself. She showed considerable insight into her own ambivalences and contradictions and a great need to explain them to herself. She spurred me on to help her to understand herself better. In doing so, she went back to her childhood fantasies, when she dreamt that secretly she was a princess, a dream that she could not share with anybody. It had no particular setting, was just an isolated image, a princess, a royal entity on her own.

In her splendid narcissism this dream-princess was what she wanted to achieve—it did not require relationships. When David attempted to make the dream into reality by treating her like a princess, she felt guilt and unease. But now, alone as a regal cleaning woman, the dream has nearly come true.

ANNE AND ROBIN

Robin's wife died two years ago, leaving him with three children, Veronica aged nine, Eric five (adopted), and Martha less than a year old. He insisted on caring for the children himself, and now lives on Social Security and studies mathematics at the Open University. He already has three credits there and can get a degree in a year and a half. By this time, Martha too will be in school. Meanwhile he tries to be the perfect mother to these children.

Robin is forty, his wife Anne was a little older. They had been married for twelve years. Their backgrounds and appearances could hardly have been more different. Robin is tall, fair, handsome in a swaggering way, looks young for his age, and underlines this by unconventional dress. His father was killed in an Army accident when Robin was ten and his younger brother eight. Robin had hardly known his father, who was always away on Army duty. He had learned from his mother and other relatives that his father, who came from a wealthy, middle-class family, also lost his father when he was ten (probably in the First World War). He was brought up by a rich, demanding, and ambitious grandfather who disowned him when he would not do as he wanted him to. Then Robin's father, who had started training as an architect, gave it up and became an odd-job-man, interested only in horses and a good life. He married a beautiful, seductive girl from a much lower social class who adored him and his "sexiness."

After her husband's death, the mother transferred her adoration to Robin, who could do no wrong in her eyes. She thought that he was as clever, as sexy, and as good-looking as his father, and told him so. His younger brother was a very ordinary boy, much like the mother's own brothers and on quite a different plane from Robin. When Robin was thirteen, his mother remarried, someone much more like the men she was used to in her own family. He was a good enough fellow, and nice to the boys, but he did not share her adoration of Robin. He made some demands on him and expressed some criticisms, neither of which Robin could take. At fourteen he ran away from home and school, and went to live with a sailor.

This was not Robin's first homosexual experience. When he was twelve, a much older man had picked him up at a football game, and asked and obtained his mother's permission "to take him home for tea, to meet my Mum" (Mum was a senile, bedridden woman). The man was a stamp collector, and Robin quite willingly let himself be seduced in return for stamps. This affair went on for nearly two years, with his mother's sanction. Robin is sure that she must have known what was happening, although it was never put into so many words. As I write, I am again puzzled by the mother's acceptance of this situation. Was it because she so adored Robin that everything he did could only be right? Or, in her love for this boy, whom she found just as sexy as her lost husband, did she identify with the man who loved him in a similar way?

How Robin met the sailor who later offered him a home I do not know. He was in the Merchant Navy but never at sea, and seemed to have had some sort of a pension. He sent Robin out to do all sorts of odd jobs to earn a bit of extra money. On the whole, they had an enjoyable time together, with quite sophisticated interests, and sometimes even had enough money to go to the opera.

Robin seemed to find girls much more difficult to approach than men, and was very unsure in relation to them. His first attempt at flirtation ended in disaster—he was beaten up by the girl's much older boyfriend. Since then he felt that it was safer to keep away from girls, and there was nothing worth remembering until he was twenty-two and met Heather, who was only seventeen. They worked together in a coffee shop, although Heather was a music student. She was rather fat, not very attractive physically, shy, and prudish. But once Robin had succeeded in seducing her, they seem to have been able to give each other the much needed reassurance that they were all right as sexual man and sexual woman. This was a great bond between these two insecure people. Although they did not marry, they set up house together, had a nice apartment and good friends. Heather worked at her music—with an allowance from her wealthy father—and Robin had a job as a draftsman. He would have liked to marry Heather, but after four years, when she came of age, her father offered her a big sum of money on the condition that she give up Robin —and she did.

Soon after this Robin met Anne, his wife. She was a painter and sculptress, and had been living with another man whom she gave up for Robin. It was love at first sight. They must have looked a very ill-assorted pair, for Anne was tiny, under five feet, with a slight hunchback and deformed legs, though a beautiful, serene face.

Anne was the first child of young parents who were not ready to welcome her. She spent the first ten years of her life in nurseries or looked after by nannies, and felt unloved and rejected. At ten, she caught polio and was badly crippled. Her parents, full of guilt for their previous lack of concern for the child, devoted their lives to help her to walk again and to regain her independence. When she was sixteen and a student at an art school, her parents went to Australia, but Anne refused to go with them. There they became wealthy and successful and started a new life and a new family, from which Anne felt excluded. There was no hostility between her and her parents, just very little contact. They were ready enough to support her financially whenever she expressed a need, and bought her a house when she married Robin.

In spite of her still delicate health, Anne was full of zest for life and had a tremendous sexual appetite. Until she met Robin she had thought of herself as a nymphomaniac—but Robin's sexual needs were as great as hers, and they were blissfully happy together. Food too was very important to both, and Anne was a marvelous cook. She enjoyed spoiling Robin and even when they were invited out she would make sure that he got the food he liked. She might even bring something along if she did not trust the hostess to provide it. Thus, Anne had taken over Robin's mother's adoration of him. She flattered his vanity and if they had any extra money at all, it was spent on clothes for him.

Their life changed abruptly when Anne became pregnant. Her health deteriorated, and she had to suffer a great deal. Robin showed little sympathy. He swaggered along, bursting with health and enjoying life, letting himself be spoiled by Anne and doing little to make life easier for her. After a few months he found the combination of pregnancy and deformity repulsive and became very rejecting, especially physically. When she had to be admitted to the hospital two months before her confinement and then had to have a Caesarean section and a prolonged hospital stay afterwards, he responded to the long separation with childish anger. When at last Anne came home with the baby daughter Veronica, the breast-feeding disgusted Robin. He continued to behave in a rejecting and selfish way, and started having affairs and staying away from home. This rejection at a time when she was particularly vulnerable and herself in need of support and mothering seems to have stirred up in Anne all her previous anxieties about being unlovable. She became severely depressed, with periods of agoraphobia, which alternated with outbursts of violent anger when she would shout and break things.

Robin was completely uncomprehending. This woman whose moods alternated between violent anger and deep depression was not the Anne he knew and on whom he had so much depended. He retaliated with anger, sometimes hitting her. It was the depression, in particular, which seemed to frighten him and drove him away from her, for fear of becoming infected by it—until one day it dawned on him that it was he who had brought it about, that Anne's despair was the result of his rejection, and that she could not go on feeding Veronica and him without feeling loved, getting fed through his sexual love. When Robin made love to Anne again, all the clouds lifted at once, and they were passionate lovers again. Anne could not do enough for Robin, and he was in paradise. They lived in an atmosphere of mutual admiration—for her sculptures, for the poetry he wrote—an admiration which strengthened their loving bond, but which was not altogether shared by the outside world. Veronica, their little daughter, was now included in this mutual adoration. She was a marvelous baby, such a confirmation of their good sexuality, and adored by both parents, in whose eyes she was the most special, most beautiful, most clever of all children.

Anne desperately wanted another baby, but since she had been strongly advised not to risk another pregnancy, they decided to adopt. They chose Eric, a very neglected, deprived little boy, who was labeled "difficult to place" and needed very special care for a long time. This was a challenge to both of them, and Anne especially responded to it with all her warmth and an abundance of maternal love. They were rewarded by seeing this poor little baby develop into a healthy, happy child.

As soon as Eric no longer needed such intensive care, Anne began to take in neighbors' children, partly to help the neighbors, partly because she had an insatiable need to care, but also to earn some money. Robin was not a very consistent breadwinner. He stayed in jobs as long as they were challenging and gave him pleasure, usually succeeded in them for a short while, but never settled down and committed himself to work. Most of the jobs were far below his intellectual potential. Anne and Robin were both bad managers, spending money for what gave them pleasure rather than for what was most needed. In spite of the growing family, Robin continued to remain at the receiving end of Anne's spoiling, and it seemed to give her great pleasure to spoil him.

When Eric was over three years old, Anne began to pine for another baby of her own, and in spite of all the medical warnings, she got pregnant again and had a miscarriage, followed almost immediately by yet another pregnancy and the birth of Martha. This time Anne's pregnant body and later her breast-feeding were exciting and thrilling to Robin and he wanted to share this with the baby, by literally sharing the milk. Anne breast-fed for six months, and did all the work in the house, for the children and for her spoiled husband. The family lived on a wave of elation in spite of the fact that Anne's health steadily deteriorated. Martha too was a special baby, very lovely and flourishing—but her mother died before she was a year old.

Anne's medical history, as seen through Robin's eyes, is most confusing. It indicates that patients and their relatives only see and hear what they want, and that doctors are willing to collude with their blindness and deafness.

Anne, as we know, had been warned of further pregnancies, and since Veronica's birth (when this warning was given), her health had steadily deteriorated. In particular, she suffered increasingly from what had been diagnosed as piles. When Martha was six months old, Anne's pains became unbearable, and her G.P. arranged for her to see a specialist at the local hospital. The verdict was immediate admission for an intestinal operation. Diagnosis after the operation: cancer with secondaries which had affected the liver. This was revealed to Robin, who seemed to have heard only the comforting comment that the intestinal operation had been one hundred percent successful, and that a life expectancy of five years was possible. He shared this news with Anne, and they planned for five years. Robin insists that Anne was in excellent health after her discharge from the hospital, because the operation had been so successful. He did not seem to notice any deterioration, and Anne went on doing her jobs with the assistance of a housekeeper—but could no longer breast-feed Martha.

Two months after her discharge, Anne collapsed in great pain on an outing to see a cowboy film (Robin's favorite). Only then did the G.P. warn Robin of her impending death, only then was he able to notice how desperately ill she was. He gave up his job to be with her, and she stayed at home for another six weeks, mostly in bed, and was admitted to the hospital only for the last ten days, when the pain could no longer be coped with at home. During these last two months, everybody suddenly came to their help, their G.P., the District Nurse, who "could not do enough," and neighbors, whom the family had not known in the past, took over the children. Robin felt very supported; the care for the children and the house were taken from him, and he did not move from Anne's side. In the hospital, where she had a room to herself, he stayed with her day and night—especially during the last three days when she was unconscious. He wanted to be alone with her and resented any interruption, even the nurses looking in. Although he felt that the moment of her actual death was frightening and repulsive, he would not share it with anybody, and later said, "If it had not been for the children, I would have died too."

A couple of whiskies helped him to regain his equilibrium, and he went straight to his children, who were staying with neighbors. He told them that their mother was dead, and that they would not see her again. It was important to him to make it clear to them (and to himself) that this was a final separation. In the following weeks, he talked to the children a great deal about their mother, and grief and tears were mixed with jokes. He distributed some of Anne's belongings among them, and he himself began to wear a favorite cape-coat of hers. But he did not mourn—"How can one, with children about?"

It was Eric who responded to his mother's death with immediate distress and severe regressive symptoms—wetting, soiling, stealing. He had furious temper tantrums, and through provocative behavior constantly asked for punishment. Robin showed endless patience with him, and a surprising amount of understanding. The nine-year-old Veronica remained calm and controlled, helping her father as best she could, especially looking after Martha. With her help, and a housekeeper, he coped extraordinarily well with Eric, the small baby, and everything else that was expected of him. At times the stress was too great, and then Robin developed inexplicable pains, migraines, physical symptoms which made it possible for him to call for help to neighbors, friends, and his own mother. But he always rallied again, there was never any sign that he might give up, never any attempt to hand the situation over to helping services. He did not even call a child guidance clinic for Eric, who almost immediately after his mother's death had to be transferred to a remedial class in school.

Now, two years later, Eric has recovered. He is top of his class in the junior school, with a special interest in "sums"—probably because he identifies with his father's new interest in mathematics.

It is Veronica, who had been so helpful to Robin, who is now worrying him. At the age of eleven, she is too adult, too responsible in many ways, but she does poorly at school and lately has started to have frequent bouts of depression. It cannot be easy for her to take so much responsibility for Martha, whom she often blames for her mother's death. "If it was not for Martha, Mummy would still be alive." This feeling must stimulate her destructive fantasies and impulses toward Martha. Sometimes she comes into her father's bedroom at night with inconsolable crying-fits: "I want my Mummy." Robin is becoming aware how much these visits frighten him, as he remembers Anne's depressions doing. Instead of sharing Veronica's grief, he dissociates himself from it. "It is a waste of time to be depressed." He must also be scared by sexual feelings which may be roused by Veronica's night visits.

It helps to understand Robin's defenses against depression if we know that he too had suffered quite severe depressions during his adolescence after he had left his mother. They stopped completely when he met Anne and did not recur until after her death. In both cases, one might interpret them as a response to the loss of a caring, adoring mother. But there may also be another interpretation. I do not know at what cost to his mother, or to his "unimportant brother," this fatherless boy managed to remain so gay and sunny throughout his childhood. In his marriage he seems to have projected his depressions onto Anne, and disowned them—and her—completely when she expressed them. We know that no one can ever be just the victim of another, and Anne had strong depressive elements inside herself. But when she became burdened with Robin's projected depressions in addition, she expressed a double dose, which frightened Robin off.

Now that Robin once again has periods of severe depression, he tries to explain them "rationally" to himself and others as feelings of guilt that he did not insist earlier on a specialist's diagnosis for Anne and that he colluded with the dangerous wish for another baby. He also tries to keep the depression at bay by idealizing Anne and their marriage: "Anything nasty is too painful to remember." He will not allow himself—or anybody else—to criticize Anne. In our talks, whenever we came near pain, he started to laugh, to grin, insisting that "one must look at the bright side of life." Yet he begins to see that his denial of his own depression might affect Veronica. If the adult Anne had to be more depressed because he refused to accept his depression, if she could be so strongly affected, how much more powerfully could it affect a growing child?

One can now see in Robin's new insights signs of maturing, alternating with childish denial—for example, he says, "Money is quite unnecessary." He shows adolescent rudeness in any slightly frustrating situation and an almost touching vanity (after reading my notes, which I was afraid might upset him, he was delighted because I had described him as handsome). His overriding need is "to please Anne." She had always regretted his lack of formal education and had wanted him to study. Immediately after her death, he applied to the Open University for an arts program (Anne's choice for him). When he did not get in, he decided on mathematics. When I saw him two years after Anne's death, he was enthralled with his subject, which had opened new horizons for him, and insisted that it was "just like poetry."

Anne had been "a perfect mother" and a marvelous cook—he has become an outstanding cook, and enjoys it, and he tries hard to be a good enough mother. Anne was so good, so helpful to everybody—Robin now plans to teach mentally handicapped children, and is taking a special course to enable him to help deaf students to learn mathematics.

Everything he does appears to be motivated by the wish to please Anne and to identify with her. He is often aware of her presence: "It makes me feel cold, yet sustains me."

What will happen when the children become older and less dependent on mothering, when the university course is finished and Robin is no longer a student, we do not know. Will he then be able to become a father (rather than a mother), an adult and breadwinner, committed to regular work, and sufficiently in touch with reality to accept that he·cannot do without money? Will he be able to become a person in his own right, develop his own potential rather than remain a shadow of Anne? Can he externalize her sufficiently to see her more realistically and stop idealizing her? Will he manage not to become too dependent on Veronica—emotionally and otherwise—and enable her to make a normal separation from him when she grows up?

While we cannot find the answers to our questions about the future, it may be interesting to speculate why these two people, so different in every way, with such extreme opposite personalities, chose each other, and were able to sustain their passionate emotional commitment in spite of violent ups and downs? Did they want to get in touch with the characteristics in each other they had not been able to develop themselves? Robin with the responsible, caring adult, Anne with the lighthearted, charming adolescent which she herself had never been able to be? Robin provided her compulsive drive to have babies to care for with a permanent charge—and her need may have contributed to his inability to grow up. Was she, tiny, crippled, and handicapped, able to feel valued and attractive through the love of this tall, healthy, vigorous man, who in turn was not very sure of himself in relation to women? Was the fact that he could make her feel good, in spite of all his childish and irresponsible behavior, an affirmation of his own reparative drives—which he later could express toward Eric?

After the difficult period through Veronica's birth, which stimulated Robin's envy and jealousy of Anne's function as a mother, he could experience the satisfaction that he could mother her through his sexual love, and this seems to have enabled him to share Anne, his "adoring" mother, with other loved children, even support and value her maternal drive for others. Without this support, Anne could not have devoted so much care to Eric, the poor deprived baby. His great need and deprivation must have touched very different chords in his adoptive parents: Anne could identify with his physical handicaps and deprivation, Robin may have wanted to pay restitution for his own greed and demanding ways. They could unite these different drives for the benefit of this baby, and enable him to grow and develop through their care and affection.

It seems that after Anne's death it was Eric's grief and regression which mobilized Robin's potential for mature responses, which—once brought to life—he could then use freely in his work and in his family. While Anne was alive and could do it for him, he had not bothered. She had to die before he was able to get in touch with the caring, repairing aspects of himself.

Considering Robin's childish behavior until shortly before Anne's death, his present attitude shows a stupendous recovery—a successful resolution of a mother/child relationship, in which his childish aspects could become maternal. Ultimately, it still poses the problem: Will Robin ever be able to become a father, for which he has no pattern for identification?

DISCUSSION

The stories of the three couples, Marion and Tony, Yvonne and David, Anne and Robin, are very different, as indeed were the six people and their marriages and families. Nevertheless, they have certain features in common. In all three marriages there was considerable conflict and stress but also a great degree of mutual emotional involvement. We get the impression in all of them that the partner who died had been exploited by the other one, but also that he may have had an investment in keeping the situation static, needing the other one to be immature and dependent as the complement to his own strength and superiority. These marriages remind me of Genet's play *The Balcony*, which makes the point that there can be no judge without a criminal, no bishop without a sinner, no general without a subaltern.

In all three marriages, the surviving partner suffered a severe sense of loss and was deeply disturbed by the bereavement. Tony had a grave relapse into illness and almost died; Yvonne was inconsolable and felt that she was going completely to pieces; Robin went on living only "because of the children." Yet after a period of mourning, disturbance, being unsettled, the bereaved not only appeared to have gained in strength but all expressed in words and deeds that they felt stronger, liberated, freed, more themselves, more able to cope with life than they ever had been while their partners were alive. This change occurred in spite of the fact that each of them had been very dependent on his partner's support, indeed had demanded it as a right without which he could not live. Yet when this support was no longer available they found some strength inside themselves. Although they idealized and loved their dead partners, they made one feel that these people had stood in the way of their own growth, had robbed them of their potential for maturity.

In spite of the similarities, there were also many differences among the three couples, and it may be precisely these that can suggest to us the varied ways of finding a satisfactory solution to bereavement. One of the differences is age: Tony and Robin were in their late thirties when they lost their wives, Yvonne was sixty-six when she lost her husband. The two men had young children who motivated their mother-substitute solutions and Yvonne was offered a home by her married son. While these external factors inevitably affected the solutions to the three bereavements, let us now consider some factors arising out of their inner worlds.

Marion and Tony had within their marriage the imprint of all the roles which make up a family. They both had had an important relationship with their mother and father, were mother and father themselves, had a son and a daughter. This wide range of tested out relationships may have contributed to their ability to contain their anxieties about their appropriate sexual roles, their mutual resentment and confusion about what to expect from each other. The fact that both had lost the parent of the opposite sex at an early age, and had been offered satisfactory replacement for this parent, helps us to understand why Tony, after due mourning, was able to replace Marion and to help his daughter to accept her stepmother.

Yvonne throughout her life had been an excessively self-contained, narcissistic person. She maintained these characteristics in her long and devoted marriage to David, but, uplifted by his adoration, was able to give affection and care to her sons. Yet fundamentally she was always—as a child, a young woman, a wife, and a widow —a single person, complete in herself. It was through these same characteristics of selfishness and self-containment, and in spite of her distress and deep sense of loss, that she found a solution for her life after David's death —one that also repaired some of her extreme ambivalence toward her parents, and thus added to her sense of liberation.

In the family of Robin and Anne there was only one role pattern: that of mother and child. Both partners' early experiences had set the scene for this restriction. Anne had never felt like a member of her family, she had always felt alone, an unloved and isolated child. In her marriage she lived out her fantasies about mothers and babies.

Robin had only experienced a relationship with his

mother—his father remained an idealized image without living reality. It is not surprising, therefore, that in Robin and Anne's family one does not become aware of the existence of a father, each of the partners taking turns as mother or baby toward the other.

When Anne died, Robin gained some strength from being able to give up being the child and become a mother, largely through his idealization of Anne. At present, while the children are small and he is a student and supported economically by others, the situation fits an accepted definition of motherhood.

Of the changes brought about by bereavement in these three families, Robin's is the most spectacular, yet it also seems to be the most precarious. By his strong identification with Anne, by becoming Anne in a way, introjecting her into himself, he has avoided losing her and has not mourned. He needs to externalize her and mourn her loss before he can become a more fully integrated person.

Idealization of the dead partner can also be one aspect of projection. Everything that is good and worthwhile is projected onto the partner and lost to the survivor, who can keep in touch with it only by giving up his own identity and assuming the identity of the dead partner.

If two years after his bereavement Robin was trying to cope with his grief and guilt by idealizing his lost wife and their marriage, we must ask ourselves whether after a due time lag he will be able to see her more realistically and become a more independent and better integrated person. His mother, who had idealized her dead husband, had transferred this idealization onto Robin, who was ten when his father died. After three years of widowhood, however, she had been able to remarry a man who was much more familiar to her than Robin's father, who fitted her own parental background, and with whom she seems to have been able to build an externally

and internally more realistic and secure life and a partnership which did not seem to demand idealization. Perhaps this bodes well for Robin.

In previous chapters we have discussed processes of
projection in close emotional relationships, through
which one person projects aspects of his own personality
into another and vice versa. To risk a broad generaliza-
tion, we might say that in the marriages of Marion and
Tony, Yvonne and David, and Anne and Robin similar
processes were at work. Their stories, therefore, may
help us to understand how a weak and dependent husband or wife may gain strength through the death of a
partner whose need was to take the role of the parent, the
provider, the responsible one. This partner may have
achieved his strength at the price of projecting his weakness and dependence onto the other, who colluded with
the arrangement because it fulfilled a need of his own
and was gratifying to him, and who therefore played his
part in maintaining the mutual projections while his
partner was alive.

When these couples first chose each other, there may
well have been hope—conscious or unconscious—for a
future interchange of roles, for sufficient flexibility not
to get stuck in predesigned role distributions. If this had
happened, then the more dependent partner might have
become able to gain confidence in his own potential for
strength, and the apparently maturer partner might not
have needed to remain quite so defended against his own
weakness and dependency needs. He might have recognized these qualities as the gateway to his sensitivity and
imagination. In the three marriages we have studied,
however, this hope was not fulfilled while both partners
were alive. The crisis of bereavement was needed to
reactivate and renew the original hope or therapeutic
drive for growth and self-integration. Thus, after the loss
of his partner, the survivor achieved some aspects of

what the couple could not achieve together.

We all know couples where one partner is full of vital-ity, bursting with life and energy. He—so to speak—runs the show, while the other partner is passive and withdrawn, an observer more than a participant. Friends and relatives of such couples may ask them-selves: How could the passive and apparently weak one ever survive if the strong one should die? Then this happens, the more active partner does die, and the other one blossoms out. He duly mourns his spouse, is full of praise and loving memories, but after a lapse of time, he takes over the partner's jobs, activities, interests, and friends, and with it all gains a "new lease on life."

Couples who are more secure in their autonomy, where each is relatively in touch with the reality of his personality and that of his partner, can use their comple-mentary roles during their marriage for mutually en-riching relationships. Yet fundamentally the same dy-namic processes of projection can be observed during the lifetimes of both partners, the same healing growth pro-moting withdrawal of projections may become possible after bereavement.

One such couple was Andrew and Ruth, neighbors and friends of mine. Ruth was the lively, outgoing one, liked by everybody, deeply interested in people, exuding warmth and concern. Andrew, intelligent, interested in many things, preoccupied with plans and ideas, was more withdrawn and prided himself on being "a loner," but was content to let his wife and children fill the house with guests and callers. He nursed Ruth devotedly through a long illness and was very depressed, with-drawn, and silent after her death, but he sometimes came over to tell me about his dreams.

This he had always liked to do—a rather amusing fea-ture in a man who otherwise completely refused "to have anything to do with the unconscious." Now that he could not express his feelings in any other way, recounting his dreams had become an urgent need. He had had vivid dreams since Ruth died, which frightened him and which, in essence, were always the same. He always had to get with great urgency to an appointed place and made tremendous efforts to do so. But he always failed, there was always some obstacle, an abyss, no bridge. One evening he was particularly upset about this "absurd" dream. This time (in his dream) he had made the most careful preparations to get to the appointed place, and it looked as if he was going to make it. He could see his goal, it was quite nearby, but he could not get there, there was no bridge.

Until that evening I had never commented on his dreams, but this time I said, "While Ruth was alive, she was your bridge to life, to other people. You got where you wanted to get through her. Without her, you feel that you can't make it, so you want to get to a place where you might find her, but there is no bridge." He was silent. After a few minutes I added, "In your last dream you got so near where you wanted to get—perhaps you can make it after all." Again he remained silent and after a while started to talk about something else. When, half an hour later, he wanted to leave, he could not get out of his chair, simply could not move. I thought that he might have had a stroke or an hysterical paralysis and called his doctor, who diagnosed a sudden gout (he had never had symptoms of this before) and helped him back to his home and bed.

Andrew was ill for about two weeks and it soon became apparent that he had undergone a crisis, a turning-point which enabled him to build his own bridges—and to make good use of them. He is now surrounded by people who ask for his help or who simply enjoy his company. His guest room is always occupied, as it was while Ruth was alive. He has taken over her role without giving up his own, and has become a much easier, more integrated person. I happen to have objective corroboration for this because we have the same talkative cleaning lady, who constantly entertains me with stories about the great changes in the apartment across the road: "Mr. Calder never used to say a word to me but now he comes into the kitchen, has a cup of coffee with me, and tells me jokes. Just as his wife used to do." When I embarked on this book I asked Andrew's permission to tell this story. He could not remember anything except, after some digging on my part, that he had had an attack of gout. Otherwise: "Well, write whatever you like, it has nothing to do with me. I always was a loner and I always will be a loner." And with this he went off to do some shopping for his next group of guests.

This story tells us something about projective processes, and also about the resistance to acknowledging changes in oneself. In marital work we are only too familiar with our clients' frequent statements that things at home are so different now because the partner has changed; they themselves have not changed at all.

Warned by this experience, I watched out carefully for changes in myself after my husband's death. He was always the cautious, thoughtful one, who would consider everything from all angles before making a decision, and these slow, careful considerations sometimes drove me crazy. I liked to make quick, intuitive decisions, take a leap and see where I might land. Sometimes this proved to be right, but often not. Now I can no longer afford to take such thoughtless chances. I have to incorporate some of Fritz's careful weighing up, and I know that I have become less impetuous and considerably more passive.

Whether this change has come about because of my changed life situation or because I have been able to withdraw some of my projections and make the projected bits my own may be a point for discussion. But since I feel enriched by this change rather than burdened by new demands I have to fulfill, I would attribute my own and my neighbor's changed attitudes to our ability to take back projections, and all that they had made of them, from our dead partners, and integrate them within our own personalities.

Thus, whenever it is possible to withdraw projections after the death of a partner, bereavement, however painful, may not only be a loss, but may also bring a gain, one that the bereaved may find difficult to acknowledge because it contradicts his pain and grief and sense of loyalty to the deceased. The crisis of loss may become a turning-point, and the bereaved may emerge from a completed mourning process as a more independent personality.

But only if not too much of the self was projected onto the now lost partner, and if the projection was not too rigidly maintained, can withdrawal be achieved. Otherwise the bereaved cannot become separate enough from the lost partner to bury him truly, for what has been lost was part of his own personality. To compensate for this impoverishment of the self, and to avoid angry hating feelings, the survivor may introject an idealized lost partner. Or he may see the deceased as one who has robbed him of what was his own, and by defending himself against insight into his own collusive projection may block any loving memories. In either case, bereavement may lead to prolonged pathological mourning, depression, or breakdown, and an inability of the bereaved to reach out toward a life of his own.

5

Bereavement in Marriages Based on Identification: How Can the Survivor Survive?

In the previous chapter we tried to understand the responses to the loss of a spouse in marriages based primarily on projection, marriages in which differences could be tolerated or even encouraged, and in which each partner maintained his individual identity. In such partnerships the adjustment to bereavement is likely to be determined by the survivor's individual strength and flexibility rather than by age, for people can learn and change up to their last breath. After the loss of a partner whose personality has been complementary, the survivor may be able at any age to take over some of the attitudes and characteristics of the dead person that had been vital to their joint lives together.

In situations in which the bereaved finds it difficult or impossible to survive the lost partner, however, or can only survive at the cost of a severely diminished life, the factor of age may be important. The question that arises here is whether the survivor's inability to accept the final separation is due to a particularly strong identification with the lost partner or to the fact of old age with its dependent and regressive needs which may make separation an insurmountable threat. It is not easy to distinguish between these two kinds of helplessness.

The classic example of an old couple who after a long and happy life wanted to die together is Philemon and Baucis. In the legend they were granted this special grace in return for their hospitality to Greek gods, who turned them both into trees at the same moment. But the fact that they became two different kinds of trees may indicate that these old people maintained their distinct individuality in spite of their closeness.

In real, modern life, one such couple who became ill at about the same time were both nursed in different rooms by different people, were for weeks without any direct contact, and died within twenty minutes of each other. For them too a wish was fulfilled.

It has frequently been observed that dying people recall earliest childhood memories or return to an almost forgotten mother tongue. It may help to face death and bereavement with less bewilderment if these phenomena can be understood and accepted as an aspect of regression. The pain and confusion that result when regressive phenomena are not acknowledged as such, especially in situations of death, bereavement, or illness, are extremely disturbing for all concerned.

A friend of mine had undergone a leg operation which was healing well until he suffered a severe heart attack and was resuscitated. The necessary medication resulted in a reopening of his wound, an infection, and a leg amputation. For days he wavered between life and death. When he returned to consciousness, this man, whose mother tongue was German but who was fluent in English, could speak only German, which neither the doctors nor the nursing staff were able to understand. Apparently unaware of this kind of regression, they assumed that his brain had been damaged and that he was mentally deranged. His wife and family, already shattered by the tragic course of events, were in agonies of distress when informed of this diagnosis. Could they wish for this beloved, highly intelligent man to survive at that price? Naturally the patient was confused for some days, and it was only when he regained physical strength that the doctors realized what was happening and the diagnosis was revoked. Although this man has suffered considerable physical damage, he fully recovered his mental potential and his intellectual performance was completely unaffected. It is important to be aware that the loss of a limb, an important part of oneself, may bring about similar responses to those observed in bereavement: depression, grief, anger, searching (the latter stimulated by phantom pains). My friend's relapse into his mother tongue after the amputation can therefore be understood as regression, which is an essential aspect of bereavement.

The often confusing phenomena that we observe in the dying may vary from infantile regression to a sense of omnipotent power, and may be difficult to understand or respond to.

The husband in one couple had been suffering from Parkinson's disease for many years, and was in a very advanced phase of the illness when, without any warning, his always strong, healthy, active wife had a severe heart attack. She was admitted to the hospital where she was daily visited by her husband and two daughters. She did not talk about dying, but made it clear that she expected to die. When her husband visited her, they had relaxed, affectionate talks and never touched on any plans for the future. With her daughters, she talked about her life and her relationship with them and their father, asking for their reassurance that she had been a good wife and mother. To her daughters' surprise she never expressed any anxiety about what would happen to her helpless husband without her. It seemed as if she knew that he would not survive her for long. After she had died, the husband wanted to hear again and again the exact details of her last hours, as if he had to make quite sure that she was really dead. Once he had accepted this fact, he was calm and composed, and, with help, able to attend her funeral. Then with surprising energy he began to settle his wife's and his own affairs, insisted on choosing the headstone for her grave, and seemed to be relieved and happy once this was accomplished. That same day a neighbor, who had been abroad at the time of his wife's death, called to express her sympathy. She was surprised to find him so cheerful. When she said good-bye, he supported himself on her arm, saw her to the door, and said, "I will be going now too." The next day he went into the hospital and died peacefully within a week.

Examples of old couples dying at nearly the same time came my way while I was writing this book, and I could not ignore them. My main intent in this chapter, however, is to explore how far the mechanism of identification in marriage may affect the ability of the bereaved to survive the dead partner. I had in mind those couples who throughout their lives could not tolerate separations, and who had always been unsure of their own identities. It seemed that such couples would have great difficulty surviving the final separation, the loss of their partners through death. The case histories which follow will illustrate this problem.

JOHN AND EVE

John was one of five children: two older sisters, a male twin, and a younger brother. From early childhood, it was he who was always the responsible, reliable, sensible one, the peacemaker, the arbitrator among his siblings. He was liked at school and by his peers, yet was somehow withdrawn, not very communicative, never adventurous. It was his twin who did all the talking, risked all the adventures. Yet the two were inseparable, as if they were two halves of a whole.

Soon after John and his twin left school, war started and all three brothers joined the Royal Air Force. When his twin brother was killed in action, John acted as the comforter of the whole family, as calm and responsible as everybody expected him to be. Although his attitudes and behavior had not changed, he himself had; life had gone out of him, and he never was a full person again.

On leaving the R.A.F., John chose to study medicine —to help others, to cover up wounds had always been his main concern, more pressing now, after his loss. But he was deprived of fulfilling this vocation. After a few terms he had to give up his studies because his father committed suicide, and there was the family and the business, a pub in the north of England, to be looked after. His father had always been somewhat unstable, and had in many ways provoked his wife's dominance. He had got used to drinking too much and had neglected the business, which was in a bad way. Money was short, and the parents' marriage, which had never been good, had badly deteriorated. After a fight with his wife, the father disappeared, and was found a few days later in the hills, shot in the head.

The mother decided that the two brothers should take over the business and try to get it going again. The younger brother, however, soon found that the irregular hours of work, the strenuous business, and most of all his bossy, interfering mother did not suit him. In spite of his mother's scenes he gave it up, married, and moved as far away as possible, making it quite clear that he had to escape from the strangling family ties. But John stayed, although he hated it, and now took sole responsibility for the pub, his mother, and his two sisters who had remained unmarried.

The father's death had completely upset the whole family and all their hopes for a different and better life. Even though they lived in a poor neighborhood, John's family had had considerable academic ambitions; education was their one big goal. All the children had done well at school and had aimed at university careers. John, as we know, gave up his studies to take over the pub. His younger brother had been just at the point of going to a university at the time of his father's death. Although he stayed in the business for only a short time, he gave up his plans to study, partly because he could not now hope for any support from his mother, and joined an engineering firm. The two sisters had completed their training as teachers, but the younger one had a nervous breakdown soon after her father's death, stopped teaching, and looked after the household. Only the older sister pursued her teaching career. She did extremely well, becoming head of a department, and today holds a good position. But this one achievement, by a female, did not change the total picture of the family, which was one of defeat —a defeat which spurred the mother into further battles. She felt that she had to control everything to avoid further catastrophes, and her tyranny became intolerable, bordering on insanity.

That was the situation in which John worked and lived, calmly and responsibly, helpful and friendly to everyone—until, ten years after his father's death, he married Eve. He was then thirty-four years old and Eve was twenty-nine. They had known each other from childhood, and had courted for several years.

Eve was the youngest of three sisters. Her father had committed suicide when she was a few months old. He was a Scottish Protestant who had been disowned by his family when he married a girl from a very poor, newly emigrated Irish Catholic family. The young couple had gone to live with the girl's parents in a very cramped, depressing tenement house, under stringently poor conditions. The father was crippled with arthritis and rarely able to work, the mother was not a very efficient breadwinner, and the young husband worked in a brewery which went bankrupt just when his wife was pregnant with Eve, her third child. It was a difficult pregnancy, with all sorts of complications, and there were already two little girls, aged seven and three. In this desperate situation the father scratched their last money together and went to America, where he had relatives, to try his luck. After six months he gave up hope and booked a passage home, but did not return to his family. They later learned that he had shot himself when he got off the boat.

It is not surprising, therefore, that Eve started her life as a vulnerable, delicate little girl, though she was pretty and attractive, and the darling of the middle sister, Mary. Mary was intelligent and independent from an early age. She became fiercely protective toward her little sister, and fought passionately with her dominant, restricting mother, who, she felt, was determined to undermine and destroy her daughters' identities.

Eve's loyalties were always torn between this loving, admired sister and her dominant, feared mother, on whose care she depended. As a way out of this dilemma, she seems to have chosen to remain delicate and dependent, yet sweet and charming. This combination secured her the devotion of her mother, a formidable woman who could only love when she was in control, and at the same time the affectionate concern and protection of Mary.

John's and Eve's families lived in the same neighborhood. Eve and her sisters, John's two sisters, and the girl who later became John's brother's wife all went to the same school and knew each other well. They were like a big female clan. For Eve, this was an extension of her family situation, which, except for her mother's by then bedridden father, was all female, with never a male in sight. On leaving school, Eve first entered the Civil Service, the career her oldest sister had chosen. When after a few years she became dissatisfied, she decided to go to the University, where her gifted sister Mary had done outstandingly well. While a student, Eve became ill with a rare blood disease, which made her vulnerable to infections and increased her dependence on her family. In spite of her illness, she managed to finish her studies and graduated at twenty-five. But when she was faced with finding a job, earning a living, and taking responsibility for herself, the illness flared up again and she almost died. She survived only through intensive cortisone treatment. She was advised to avoid too much strain and took an easy secretarial job. Her anxieties about standing on her own feet were probably aggravated by the fact that Mary, who had always been her greatest support, emotionally and intellectually, had meanwhile married a brilliant scholar and lived with him abroad.

Although Eve was twenty-nine when she and John got married, she had been hoping for several years that he would propose to her. He had taken his time, however, knowing how strongly opposed his mother was to the marriage of any of her children. When he decided to marry Eve, his mother refused to see her, did not come to the wedding (nor did John's sisters who were dominated by her), and would not acknowledge the fact of the marriage. She had done the same when her younger son got married, but that couple had insisted on leading a more separate life. The mother refused to meet the wife, but later took some interest in their children—thus the total situation was not quite as absurd. But John and Eve did not or pretended not to mind. John continued to see his mother daily (the business was in the same house), paid the rent, did the repairs and looked after his mother's and sisters' welfare, just as before his marriage. The young couple never made any real attempt to fight the mother's antagonism, and during the fourteen years of their marriage mother and daughter-in-law met only by chance.

Yet John and Eve adored each other. They lived in a tiny, ugly grey house, without any color, comfort, or cheer, caring for each other, completely devoted to each other, worrying about each other's health (John too had many ailments but never did anything concrete about them). John called Eve "my pet," and her sister Mary, to whom I owe this story, says that in their little house they always reminded her of two grey squirrels from a Beatrix Potter book. Both were of gentle disposition, and lived a very quiet, withdrawn but contented life, conscientiously sharing the household chores. They had few friends and hardly any social life, justifying this by Eve's delicate health and John's inconvenient working hours. One felt that this restricted life was what they really wanted, and that they had no strength, no vitality left after doing what was required of them in John's work and in their little household. This withdrawn life apparently also helped them to avoid conflicts with John's family, and enabled him to contain his divided loyalties between his mother and Eve, just as in the past Eve had used the restrictions imposed on her by her delicate health to avoid conflicts in her own parental home.

Unable to have children after five years of marriage, they adopted a little girl, encouraged in this step by Mary, who had very successfully adopted two. In addition to her career, Mary was a devoted mother and an excellent born homemaker. But for Eve, the demands of a strong, healthy little girl were a great strain. In spite of John's help with the baby, as with everything else, she could not cope and became increasingly dependent on her mother and sisters.

It was striking how, in spite of the almost claustro-phobic closeness of this couple, they each continued to play the same roles in their respective families that they had before their marriage. Eve remained the delicate, dependent darling, and her demands for help and sup-port were always unquestioningly accepted by her mother and sisters. John remained the dependable, duti-ful son and brother, quiet but pleasant to everyone, ap-parently without any needs of his own. He never com-plained of his lot (although he made it clear that he disliked working in the pub), yet gave the impression of feeling somehow cheated, that all his good behavior, his unshakable concern for others, had brought him so few rewards.

John and Eve had used their marriage as a fortress against all the hate, anger, and destructiveness which had dominated the lives of both their families. Neither of them had ever been able to fight against these frighten-ing powers or break away from them, but had passively endured them. They were caught in a net of passive endurance which kept them tied to their families and strangled all drives to develop their own identities, strengthen their autonomy. Inside their fortress there was no need to fight, and no stimulus toward change and growth.

After fourteen years of marriage, when Eve was forty-three and their little girl nine, Eve had a recurrence of her disease, which quickly led to complications. She had to be admitted to the hospital and died within ten days. Almost immediately after Eve's death, John, who during her illness had spent every free minute with her, moved with his little girl into the home of his mother, who was by now senile and cared for by her daughters. He showed no signs of mourning and continued life as before, calm and responsible, concerned only for others. This was what everybody had expected of him. The only startling thing was that this quiet, controlled, and apparently so rational man let it be known, in his usual matter-of-fact way, that he talked every night to his wife.

Four months after Eve's death, John's mother died, and again he did all the right and expected things and continued life as before. Two months later he contracted infectious hepatitis, and died within two weeks. The orphaned little girl stayed on with his sisters, who both knew and cared about children and made her the center of their lives. She seemed happier and more content in this all female household, where she was loved and wanted, than she had with Eve and John.

How can we understand this marriage, and the lives and deaths of Eve and John? We know that Eve was born under extremely difficult circumstances. Her mother had been in poor health and felt acute anxiety throughout the pregnancy and her baby's early life. At the time of Eve's birth, her father had felt so hopeless and depressed that he could not continue to live. The situation in the grandparents' home, which they shared, was not only extremely poor but burdened with anxieties, as the grandfather's health deteriorated and he became bedridden. The "destroyed" father and the helpless grandfather were the only male images transmitted to Eve in this otherwise all female household. Her oldest sister remained unmarried and completely submissive to their mother, although she later became the main breadwinner, and had a good career in the Civil Service. Mary, the middle sister, Eve's champion and her exact opposite, was in constant rebellion against their mother. She left home as soon as possible, made a good marriage and a successful academic career. She managed to break away from home, as did John's younger brother, while all the other members of both families remained caught in the defensive net, defended against change in a changing world.

We have seen what defenses Eve developed to cope with her divided loyalties and the ensuing conflicts between the strong, admired sister and the dominant, possessive mother on whom she was dependent—and how these mechanisms later helped her to tolerate her mother-in-law's rejection and, with John's support, to withdraw from life and avoid conflict. One sees this young couple, hardly venturing out, excluding the world, wanting nothing but each other, in the security of their shell, in which they could, in an odd way, continue their childhood situations.

On the face of it, John and Eve were extreme opposites. Yet they were halves of a whole, just as John and his twin and Eve and Mary had been. They developed their apparently very different characteristics—Eve so dependent, John so dependable—in the face of very similar parental patterns. Both had experienced weak, vulnerable, ineffective fathers and very dominant, bossy, restrictive mothers. Both had managed to develop defensive mechanisms which enabled them not only to survive and avoid conflicts, but to remain loved and loving.

When they found each other, they built a protective shell around themselves, but continued to play their well-developed roles both inside this shell and outside in their respective families.

It seems that their marriage was another defense which enabled them both to remain what they were, without the pains involved in change or the dangers of responding to aggression and destructiveness, their own and that of others. To avoid this must have been vitally important for John and Eve. Not only had they both endured their dominant and destructive mothers, but they also had lost their fathers through violent deaths, suicides with no explanations, no farewell to the families. John and Eve's response to this shared fate was a shared withdrawal from a threatening world and from their own destructive fantasies.

Mary, Eve's sister, told me that despite Eve's delicate health and frequent illnesses, her death came as a tremendous shock to all who knew her, most painfully to herself. On the other hand, although Mary had always admired John's strength in all adversity, she realized what a terrible loss Eve's death was to him, but had taken it for granted that he would stay alive for the sake of his little girl. Yet his sudden death did not surprise her; it gave her almost a sense of relief that John was able to give in and do—for once—what he wanted. It seemed the natural solution for this man, who throughout his life had always been forced to give up what he loved and wanted—his twin brother, who had been his other half, his career, his aspirations, his autonomy. Eve and the affection and safety in their peaceful little house were the only comfort life had offered him. There they had lived in joint repudiation of terror and violence, in a collusive flight from life and from any assertion of their own autonomy. In their avoidance of activity, they lived a dead life, yet one which provided shelter for both of them as long as they could be the other half for each other.

John could not face living once again without his other half. He waited until his mother was dead and he could see his little girl well settled with his sisters, whose lives had found a new meaning through their devoted care for the orphan. He was no longer needed for either, his sacrifices were unnecessary. He did not take his life, but readily succumbed to the first illness which enabled him to leave it, and died in the same passive, accepting way in which he had lived.

We may be sad about the poor limited lives of these two people, but we cannot mourn their united death,

which seems as right for this self-contained young couple as it did for the fulfilled lives of Philemon and Baucis.

John and Eve, in their joint flight from life and autonomy, are possibly exceptional. However, it is quite
common in marriages that one partner, most often the
wife, has lived entirely for the other, has given up her
own career, her own interests, her own identity in support of her husband. Often we hear divorced women
resentfully protest, "I gave up everything for him—and
now he has left me." For the widow who feels like this,
the task of surviving may be beyond her resources, especially since the repressed anger and resentment about
her self-sacrifices may lead to self-destructive impulses.
If she can feel that the denial of her own needs has been
worthwhile, gratifying to herself and her husband, and
if she can find a sense of value in herself, she may be able
to make a new life. If not, her feeling of futility, of being
useless, her resentment about her wasted life may make
it impossible for her to continue it. In any case, the
degree of ambivalence, an inevitable factor in all bereavement, is likely to be stronger in this than in other
mourning situations.

The stories of Mrs. Green and Mrs. White illustrate
this dilemma.

MRS. GREEN

I know about Mrs. Green through her daughter, a very
successful professional, who came to me because during
her three years of marriage she had had several miscar-
riages. She was beginning to wonder whether the mis-
carriages were an expression of an ambivalent attitude
toward having children. Her sister, who was three years
younger but had married before her, was also still childless, and although she was in many ways very different,
she seemed to have similar problems. Could it be that

both daughters had taken over their mother's very ambivalent feelings about being a woman, a mother?

The mother herself had given up her career when she married the father, whom she had met at the university where they were both history students. She was two years older, but at the time they met, she had been made to feel that she would never get far with her studies and was sadly discouraged, while he, undoubtedly much more gifted, had already been earmarked for a brilliant career. As soon as they decided to get married, she gave up all ambitions for herself. After the marriage she used everything she had, any money she could earn in teaching jobs, any skill she had acquired in their mutual field of work, all her mothering and caring, and later, when he became a prominent internationally known historian, all her gifts as an untiring hostess to support him and to further his career. It seemed that she had no needs, no interests, no friends of her own. She totally fitted into his pattern. To be needed by him seemed to be the essence of her life, and he constantly confirmed his need for her. For example, he would say that he could not write a word unless she was sitting opposite him at the table. Yet, in fact, he did not make it possible for her to participate in his work. Her own ambivalence surfaced sometimes in sudden attacks on his work, in a belittling of his achievement. At the same time, she often behaved like a little girl, as if she were his pupil rather than his wife. She never admitted that she was two years older and talked of an age difference of a few days.

The father's life involved a great many social engagements, receptions, conventions, and entertaining, and it was important to both parents that the mother be included—always as his shadow or his hostess, never as a near colleague, somebody who, after all, had shared his studies. Although she would never miss any of these social occasions, she did sometimes explode with rather bitter jokes about her part in them. She confided to her daughters that she found it difficult to go to these parties, and said that she was a hive of nerves while there.

She was taller than her husband and stooped in order to appear smaller. Her daughter sadly recalls that she could never be proud of her mother, who stood and dressed badly and looked old for her years. She wonders what her father might have felt on these occasions. Although the mother took no trouble over her appearance, she was highly critical of it. Her daughter found snapshots of hers with denigrating remarks, such as: "Why do I have to look so coy?"; "What an unbecoming dress"; "I ought to have kept in the background." But even without any comments, the photos show an uncertain, rather anxious-looking woman, lacking in self-respect and dignity. The sole exception is one taken in college with her roommate, dressed up in a crazy mixture of clothes for a carnival. She was known as Peter in college—and so far as one can guess from this snapshot and from the stories she told about this time and this friend, she was full of life and fun then. Did she give all this up for her husband or for her womanhood?

None of her doubts ever came into the open. The couple were inseparable and their two daughters were included in the family closeness and colluded in the established pattern, in which the father was the center of the universe. This near-claustrophobic closeness of the small family strongly contrasted with but was unaffected by their lively social life. The daughters both felt the contrast in the insistence on this close tie and the lack of real interest in them as individuals. Yet they were very distinctly different women: the older one was predominantly intellectual; the younger had only feminine interests. Were these differences ignored by the parents because they could not risk having any between themselves? Another contradiction which puzzled the daughters was that despite their father's unquestioned dominance and prominence, their mother not only shaped their lives and images of themselves, but also gave them the feeling of some hidden strength. They would joke about mother's "secret weapon," which she used cunningly while pretending to be helpless and weak. Part of this weapon was her ability to scrape together secret funds (the family was always badly off financially), which she disclosed in moments of crisis, always for her husband or the family, never for herself.

The daughters attributed the claustrophobic closeness of their family largely to the fact that the parents, who both came from New Zealand, had never really settled in England, where they moved after eight years of marriage when their father was on the way to becoming "a prominent man." They had been childless for seven years, so that my informant was just a year old when they arrived in England. The parents never stopped longing for New Zealand, which remained "home" for them and where they both had many relatives.

The father's parents came from large and very successful professional families, and he felt himself to be a member of this large intellectual clan even though he himself had only one brother, and his father was a modest Baptist minister. When he was fifteen he went to live with an uncle who was head of a college, to which he was admitted as a preparation for the university. He was earmarked for a successful academic career from the start.

The mother's parents also came from large families (her mother was the youngest of thirteen). Both these parental families were very supportive, and from the age of three, the mother, who was an only child, was sent to one of them for the summer months, traveling alone by boat with a cardboard label containing names and addresses hung around her neck. However much she may have enjoyed the country holidays with her relatives, the foundations for her feelings of inferiority and inadequacy were probably laid there.

The mother's father managed a small bakery, but his wife had other dreams—and great ambitions for her only daughter. It was largely her drive which secured the girl a university education. That Mrs. Green failed to fulfill her mother's ambitions must later have made her husband's outstanding career doubly important to her. Through him she could fulfill her own and her mother's dreams, and give meaning to her life.

No wonder, therefore, that he became the center of her life, and that the children often felt in the way, a nuisance—especially while they were little and needed her time, love, and presence most. She made no bones about the fact that small children bored her, and would later say to her growing daughters, "Don't you ever expect me to be a doting grandmother."

Mrs. Green had always been rather delicate but denied any need for rest and care, and was determined to keep going for her husband and family. Her husband, however, was very robust and strong until he had a heart attack two years before his death. He tried to ignore this; like his wife he rejected any care and would work hard in the garden on Sundays, digging and chopping wood. His daughter recalls a hospital visit for a checkup on which she accompanied him. He was running vigorously along the corridors, and she could not keep up with him. When she begged him to slow down, he said, "When I am running, they can't say I am ill." He hated comments on his health, and his sudden death from a coronary came as a great shock to the family. The mother had really been more ill than he; it was her health about which the daughters had worried.

It was not a surprise when their mother had a stroke immediately after her husband's funeral. While the doctors were still disputing whether she could be nursed at home, she had two more strokes in quick succession and was admitted to the hospital. She lived for another five months, paralyzed and with a severe speech impediment but fully conscious, except that she refused to accept the fact of her husband's death and disputed every proof of it. She had her own certain evidence that he was alive, for he visited her at the hospital, flying in through the window. As this was the only symptom of delusion in her otherwise rational behavior, her daughters and friends accepted it as a sick woman's valid defense against the shock of loss. This attitude was maintained for about four months after her husband's death, until the day when the family lawyer called on her to discuss the will and estate. He arrived at ten o'clock in the morning and found her fresh and lively. As soon as he tried to discuss the estate, which was, after all, evidence of her husband's death, she became completely unable to speak. At this moment she accepted that her husband was dead, and then made no further efforts to live. She deteriorated rapidly and died within a month.

MRS. WHITE

Mrs. White, a very attractive woman in her fifties, came to see me in a state of acute anxiety a few days after the second anniversary of her husband's death. She had traveled to London from Chile, where she lived, in the hope that this would help her to feel better, as London had always been a happy place for her and her husband Paul. She had met him in London, while she was an art student and he was training as a journalist. They had both loved London, which they often revisited with great happiness. But this time London had let her down, she felt restless and frightened, could not sleep or eat, did not want to see her friends, everything and everybody seemed hostile and threatening.

Mrs. White had been the only child of parents who adored her and each other. Her father was a successful businessman, whose international business centered on their big, beautiful home, and his wife was the hostess for his many customer/friends. Their daughter fitted in happily, but in her late teens she felt the need to get away, to develop her artistic talents and discover herself more. Hence the decision to train in London. Her parents, though sad to let her go, supported her in every way, and she had two very happy years in London.

When she and Paul decided to get married, they returned to Chile, where, by chance, Paul also had spent most of his childhood. Her parents were delighted to welcome him into the family. Her father had a charming small house built for them, next to his own big one. After a year, Paul agreed to give up journalism and become his father-in-law's business partner. The Whites had two children, a boy and a girl, both healthy, happy, attractive, and intelligent. Life was very good—without a flaw. She herself had given up her interest in art and lived in her three-generation family. She was happy to "fit in," feeling that this was right for everybody concerned, and there was nothing she missed.

The couple had been married for twenty years when both of Mrs. White's parents died in quick succession. Her father had a rapidly progressing cancer, and her mother died a few months later of a "broken heart." It seemed at the time that it could not have been otherwise, the two had been so close, so much one.

At about the same time, Mrs. White's children were beginning to leave home. The daughter went to Paris, to an art college, and later married a French colleague. She now has two children and lives in France. The son lived in Boston, studying law, and had a serious girlfriend.

For business reasons, Mr. and Mrs. White moved into the parents' house. She took over her mother's role, which was familiar to her. She became hostess to her husband's friends, accompanied him on his wide travels, and shared everything with him. She wanted nothing more, and they were very happy. In spite of being so tied to the business, they had marvelous vacations. For their thirtieth wedding anniversary, they went to Mexico and had a wonderful time together. Then one night, without warning, her husband called out for her—he was not well, and within minutes died in her arms.

She could not comprehend it, could not let him go, was quite unable to do anything. The hotel manager called her son, who took over. He did everything that had to be done for the father's funeral and memorial service and decided to come live with his mother. He gave up his law practice and took over his father's business and role in the house. Mrs. White does not know for how long she stayed in her numbed apathy, many months she thinks. When she began to live again with some degree of consciousness, there was her son in her husband's place, and she turned to him in every way as she had to his father. Sometimes she called him by her husband's name.

Then, after the first anniversary of Paul's death, she began to feel that her son was depressed, that he did not really like the business or the house, that his girlfriend was angry with him for having given up his own life and jeopardized hers, that things just were not right. What was she to do? How could she, or the business, survive without him? She became restless, had all sorts of physical ailments, became increasingly unsure of herself, frightened, desperate. It was then that she decided to come to London, and later to visit her daughter in Paris. But now that London had been such a disappointment she felt unable to do this either. Would it be best to return home and be miserable there?

During Mrs. White's five-week stay in London I saw her ten times. Her panic subsided during our first talk, in which she made me feel that she was very near to finding her own solution and needed only some support in clarifying and facing it. Although she had been as closely identified with her husband as her parents had been with each other, she had rejected her mother's solution—not to survive her husband. What she had to face now was that she had avoided mourning her husband by replacing him with her son as soon as she "came back to life" after the period of numbness, apathy, near unconsciousness.

In this attempt to avoid the pain of grief, she transferred onto her son some of the feelings she had had for her husband, identified with him in the same way, and put him into the same roles. By doing so, she never internalized her lost husband, a necessary prerequisite to mourning, and therefore never completed her mourning process. Only when she realized that what had felt so right in relation to her parents and her husband felt wrong and destructive in relation to her son, who had his own life to live, was she able to give up the longed for solution of repeating her familiar pattern of identification. Her flight to London was an unconscious attempt to break the vicious circle, to give up the protective cover and face her loss, pain, and grief. Her anger with London, her feeling of hostility and persecution, became an expression of a delayed mourning process, in which she felt helped and supported by her sessions with me.

She wondered if she would have been able to survive if her son had not accepted her transfer of feelings onto him—or whether she would have died, like her mother. But in talking about it, she felt that even at the moments of greatest despair, she had always known that she wanted to live and that she had enough strength to do so. She felt sad that she had so "misused" her son, but "eternally grateful" that he had helped her in the transition to life without making her feel that she had irrevocably damaged him.

After five weeks she went to Paris to see her daughter and her family. I got a postcard saying that she was delighted with her daughter's life, her artistic achievements, and most of all with her grandchildren. Three months later she wrote from Santiago that she had found an apartment in an artists' colony and had taken up painting again. Her son was in the process of selling the big house, handing the business over to a partner, and returning to his previous law practice. He was planning to marry his girlfriend. A year later she wrote a short note to say that all was going well, and that she herself was thinking of remarrying, an old artist friend who was widowed. "We have much in common but, don't worry, I have learned my lesson," which I read as meaning: I have found my own identity and am not giving it up again.

On the face of it, the stories of Mrs. Green and Mrs. White were similar. They were both only children, very close to their parents, had both trained for careers different from their parents', which they gave up when they got married, and from then on used all their accomplishments and resources to support their husbands in their work. Both husbands colluded with the existing pattern of identification with the parents, and accepted the parents' projections on them. Mr. Green became the successful academic his mother-in-law had longed for. Mr. White became the ideal partner and successor in his father-in-law's business. Both women were in their fifties when their husbands died unexpectedly, and both had two children who at the time of bereavement had left home but were available and supportive to their widowed mothers. Neither of them was faced with serious external problems. Both were deeply shocked by their husbands' deaths, could not acknowledge the reality of their loss, and felt their own existence threatened.

Mrs. Green succumbed to this threat and died soon

after her husband. Mrs. White, after two years of confusion and struggle, achieved an independent existence and built a new life. Is there something in what we know of these two women's previous histories to explain these differing solutions to bereavement in apparently similar situations?

From the age of three Mrs. Green was sent off each summer by boat, all alone, to travel to relatives. These vacations were presented to her as a pleasure and a treat, but the little girl, who for the rest of the year lived closely with her parents, may well have felt rejected and have been very scared. This confusing situation made for insecurity in her inner world, and was difficult for a small child to assimilate.

Later when she left her father's bakery to go to the university she again was offered independence and growth but felt that she was being sent away to fulfill her parents' needs, especially her mother's ambition. How little this move expressed her own needs we can see from the readiness, almost relief, with which she gave up any attempt at a career of her own after her marriage.

What sense of identity Mrs. Green had was built on her identification with the projections of others, and it was this method of relating which she transferred onto her husband. He was ideally suited for this role, for he was the exact fulfillment of her mother's ambitions. By providing this successful son-in-law, she gave her mother the gratification she had failed to give her directly. From then on she saw her role as strengthening and supporting this source of satisfaction, for herself and her family, by abnegating herself. As an autonomous person there was nothing for her to do. Immediately after her husband's death, she had a stroke, but continued to live as long as she could deny the reality of his death. When this was no longer possible, she died.

Mrs. White also had lived in close identification first

with her parents and later with her husband. But she had had more emotional security in her early life. When, in adolescence, she wanted to go abroad and study to be an artist, she did so with her parents' support. When she brought her husband home, the young family patterned their life on that of the parents, on the basis of mutual support and affection. In this "ideal" three-generation family there appeared to have been little strain and conflict, little opportunity to learn to tolerate frustration. When Mrs. White's father died, and her mother followed him within weeks, Mrs. White and her husband immediately moved into the parents' house and unquestioningly assumed their role in the business and in society. The pattern of fitting in, of cooperative identification, was continued without apparent effort or pain, and without any struggle for individual autonomy.

At the unexpected death of her husband, Mrs. White's world was shattered. After the first phase of shock and numbness, she attempted to rebuild it by replacing her husband with her son, resuming the same pattern of identification with him in denial of pain, mourning, and loss. Two years later Mrs. White became aware that her familiar pattern of relating was inappropriate to her new situation. It was at this point that she accepted the reality of her husband's death and began to mourn.

In her delayed mourning process Mrs. White was able to fall back on the internalized "good" parents and her happy early life. This enabled her to test out her inner resources and gain the strength to complete and survive the task of mourning.

Mrs. Green, on the other hand, who in many ways had also tried to avoid conflict by identifying with the important people in her life, was too unsure of her own autonomy and worth to face the loss of her husband. She could not draw strength from internalized "good objects," which might have enabled her to survive, and died.

It seems, therefore, that these two women's different responses to their in many ways similar bereavement situations can best be understood in terms of their early experiences.

6.

Processes of Mourning and Grief

An increasing number of psychological studies in recent years reflect a growing interest in grief and bereavement. This trend appears to be due partly to an attempt to break down social taboos about death and mourning. Recent uncertainties about boundaries between mental health and mental illness also may have made it more urgent to conceptualize distinctions between normal and pathological mourning, and between grief and illness. However, since the nature of mourning is so manifold, and the reactions of individual personalities vary so widely, a comprehensive definition is difficult to find. To cope with this problem, attempts have been made to break down the process of mourning into observable phases, and although the number of phases and the emphases on them varies in different studies, a picture is now emerging which is helpful for understanding and assessment.

All studies agree that *shock* is the first response to the death of an important person, and that shock will be particularly pronounced at sudden unexpected death. It may find expression in physical collapse (as with Tony and Mrs. Green), in violent outbursts (such as Yvonne's), or in dazed withdrawal, denial, and inability to take in the reality of death (Mrs. White).

Mourners often complain that they were not prepared for what it would be like: "Why did nobody warn me that I would feel so sick . . . or tired . . . or exhausted?"; "Nobody ever told me that grief felt so like fear"; "I wish I had known about the turmoil of emotions." But can anybody tell or warn, can books really help? Or is grief one of those emotional learning situations in which theory makes sense only after the experience?

Yet here I am, writing a book about grief and mourning, hoping that even if it does not help the problems of immediate bereavement, it may help toward creating a climate in which these are not increased by the bewildered and uncomprehending responses of others. And that, once the state of shock and confusion is over, the mourner's shame and anxiety about his irrational behavior may be lessened by the knowledge that this is the universal and natural response to grief and loss, and that he is not only entitled to have and express these feelings, but that it would be wrong and perhaps harmful not to do so.

The attempts of the bereaved to cope with this first phase of shock and confusion will vary with his temperament and situation. He may be completely numbed and apathetic or he may be overactive. For physical shock, rest and warmth are the recognized methods of treatment, yet the most frequent advice given for the emotional shock of grief is to "keep going," "get busy." This "remedy" may not only set the scene for a denial of loss and pain and subsequent pathological development, but it is likely to lead to all sorts of disasters. I know from my own experience and that of others the frightening and exhausting results of the innumerable blunders of those first busy days—the things mislaid, lost, wrongly

addressed, and so on, and the agonizing attempts to retrieve them. For example, having collected my husband's
most important papers from his lawyer, I managed to
throw them into a strange letter box. Why, then, this
advice to "get busy"? Does it express the adviser's fear
of getting involved in the mourner's pain? Geoffrey
Gorer says, "Giving way to grief is stigmatised as morbid, unhealthy, demoralising. The proper action of a
friend and well-wisher is felt to be distraction of a
mourner from his/her grief."[1]

There may also be in this desire to distract a recognition that the newly bereaved who finds it difficult to rest
and sleep even at night is unlikely to be able to relax, and
therefore it is better to "keep going." The mourner's
restlessness may be his anxiety about having to acknowledge that he is alone, abandoned. What he may need most
is the physical comfort of another person's presence, and
in our modern condition of isolation such comfort often
is not available.

The most common "solution" for widows and widowers is to fill the empty space in the double bed with a
child. As the need for warmth and comfort will last
beyond the usually short phase of shock, this "replacement," which may well meet the child's conscious or
unconscious wishes to take the place of the dead parent
in relation to the living one, may induce a situation
which later could become difficult to resolve, and could
lead to neurotic problems and dependence. Often a pet
is used to mitigate the misery of lonely nights. A more
satisfactory solution was found by one widow, who after
an initial period of sleeplessness could happily go to
sleep cuddling a bolster, just like a baby who needs a
teddy bear to go to sleep without his mother. Why not

1. *Death, Grief and Mourning in Contemporary Britain* (London: Cresset Press, 1965), p. 130.

acknowledge and satisfy without shame the baby needs stirred up by bereavement?

Usually the phase of acute shock lasts only a few days and is followed by what one might call a *controlled phase*, in which arrangements have to be made and the funeral faced and endured, and during which the mourner is surrounded and supported by relatives and friends. This period of support and the form it takes vary not only according to tradition, culture, and social and religious group, but also in the interpretation of the supportive function. This may support the mourner's super-ego with expressed or implicit demands for mature behavior or it may support the mourner's regressive needs with the expectation that he give vent to grief. In either case the presence and sympathy of others, the "special" position in which he finds himself, will give the mourner a sense of safety. He may literally feel that the others will see to it that things do not get out of control, that life goes on.

The real pain and misery makes itself felt when this controlled phase, and the privileges that went with it, is over, and the task of testing reality, coming to terms with the new situation, and the painful withdrawal of libido from the lost person begin. It is then that the mourner feels lost and abandoned and attempts to develop defenses against the agonies of pain. *Searching* for the lost person, an almost automatic universal defense against accepting the reality of the loss, may go on for a long time. C. M. Parkes quotes from a catalogue to an exhibition of the works of Kaethe Kollwitz:

Over a number of years, K. Kollwitz worked on a monument for her young son who was killed in October 1914. His death became for her a sort of personal obligation. Two years later she noted in her diary: "There is a drawing made, a mother letting her dead son slide into her arms. I could do a hundred similar drawings, but still can't seem to come any closer to him. I'm still searching for him as if it were in the very work itself that I had to find him."[2]

Searching is the principal behavior pattern evoked by loss. Children and animals search for the absent object. The bereaved adult, even if he is aware of the irrational component in his behavior, keeps on searching for his dead, during unguarded moments, in hallucinations, and especially in his dreams. My neighbor Andrew ("Discussion," Chapter 4) is a vivid example. Again and again in his dreams he tried, with great urgency, to get to a place where he might find his lost wife. His dreams were a wish for a miracle.

Most people are not aware of their need to search but express it in restless behavior, tension, and loss of interest in all that does not concern the deceased. These symptoms lessen as bit by bit the reality of the loss can be accepted and the bereaved slowly, slowly rebuilds his inner world. Yet I wonder whether the impulse to search for the lost person ever completely disappears. Even for those bereaved who have successfully built a new life, search for the lost love object persists at moments of great strain, weakness, or illness, just as the dying person often recalls memories of his childhood and appears to be searching for his first love objects, his parents.

As the bereaved becomes more relaxed, and tension, frustration, and pain decrease, *searching* may lead to *finding* a sense of the lost person's presence. C.S. Lewis says in *A Grief Observed:*

... as I have discovered, passionate grief does not link us with the dead but cuts us off from them. This

2. Colin Murray Parkes, *Bereavement: Studies of Grief in Adult Life* (London: Tavistock Publications, 1972), p. 39.

becomes clearer and clearer. It is just at those moments when I feel least sorrow—getting into my morning bath is one of them—that H [his wife] rushes upon my mind in her full reality, her otherness. Not, as in my worst moments, all foreshortened and patheticised and solemnised by miseries, but as she is in her own right. This is good and tonic.[3]

For me it took years before I could experience this "tonic" of Fritz's presence, and it is a wonderful surprise that this is increasing as time goes on. It happens most often on waking (when he used to come in with my breakfast tray, and now does so in my vision) or at night, when I go to sleep. It has nothing of the supernatural about it, and is a reassuring, gratifying experience which feels absolutely realistic. Other widows have told me of the same experience and of it becoming more frequent as they relax in their new life and the "pining" stops or at least decreases. For whatever the mitigating experiences, depression and despair will come and go, reappearing—if all goes well—at longer intervals, staying for shorter spells. If mourners can accept and understand this, they will feel less pain and anxiety about "relapses."

There are no timetables for what have been called phases of mourning, nor are there distinct lines of demarcation for the various symptoms of grief which find expression during these phases. For the bereaved, the most alarming and bewildering aspects of grief are those in which he can no longer recognize himself, for example, the often irrational anger and hostility, which may be quite alien to the mourner's usual behavior and may make him feel that he is going insane. I still remember with shame my own completely mad anger when an otherwise loved relative carried an umbrella for an occa-

3. London: Faber and Faber, 1961, pp. 44–45.

sion on which I found it inappropriate. Anger and hostility may take quite irrational forms and be directed not only against the medical people who looked after the deceased, but against the nearest and dearest, including the dead person himself. They express the ambivalence of the mourner toward all these people but most especially, and most painfully, toward the lost person who is causing him so much distress by his abandonment. One of the aspects of this distress is that neither the love for the lost person nor the person himself was perfect. "A stable adjustment to another's death involves assimilating both the loved and the hated elements of his personality. As a consequence the bereaved must experience some self-hate, some self-accusation, some guilt."[4]

Here we can perhaps see most clearly the repetition of childhood responses toward the loved parent who, when he leaves the child, is hated and becomes the object of murderous fantasies. Ambivalence toward the absent mother or the dead person is more than just mixed feelings about them. Mixed feelings may be based on a conscious, realistic assessment of the imperfect nature of these people; ambivalence only becomes a conscious process with difficulty, by overcoming resistances. Its pain is caused by contradictory and interdependent feelings of love and hate for the same person. The infant has to cope with the terror that his hate will kill his mother, and that he will then lose her forever. The adult mourner who has lost his loved object forever relives the infantile terror that his hate and lack of love have brought about the loss.

Ambivalence is inseparable from guilt, and there is always guilt at the death of an important person—guilt about what has been said or not said, done or not done, justified guilt and guilt which has no rational justifica-

4. John Hinton, *Dying* (Penguin, 1971), p. 181.

tion. Perhaps the most painful and confusing guilt is about the moments—however fleeting—of triumph that the other one is dead, and I am alive! Yet just as with mixed feelings, guilt can also be based on realistic regrets about insufficient care and concern for the dead. Often it is a mixture of justified and unjustified feelings, and it is this mixture which makes it so difficult to live with guilt.

We all know situations in which a mourner who has behaved very badly toward the person who died can find relief for his guilt only by devoting his life to paying restitution. Uncle Jack, the uncle of a friend of mine, was such a person. While his wife, Molly, was alive, he had given her a miserable time. Until she married her grumpy, bad-tempered husband, Molly was a lively and charming woman. The couple had two sons and lived in Yorkshire where Uncle Jack bought farms and converted them into small holdings. Before or during the conversion periods, he lived with his family in makeshift arrangements. Their home was sometimes in the manor house, empty, barely furnished, with splendid marble fireplaces but no money to provide heat in the winter; sometimes they had to make do in shacks on the building site. In either case, they were always on the move, never settled, never had a comfortable home. The frequent moves also involved frequent changes of schools for the boys and, as a result, poor educational records, which contributed to their insecurity and aggressiveness.

In addition, there was never any money, not so much because Uncle Jack did not have any as that he needed what he had for new conversions and persuaded his wife that he could not spare anything for the household. It was she who had to earn what the family needed, and as a trained schoolteacher, she managed to do this. But the frequent moves naturally also affected her jobs, and made life unbearably hard, especially since her husband never acknowledged the difficulties he made for her. Whenever she had a problem finding a new job or had to accept an inferior, badly paid one, he blamed her incompetence.

There was no sign of love or mutual concern between the parents. The only affection in the household was between mother and sons. The boys were sorry for their mother and hated their mean, bad-tempered father.

The gay, beautiful Molly, turned into a sad, prematurely aged wife, and at the age of fifty suddenly, without fuss, she died of a stroke in her classroom.

From the moment of his wife's death, Uncle Jack was desolate. He immediately stopped all work, lost all interest in his farms, and bought a house next to the churchyard where Molly was buried. In one of the ground floor rooms he had a special window made so that he could look out on Molly's grave. He had the most expensive, most impressive memorial built for his wife, whom throughout their married life he had neglected and humiliated. Now he liked to think and talk of her, as of a cherished, very special, very important person. For the rest of his life, six full years, he sat by the window staring at her grave.

When Uncle Jack died, not yet sixty, he had not really been ill but simply gave up his futile life. His one wish was to be buried next to his wife, and to share with her the V.I.P. memorial which he had built in idealization of her and which was to reflect some glory on himself. Such idealization of the deceased may express an attempt at restitution and a defense against the pain of guilt.

Often idealization is closely linked to identification with the lost person. Identification appears to be a feature in all cases of bereavement, varying only in degree, and can be seen as one aspect of the necessary task of internalizing the lost person. It gives comfort to the mourner, makes him feel close to the deceased, and thus mitigates somewhat the pain of loss. Robin (Chapter 4) not only wanted to please Anne by doing what she used to do or wanted him to do, he was also aware that he felt much better if he was like Anne, whom he saw as perfect since her death.

It is well known that mourners often get the illness which led to the death of a close person. Habits and interests of the deceased may be taken over indiscriminately. A woman in her forties was never interested in gardening before losing a brother who had been a passionate gardener. After his death she compulsively got up every day at sunrise to tend the garden, since she felt this was what her brother wanted her to do.

A hitherto rather dull wife whose witty husband had died surprised herself and all around her by her newly acquired gift of repartee. She tried to explain this by saying alternately, "I have to do it for him now" or, "It isn't really me, he speaks out of me" (like a ventriloquist). This same woman, partner in a very good, loving marriage, told me that she had always been amused by her husband's patient peeling of the top of his boiled egg, while she used to cut it off. "Now," she said, "I just cannot bring myself to cut the top off, I have to peel it off patiently."

Another woman, who had always been upset (and often nagging) about her husband's bad table manners, developed these same manners after his death. Freud says: "If one has lost an object or has to give it up, one often compensates oneself by identifying oneself with it."[5] Identification with those aspects of the bereaved's personality which have been previously rejected (such as

---

5. Sigmund Freud, *New Introductory Lectures* in *Complete Psychological Works of Sigmund Freud (Standard Edition)*, trans. and ed. James Strachey (London: Hogarth Press, 1953–66), vol. 22, p. 86.

the bad table manners) may be an attempt at restitution, at repairing the rejection. Identification and restitution, anger, hostility, and guilt may all be interwoven during the mourning process. There are no distinct boundaries or timetables. Identification with the lost object, in Freud's sense, is a filling up, a replenishment of the self, in order to become a stronger, better integrated, more separate person. It is quite distinct from the identification with a marriage partner that I have been discussing in previous chapters, which implies a weakening, a giving-up of the self.

Perhaps the most important and critical, and also the most painful and bewildering, phase of grief is *regression*, which I discussed more fully in Chapter 3. People who believe strongly in self-discipline and control may be puzzled by regressive behavior in themselves and others. The bereaved may feel frightened and ashamed of the childish and irrational actions which neither he nor the people around him seem able to understand. What he needs most are sympathy and loving acceptance, which will make him feel secure. If these are lacking, the mourner is in great danger of getting stuck in the regression which may then lead to illness. The fear that the regression will last forever probably causes anxiety to all bereaved people. In my case material as well as in encounters I have not reported, people have said, "I felt like I was going insane"; "I was terrified that things were beyond my control." The terror of these people is not just because they behaved in a childish way, but because of the compulsion to do it.

We have seen earlier how in grief the mourner falls back on methods which in childhood helped to control and master pain. Regressive behavior is one of these. The three-year-old who starts wetting and soiling again after the birth of a rival sibling is asking for extra care and attention. Both the small child who wants to be a baby again and the adult in pain learn to use regression in their new situation to gain comfort and love. If the desired response is forthcoming, the toddler can move on and make a step toward growth, become the "big" brother or sister. The regression of the adult mourner can alternate with expressions of exceptional maturity and self-discipline (as in the case of the woman who gave in to her most infantile needs when she wrapped herself in a soaking hot bathtowel, but showed outstanding strength and control by reading one of the lessons at her husband's memorial service). Regression in grief must be seen and supported as a means toward adaptation and health.

THE PHASE OF ADAPTATION

There are two points on which all studies of grief and mourning agree. I have already mentioned the first, that shock is the initial response to bereavement. The second is much more difficult to define. It is the fundamental importance of being able to mourn and to "complete the mourning process." What exactly does this mean?

We have seen that the course of mourning cannot be predicted because it depends on many factors, such as the relationship between the lost person and the survivor, the circumstances of the death, the external situation, and the inner resources of the bereaved. Therefore, however much we learn about patterns of mourning, they will take different forms with each individual. The precondition for a person to "complete" his mourning process must be that he is allowed to mourn in his own way and time.

There is no norm for mourning and no norm for adaptation; nor can there be any definite time limit for either. The time mentioned in studies for the various phases and for the total process of mourning is too short to fit the needs of many mourners. One year, comprehending the full circle of the seasons with their birth and death symbols, may be the most meaningful "objective" period of time for the completion of the mourning process, although I have known mourners who after the loss of their partners suffered from episodes of depression, despair, and regressive setbacks for well over two years and later made exceptionally good adaptations to a new life. Even then, periods of despair and grief as well as searching may recur in special external or internal situations, such as an anniversary or illness. These recurrences should not be regarded as pathological. The only valid criterion for pathological grief is that the mourner is unable to cope with his life. In any case, there is never just a continuous progress with a definite date for adaptation, and periods of apparently good recovery may well be followed by periods of pathology.

Recovery from the wound of grief has been compared with recovery from a physical wound. Physicians can alleviate pain and support the natural healing powers of physical wounds, but for the wound caused by the loss of a loved person there has been great uncertainty in our time and culture as to how far and in what way help can be given. In the loneliness and isolation of modern society every mourner needs special sympathy and support from the people around him.

The mourning process involves the healing of a wound. Once the physical wound has been safely covered by healthy tissue, the process is completed and the patient does well to forget all about the injury. In mourning, however, the cause of the injury, the loss of an important person, must not be forgotten. Only when the lost person has been internalized and becomes part of the bereaved, a part which can be integrated with his own personality and enriches it, is the mourning process complete, and now the adjustment to a new life has to be made. The bereaved who has never been able to face his own death cannot successfully make this adjustment. Samuel Johnson said: "Our fear of death is so great, that the whole of life is but keeping away the thoughts of it." In 1755, after his wife's death, he wrote: "I have ever since seemed to myself broken off from mankind; a kind of solitary wanderer in the wild of life, without any direction, or fixed point of view; a gloomy gazer on the world to which I have little relation."[6] Repressed or delayed mourning may contribute to such a condition, and may lead to an impoverished life.

In his major contribution to the theme of grief in "Mourning and Melancholia," Freud makes clear that

> although grief involves grave departures from the normal attitude to life, it never occurs to us to regard it as a morbid condition and hand the mourner over to medical treatment. We rest assured that after a lapse of time it will be overcome, and we look upon any interference with it as inadvisable or even harmful.

"What is the task which the work of mourning performs?" Freud asks—and answers, "The testing of reality, having shown that the loved person no longer exists, requires forthwith that all the libido shall be withdrawn from its attachments to this object." In other words, faced with the fact of death, the bereaved has to withdraw his emotional attachment from the deceased.

Freud then speaks of the struggle which arises from this demand, a struggle which can be so intense "that a turning away from reality ensues, the object being clung to through the medium of hallucinatory wish-psychosis." The difficulty of facing another's death is sometimes so strong as to make the acceptance of reality impossible.

6. James Boswell, *Life of Johnson*, R. W. Chapman and J. D. Fleeman, eds. (Oxford University Press, 1970), pp. 416, 196.

An example of hallucinatory wish-psychosis would be Mrs. Green's vision of her husband flying in through the hospital window to visit her. But as Freud says, "The normal outcome is that deference for reality gains the day . . . Why this process of carrying out the behest of reality bit by bit, which is in the nature of compromise, should be so extraordinarily painful is not at all easy to explain in terms of mental economics. It is worth noting that this pain seems natural to us."[7]

Melanie Klein, whose contribution to the subject is pre-eminent, goes some way toward answering Freud's question about mental economics:

> The pain experienced in the slow process of testing reality in the work of mourning seems to be partly due to the necessity, not only to renew the links to the external world and thus continuously re-experience the loss, but at the same time, and by means of this, to rebuild with anguish the inner world, which is felt to be in danger of deteriorating and collapsing.[8]

In "Mourning and Melancholia" Freud stresses as the paramount task in mourning the withdrawal of libido from the dead person, and lays no emphasis on the other, perhaps even more important part of the task, that of internalizing the lost love object. This is probably because his concern in this work is to contrast the relative normality of the process of mourning with the relatively pathological state of melancholia. At that time, Freud was not primarily interested in mourning as such. Later on, in *The Ego and the·Id* (1923), he put forward the notion that the withdrawal of the libido that attaches one

7. Sigmund Freud, *Standard Edition*, vol. 14, p. 244.
8. "Mourning and Its Relationship to Manic-depressive States," *International Journal of Psycho-Analysis* 21 (1940): 125.

person to another can only take place when the lost person is reinstated with the Ego.

Abraham, in his *Short Study of the Development of the Libido*, says, "The loved object is not gone, for now I carry it within myself and can never lose it."[9] This process of internalizing the dead, taking the deceased into oneself and containing him so that he becomes part of one's inner self, is the most important task in mourning. It does not happen immediately; for a varying span of time the bereaved is still in touch with the external presence of the lost person. Once the task of internalizing has been achieved, the dependence on the external presence diminishes and the bereaved becomes able to draw on memories, happy or unhappy, and to share these with others, making it possible to talk, think, or feel about the dead person.

From the moment life begins through all the phases of child development, human growth depends on accepting and mastering loss—loss of the safety in the womb, loss of the breast, loss, real, fantasied or threatened. Melanie Klein (in her paper "Mourning and Its Relationship to Manic–depressive States") sees the "infantile depressive position" (the sadness which we can sometimes see in the expression of a preverbal baby who seems to tell us that he is frightened and feels lost because the "good" mother has deserted him and has become "bad") as the first response to the threat of loss, a threat which rouses feelings of hate toward the loved mother, whose loss is feared. The contradicting feelings for the same person, which are struggling inside the baby, are his first frightening experience of ambivalence. They set the scene for all the future struggles in this major human predicament, to come to terms with ambivalence, and the contradicting

9. Karl Abraham, "A Short Study of the Development of the Libido," in *Selected Papers* (London: Hogarth Press, 1924), p. 437.

forces which make up the inner and outer worlds.

To cope with loss, the child has to take into itself the object whose absence frightens him—in other words, in order not to get too bewildered by the mother's comings and goings, the infant has to set up a permanent mother inside himself. If the real mother is felt to be more threatening than reassuring, or if the child feels her absence more than her presence, the internalized mother will be a "bad" instead of a "good" object. Melanie Klein sees success at establishing an internal "good" object in early childhood as a precondition for the ability to tolerate later anxiety about loss and separation. In adult mourning the fears of losing the internalized "good" parent are revived through the death of a loved person. This is what the mourner means when he says, "I have not only lost my husband (wife), I have lost everything good; I have lost myself." In the process of mourning, the bereaved will repeat the same defenses used in the infantile depressive position to master "bad" objects and the feelings they arouse, and to restore the "good" ones, in order to be able to cope with the ambivalence about the dead person who has deserted him. Just as the frightened child has to set up a permanent mother inside himself, the adult mourner has to internalize, take into himself, his loved object so that he will never lose it.

Klein's point that the child's internal "good" object is a precondition for the ability to tolerate loss and separation is taken further by John Bowlby's studies on separation.[10] Bowlby stresses the concepts of attachment and loss, and sees separation anxiety in early childhood as the main key to understanding the mourning process. Separation anxiety expresses dread of some unspecified danger, either from the outside or from mounting internal

10. *Attachment and Loss*, vol. 1, *Attachment* (London: Hogarth Press, 1969).

tension, and dread of losing the object believed capable of protecting or relieving one. The baby's first response to this threat is protest and screaming: followed, if the threat is not removed, by withdrawal, apathy, and despair.

Separation anxiety will be reactivated in all subsequent fears of losing a person to whom a deep attachment exists. It is a natural process and the basis for mourning. If a child has not experienced separation anxiety, this indicates that he has not been able to develop a true attachment, and his ability to cope with loss through mourning will be crippled. So will be his chances to internalize the lost person as part of the mourning process, and to strengthen his own identity with the support of the internalized object. In short, to tolerate separation anxiety and to mourn are signs of the healthy personality who is capable of deep attachment. Without real attachments, secure autonomy cannot be achieved.[11]*

11. John Bowlby, "Pathological Mourning and Childhood Mourning," *Journal of the American Psycho-Analytic Association:* 11 (1963): 500.

*I would like here to express my indebtedness to Colin Murray Parkes and to Yorick Spiegel, who through their untiring and sustained research have made major contributions to our knowledge in this field, and whose findings I have widely used. (Yorick Spiegel, *Der Prozess des Trauerns* (Munich: Kaiser Verlag, 1973).

I also want to mention those autobiographical publications which focus on the loss of a marriage partner and which have helped me to link the increased knowledge of processes of mourning with the individual mourner and his unique experience: C.S. Lewis, *A Grief Observed* (London: Faber and Faber, 1961); Mary Stott, *Forgetting's No Excuse* (London: Faber and Faber, 1973); Sarah Morris, *Grief and How to Live With It* (London: Allen and Unwin, 1971).

7.

Repressed Mourning

The stories in this chapter differ from the others in this book in that the focus is not on processes of grief and mourning but on an attempt at therapeutic intervention with problems which on the surface had nothing to do with bereavement.

The problems presented were as follows:

Dr. Allen had run away from her husband because she felt trapped, and both were utterly bewildered by her incomprehensible behavior.

Mr. and Mrs. Bond asked for help because the wife's sexual frustration threatened a marriage which was approaching its silver wedding anniversary.

The Cohn family came in because of the violent fights between mother and daughter and the father's involvement with them.

Mrs. Dean was worried about the behavior of her oldest son, and her inability to communicate with him.

The methods of therapy offered to these patients varied widely but in no case was there any original intention to explore bereavement situations. Dr. Allen and her husband were referred for marital therapy by a psychiatric department to which the wife had applied for admission. I saw them privately for a period of six months in conjoint, alternating with individual sessions, and had two follow-ups with the wife a year later.

Mr. and Mrs. Bond had applied to the Institute of Marital Studies, and were seen there for a limited period by a colleague and myself in conjoint sessions.

Mr. Cohn's long therapeutic contact with me was initiated by the psychiatrist who worked with his daughter, and went on for the most part in conjunction with hers and her mother's therapies with other individual therapists.

Mrs. Dean I saw privately in weekly sessions for about a year, during which time her son had intermittent treatment with another therapist. Once the pressure of the immediate crisis was removed, we had a flexible arrangement, meeting on demand at lengthening intervals. During the last five years we have just kept in touch, meeting a few times every year.

In spite of these different patterns of therapy, and the different symptoms that were presented, the problem that was soon revealed was the inability of these people to experience and express feelings and the resulting blockage in communication with the important people around them. As the therapeutic work continued, this blockage could be seen to be caused by prohibited or repressed grief from a previous loss through bereavement, which had occurred six, eight, forty, and five years respectively before the start of therapy.

These stories raise an urgent question: How many symptoms of physical or mental disturbance are caused by unrecognized repressed grief for the loss of an important person?

DR. ALLEN

Dr. Allen and her husband were both G.P.s, both in their thirties. They had been married for seven years, had no children, but were apparently very happy. They had never had an argument, never a cross word. They had much in common, had worked together, had saved and planned in order to buy a house. Moving into a home of their own, just two months before I met them, was a great achievement, a highlight of their lives. A few weeks later, without any warning, the wife walked out and immediately asked to be admitted to the psychiatric ward of the local hospital. The psychiatrist there could find no psychiatric disorder and after a session with her and her husband felt that the trouble lay in their marriage and referred them to me for marital therapy.

Our first session was very painful. Both husband and wife were utterly bewildered and hardly able to talk. The husband was angry and uncomprehending: he had always tried to make his wife happy. Why did she not tell him what was wrong? Why had she walked out without talking to him? How could he ever trust her again? The wife was depressed and puzzled by her own behavior, yet resentful of her husband's lack of sympathy with her in her misery. She did not know why she had walked out; something inside had forced her; she felt so trapped, so helpless and hopeless.

In the course of this first, difficult session I learned that the wife had been married before and that her first husband had died after a very short time. Something in the way she gave me these facts made me feel that this was connected with her present depression, and I invited her to come for a few individual talks.

She was an only child, born while her father was in the army and later a prisoner of war. She did not see him until she was seven years old. Her mother was headmistress at the school to which she went at four and a half and was always very busy. Dr. Allen was constantly made aware that she was the sole object of her mother's affection, and was allotted the special task of making her happy. Yet she also felt that she was a great burden for her hard-working mother. She was torn between wanting to be very good to please her mother, to be her best pupil, and a recurrent wish to rebel, be a nuisance, run away.

Talking about this, Dr. Allen saw how similar it was to her marriage. There too she had wanted very much to please her husband, to be a good wife, to have an ideal marriage—until she was overwhelmed by the feeling of being trapped and had to run away.

She could also recognize the need to run away in her teens. Ever since she was seven and her father had come home, she had been very torn in her loyalties between him and her mother. He was an exciting stranger with whom she fell in love, wanting to have him to herself and feeling intensely guilty toward her mother. In her teens she decided to leave home as soon as possible. To help sick people had always been her great passion; she had played "Doctor" from early childhood. She was overjoyed, therefore, to win a scholarship to a medical school, and dedicated herself to her studies.

In her last year, as a resident at a renal ward, she was in charge of a patient with kidney failure and a life expectancy of a few weeks. Frederic was much older, her father's age, widowed, with grown-up children. She fell passionately in love with him. He responded to her loving care and to the warmth of her affection with a spectacular improvement in his physical condition which was regarded as a miracle by all the medical personnel.

Just at the time when Dr. Allen had finished her residency at the hospital, Frederic was considered fit enough to be discharged. She managed to get a job at a maternity hospital in his home town and went to live with him and his children, who were about her age and made her very welcome. When Frederic was still alive after a further four months, they decided to get married. Six weeks later he had a severe setback, was rushed into the hospital, and died within a day. Talking about this, Dr. Allen said, "I felt completely dazed. Whatever was happening had nothing to do with Frederic and me—it was unreal, untrue, it just could not be. Only when my father came and I could sob on his shoulders did I accept for a fleeting moment that I had lost Frederic forever."

I saw Dr. Allen alone for six sessions in which she talked only about Frederic and their short life together. She sobbed and mourned—for the first time, eight years after his death. She said that at the time of her bereavement she had felt too dazed to mourn, and then everybody had said, "What a blessing that Frederic went so quickly, without suffering." And, "You are so young, so beautiful, you'll soon get over it." After all, she said, "I just could not be depressed or think about myself. I had to smile at my mothers and my babies." She went on living with Frederic's children. When she passed her final exams they gave a party for her, at which her present husband, George, was one of the guests. A year later she and George got married. She said that they had never considered having children, they were too interested in their work and too busy. After this statement, Dr. Allen was silent for a long while, and then started to cry. Later she told me how desperately she had wanted a child by Frederic, "even when I thought he had only weeks to live." But this craving had disappeared: "I think I have buried the wish for a child with Frederic."

A few weeks later, after a very painful session, she said, "I would now like a child by George—but I cannot ask him. If he does not respond exactly as I need him to respond, it will be finished forever." She asked me to have a talk with George, in the course of which it became clear how little he knew about his wife's first, short marriage. He had seen it as his job to cheer her up and make her forget this unhappy experience, to divert her thoughts. He adored her and wanted only what she wanted. Children—well, he would have liked a baby, but as she never expressed this wish, he had not asked her. Now he was delighted, for to have a baby was the surest proof that she would not leave him again.

Dr. Allen conceived soon after this session. She had a wonderful pregnancy, and both were very happy. But there were still moments of depression, and during the first few months of the pregnancy she found it difficult to rid herself of the fantasy that she was carrying Frederic's baby, his son, because the baby was only talked about as "he." In telling me this she recalled her adolescent fantasies about having a baby boy by her father— then quickly, and with obvious relief, spoke about her mother's joyous preparations for the baby, and her great excitement at becoming a grandmother.

In due course I was informed of the safe arrival of a girl, and soon she was proudly shown off to me. Dr. Allen was overwhelmed with joy. She could hardly let the baby out of her arms and never for a minute out of her sight. Again and again she said, "I can hardly believe that I have such a perfect baby." She giggled when she spoke of her delight at having a daughter, especially one who immediately after her birth had been such a ridiculous replica of George, "as if she wanted to proclaim to the world who her father was." Although Dr. Allen did not put it into words, she made clear what a relief it was to her that this baby girl had presented her with a reality which had finally destroyed the fantasies about having a son from her own father or from Frederic.

Later in our session she told me of a three-day period of post-partum depression after her discharge from the hospital, which had brought back to her the blackness of her previous breakdown. This had been terrifying, "but I shall be a much better doctor because of this experience." And, struggling after a long silence, she said, "It will always remain a nightmare and I still do not know what brought it about just at that time. All I know is that without that nightmare, I would never have had her. (Hugging the baby) I had to earn her by first going through the agonies of grief."

MR. AND MRS. BOND

Mrs. Bond made a frantic request for help to the Institute of Marital Studies because her husband could not give her sexual satisfaction, did not understand her, and was unfeeling and uncommunicative. The couple were in their early forties, had been married for twenty-four years (they got married very young because she was pregnant), and had two sons, aged twenty-three and nineteen. We knew from the referral form that a third son had died at the age of nine, six years before our meeting.

Mrs. Bond stressed that she had always been dissatisfied with her sexual relationship with her husband but that since she had started a business of her own, a beauty parlor plus sauna, a year ago, she had learned from her customers about the sort of sexual intercourse they enjoyed and now her feelings of frustration had become unbearable. She felt that with this business a new and liberating phase of life had started for her; she felt effective and independent at last, having always before been dependent on either her parents or her husband. We learned later that her husband had supported her considerably in setting up the business, had found the premises for her, kept her books, and had been responsible throughout for all the administrative work connected with it.

Mr. Bond was depressed and apathetic. He felt threatened and defeated by his wife's demands on him, both sexually and in every other way. He did not actually say

so, but conveyed in his whole manner his hopelessness
and his feeling that the more he gave, the more she
wanted and the less able he felt to ever satisfy her. He
was very dependent on her, feeling completely at her
mercy, and said repeatedly, "I can only function if I have
your support."

He was dissatisfied with his work but while his wife
egged him on to change jobs, she had defeated several of
his attempts. Even when very attractive possibilities
arose she found faults and put obstacles in his way. She
would not let him accept a job that involved occasional
absences from home or a great deal of driving, would not
consider leaving their present house, which meant that
he was tied to a local job, and altogether had defeated all
his efforts to change. He talked about this in a muted
voice, carefully choosing words that did not sound critical of his wife and shielding his face with his hands so
that neither we (a male colleague and I saw this couple
in conjoint sessions over a limited period of time) nor his
wife could see his expressions. His wife did not argue
with him, but commented that her objections to these
jobs were always caused by her love for him. She hated
to be without him and in her anxiety for his safety, she
could not let him take a job involving much driving. Her
own complaints about his lack of initiative and general
inefficiency were mixed with expressions of admiration
for his clever brain and his many interests and artistic
gifts, alternating with her fears that "he will lord it over
me." Talking about their sexual relationship she said
that he had always been able to get satisfaction even
when she was completely unresponsive. Now she was
very much improved, "but I'm still a long way behind
him."

Mrs. Bond's castrating, undermining attitude and her
husband's passive yet resentful acceptance of it became
strikingly clear. This is a very familar pattern of interac-

tion in couples who ask for help. Side by side with it, we were aware of much affection between Mr. and Mrs. Bond and great mutual dependence.

Their life histories confirmed that they had brought the outline for their pattern of interaction into the marriage from their pasts. Mrs. Bond had been an only daughter with a slightly older, clever, envied brother. Her mother was stupid and interfering; she despised and hated her. Her father was idealized. He was everything that a father could be and a very successful businessman. She was very close to him, and had worked in his business.

Mr. Bond's father lost his job in Yorkshire, which to this family was home, when his son had reached puberty and had won a scholarship to a school there. This was at a time of depression with much unemployment, and for the father to get another job, the family had to leave all they had cherished, including the son's chances for a grammar school education and move south, where they knew nobody and felt isolated and strange. The father, who had never had much self-confidence, could not settle in the new place and was a complete failure. His son suffered with and for him. He felt close to his father, whom he admired as a man of good intelligence, many gifts, and great integrity. He identified with him in his inability to hold his own in a hostile world, especially as he himself had difficulty adjusting to the new surroundings and new school methods. He too felt himself to be a failure in spite of his high intelligence, which added to his father's worries. The only other child, an older sister, had married soon after the move south and gone abroad with her husband, leaving the mother with two depressed men.

Mr. and Mrs. Bond had met at a dance when she was eighteen and he just twenty. It was love at first sight, a first love and a first sexual experience for both young people. After a few weeks of passionate courtship, the girl, having more or less seduced the shy boy, became pregnant. Her parents were outraged. The pregnancy was felt to be an utter disaster, and was blamed entirely on the young man. The parents insisted on a rushed marriage, without blessing or honeymoon. Immediately after the wedding, the young husband volunteered for the army, was sent abroad, and was away for four years. Whether this had been suggested to him by his wife's parents, or whether he chose it as a way out because he felt so humiliated by them, unable to stand up to or compete with his wife's love for her powerful father and successful brother, remained unclear. His wife spoke of this period as "his desertion from me." During his absence she continued living with her parents and working for her father. Her mother looked after the baby.

When soon after the husband's return she became pregnant again, her parents' fury was renewed. They blamed him for being irresponsible in having another baby without being able to provide adequately for his family. His wife too was very upset, accused him of tying her to the house and of interfering with her budding liberation.

At this point the father bought a house for his daughter, making it abundantly clear that it was to be hers. This house, for which the husband had always paid everything that had to be paid, remained very important to Mrs. Bond. When we first met this couple, she "would not dream of leaving it," although she knew that it was inconveniently situated and increased her husband's job problem.

Throughout the twenty years that had since passed, however, the couple had stayed together, had patches of considerable happiness, and there clearly was a very strong emotional tie between them. What brought them at this point to ask for help with such urgency? Although they presented an almost overclear picture of a castrating woman and a castrated man and although their life histories endorsed this, we had the feeling that we were being asked, nonverbally, to see something that was not being shown to us.

Had the present situation, in which the two older sons were leaving home, having girlfriends, and discussing marriage, reactivated this couple's anxieties about the unblessed start of their own marriage and their inhibited sexuality? The wife, near menopause, was in a sexual frenzy, insisting that she must now get the orgasm she had missed for so long—or it would be too late. The fact that the couple were now alone together for the very first time had made their lack of communication a more pressing problem. Yet, in spite of the validity of all these stresses which the wife overemphasized and from which the husband seemed to dissociate himself, we felt that what had brought the couple to ask for help at this point was too frightening to look at without "parental support." We were also struck by the silence about the death of their youngest son—known to us only through referral notes.

In response to our attempts to find the real cause for this crisis, the husband remained silent and depressed. If he spoke at all it was about his work difficulties. The wife insisted that she had only now fully realized how frustrated she was, and how unfeeling and insensitive her husband, but that the crisis had been coming on for the last six years. She recounted with many histrionics all the things that had happened. The most important and upsetting event of that six-year period was the sudden death of her father of a heart attack on New Year's night while sitting on the toilet. It was ghastly that this powerful, admired father should die such an undignified death. What a terrible omen for the new year. No wonder the shock led to her mother's mental breakdown. The mother is still, six years later, in a mental hospital, and her daughter finds the visits to her a great burden.

Mr. Bond's father had also died the same year of a brain tumor, leaving his widow unprovided for. This was a great sorrow to his son, who during his wife's dramatic account of all the terrible things that had happened during the last six years had remained silent, looking depressed. The death of their youngest son in the autumn of that ill-fated year, which must have been the most traumatic of the losses to this couple, was not mentioned by either, nor anything about him, not even— ever—his name.

At our third meeting, they talked about the forthcoming weekend visit of their two sons. Mr. Bond expressed the hope that this time his wife would make them really welcome and not complain all the time about their demands. Mrs. Bond retorted that what she was complaining about was that her husband was always monopolizing the sons and that the three of them were talking "too clever" for her. They made her feel excluded. The couple went on talking between them rather compulsively about the two sons and we felt that they could not allow themselves any pause for fear that something would come up which they did not want to discuss but which we felt was connected with the cause of their present stress. At this point, therefore, I asked whether their sons missed their younger brother very much. The couple responded with a terrified gasp and then the husband began to cry. The wife, clearly shocked, tried to go on a bit longer. In a high-pitched voice she talked frantically about her exclusion from all the men. Then, after a silence and more subdued, she acknowledged her husband's tears, saying quite tenderly that she knew that this youngest son, James, had been his favorite. Meanwhile the husband tried to control himself sufficiently to talk about James, whom he described as the most beauti-

ful, most gifted of their children. He frequently interrupted himself with sobs. The wife, obviously shaken by
her husband's suffering, still tried to lower the emotional
temperature, saying, "Yes, in your eyes he could do no
wrong, you spoiled him no end, yet he sometimes needed
his bottom spanked." When the husband, still crying, did
not respond, she went on, "And what a beautiful bottom
to spank he had," and then finally started to cry too.
They cried together for some time and we could sense
their tremendous relief to be able to do so. Then both,
in turn, told us about this boy and about his death, on the
birthday of his oldest brother, one day before his own
ninth birthday.

The parents were taking the oldest son to the movies
as a birthday treat. James wanted to come along and was
furious when his parents refused to take him, insisting
that he ought to go to bed early in order to be fresh for
his own birthday party the next day. He was very angry
and as they left the house he shouted rudely and angrily
after them.

When they came home after their outing, the house
was full of smoke and James was dead, lying on a foam
rubber mattress surrounded by fireworks. The parents
had meant these to be a surprise for his birthday party
—he must have found them, and in his anger started to
light some, setting the mattress on fire, and dying, overcome by the fumes.

Both parents must have been overwhelmed with guilt
for leaving the angry boy alone in the house and not
safely hiding the fireworks. But they never shared their
guilt or their grief. They did what had to be done but
never, never spoke of James. Now the mother said that
the boy's angry face when he was left behind had
haunted her for years, and that for a long time she was
unable to go into his room or touch any of the things that
had belonged to him. Mr. Bond cried silently while his

wife was talking. When our session was nearly up, he walked across the room to comfort her, saying how sad it was that this had been such an upsetting hour for her —as if it had been his fault. She took his hand and said tenderly, "Well, it has been upsetting for you too." We were struck that even at this moment of great emotion, when they had been so united in their pain, Mr. Bond had to make us all feel that he was to blame. We could sense how throughout their marriage he had provoked her blaming, undermining attitude toward him. On this occasion, she had not taken up the provocation but responded with compassion. They left exhausted by this emotional experience but very close and loving.

We met Mr. and Mrs. Bond for only two further sessions. These meetings confirmed our immediate observation that the sharing of grief had removed an obstacle which hitherto had made it impossible for the couple to communicate. The tragedy of their son's death had been the culmination of events confirming for each his worst fears. On some level Mrs. Bond had always been aware of her need to hurt those she loved, of her destructive impulses. She knew how upsetting her illegitimate pregnancy had been to her parents, especially her father, and how she had punished her husband by letting him carry all the blame (although she knew that she had been the seducer). She must also have felt that she had contributed to her mother's mental breakdown by having been such a rival to her, so intent on stealing the first place in her father's heart, and later, after his death, leaving her unsupported and rejected, almost as if she wanted her to be taken into a mental hospital, out of her way, and even grudging her the monthly visits. The death of her youngest son, after an angry scene, must have very much increased her burden of guilt. She was proud of this favorite child, yet had always resented his father's special love for him. On family outings, it was always James who was in the limelight. Was this why she had excluded him on this occasion?

Mr. Bond, on the other hand, was used to carrying all the blame. Throughout his life his experience had been that he had to lose what he cherished, that he was not worthy of holding what he loved. He had lost the hope for the academic success for which he was well-equipped through his family's untimely move; he had lost his drive and initiative through identification with his loved, depressed father. He was made to feel that he had damaged his wife through the pregnancies, that he had not deserved her, and he had to leave her as soon as they were married. His favorite child died through his negligence —why had he not hidden the fireworks, why had he not avoided the scene?

Each partner had been too defended against these fears, had felt too unsafe, too vulnerable in relation to the other one to risk exposure. When at last they could do so in the safety of our presence, they were tremendously relieved.

During our last sessions they told us repeatedly that talking to us and showing their shared grief to us had made them feel for the first time acknowledged and valued as a couple "by people who count." To stress this, Mrs. Bond said, "You see, we never had our parents' blessing. Now that you have given it to us, we really feel we belong together." They were now trying to find all sorts of ways to express their new togetherness. They joined a drama group and were taking joint flying lessons. In both these activities Mr. Bond excelled and his wife, when telling us about it, still used the phrase "He is lording it over me." But they were doing these things together, sharing their interests, and his "lording it" over her seemed to have lost much of its threat. One son had married, the other had fixed his wedding date. Mr. and Mrs. Bond liked both daughters-in-law and their families. Their own family had thus been extended with people who knew them only as a pair, and the feminine component had been strengthened. Mrs. Bond loved chatting with the girls while the men "talked clever." And Mr. Bond enjoyed being "made a fuss of by two pretty young things." The much fought for maleness in the family had lost its importance now that femininity could be valued and enjoyed.

In our last session the question of the house was brought up. After all, they would not need such a big place once both sons were married and they were "just the two of us." If the husband was offered a better job elsewhere, why not move—they could make a good profit on the house.

In all this Mr. and Mrs. Bond appeared to be much more relaxed and united, in spite of the fact that their fundamental pattern of interaction had remained unchanged and probably always will. With better communication and increased tolerance, now that they are able to face and share their guilt about what they felt they did to James, they may well be able to continue to make constructive use of their changing life situation and contain their anxieties about their mutual destructiveness.

THE COHN FAMILY

I got to know Mr. Cohn because his daughter, Anne, aged sixteen, had caused her parents much concern. She was troublesome at school and had constant fights with her mother, rebelling, protesting against their home, yet jeopardizing all attempts to make arrangements for her to be away. She ran away from boarding schools, cut short visits to relatives abroad, and could not even stand vacations with other adolescents.

The psychiatrist who had been treating her felt that

Anne's hostility toward and dependence on her parents should be seen not as an individual problem but as that of the family. It had become apparent that the relationship between the parents was very strained, that neither could appreciate the other and both felt attacked and unvalued. In the conflict with Anne especially, the mother felt that her husband blamed her, undermined what authority she had, and always sided with Anne. In spite of Mr. Cohn's insistence that it was his wife's problem and he was not involved, the psychiatrist felt that in some undefinable way the father was the kingpin in this conflict and that he had some unconscious investment in keeping it going.

Both parents very reluctantly agreed to accept therapy with two individual therapists, who would keep in touch with each other and with Anne's therapist. This is the background to my work with Mr. Cohn, who was then in his forties.

From the beginning I was struck by the contradicting features in this man's personality. He had an executive position in a big international firm and had obviously done extraordinarily well in his work. But his manner and appearance were those of a failure, of someone who didn't count. He traveled all over the world, met important people, but felt himself to be dull and boring, with nothing to talk about that could be of any interest to his family or others. He had a beautiful home which he had acquired with the money he earned, but this was his wife's domain in which he had no say. When they had guests, he felt like a stranger, not a host, and annoyed his wife by letting himself be waited on as if he were a guest. This was all the more puzzling because Mr. Cohn had many accomplishments and interests. He didn't value these for himself, however, and felt they could be of no value to others. He practiced them secretly, almost shamefacedly, and gave the impression of a man who felt he had no right to be alive.

It was clear how tremendously involved he was with the emotional crisis at home. Our sessions were filled with detailed reports of his wife's impossibly provocative behavior toward Anne, whose difficulties he saw entirely in response to her mother's unfair demands. "I know she is sometimes rude, but I can always see her point." His involvement with the scenes between mother and daughter was almost compulsive, and although he felt these scenes were driving him mad he could not stay away from them. Even when he traveled on business, he was preoccupied with what might happen at home, and telephoned daily from wherever he was. The expectation of approaching catastrophe dominated his life. He frequently said, "Disaster is always around the corner."

Although he so clearly demonstrated his emotional involvement with the battles between mother and daughter, he was unable to acknowledge that this might have something to do with feelings inside himself, belonging to earlier experiences in his life. He insisted that he was so upset about the scenes at home simply because he detested fights. He was beginning to see a connection, however, between his wife's bad temper, her angry and demanding attitude toward her daughter, and her disappointment in him. She often complained about his coldness, diffidence, and lack of affection, but he could do nothing about this, he simply had no emotions, nor did he want an emotional life, all he wanted was peace.

Slowly I learned something about Mr. Cohn's background. He had come to England with a youth-transport when he was fifteen after the Nazi invasion of Czechoslovakia. His Jewish family had planned to follow him but were arrested before this was possible. His father died before he was deported, all the others were gassed in concentration camps. Mr. Cohn only mentioned this as an item of information, without feeling. The most important event of his life had happened much earlier.

When Mr. Cohn was three, he and a sister one year older, were taken to the country by their father and told that their mother was ill. The father visited his children weekly, bringing them presents. After a year he came with "Mother" and took the children home. Mr. Cohn remembers that he commented on "Mother" having become much smaller. This was his one and only attempt to express his doubts of whether this was in fact the mother he had known. He never asked his father, never shared his doubts with his sister, and does not know what she thought. At no time was there any open questioning of the new family situation. Yet both children knew that their mother's parents, who played a considerable part in their lives, were not the parents of the present mother. This was never openly discussed or acknowledged. As the boy grew older, his grandfather would take him to the synagogue each year on February tenth, to pray for the dead. The grandfather never said for whom they were praying and the boy never asked.

His sister constantly fought with the stepmother, but he got along quite well with her, tried to please her and fit in. (Anne was like this sister, even looked like her. That is why he could understand her so well.) Already at that time, much to his father's concern, Mr. Cohn was passive and withdrawn. His father often reprimanded him for being so dull, so without initiative. "That boy will never get anywhere" was his father's verdict. All that that boy wanted, even then, was peace. He did not ask any questions, he avoided all conflicts, all emotions, all taking of initiative which might have led to questioning—for the sake of peace. Nor did he become an ally of his sister, who was not content to accept the cheat without arguing and rebelling. But much later, when his sister was dead, he took Anne's side, identified with her in her fights with her mother—in reality she was Anne, in fantasy she was his sister!

Telling me about his childhood and youth, Mr. Cohn said, "You see, I could get somewhere in my job, could show initiative at work, once I was away from my father and the home, but in my own family, in my relationships at home, I have the same feelings of hopelessness and helplessness which I had as a boy." He remembers vividly the day he left for England and his maternal grandmother, on kissing him good-bye, reminded him with much emotion always to say his prayers on February tenth. "I almost fainted. I thought: Now the truth comes. I could not bear it and I rushed down the stairs."

In England he met a distant relative who told him that his beautiful, talented, and very emotional mother had drowned herself in a state of mental disturbance. He also learned how much his father had admired his wife's integrity and intelligence, but that he had not been able to cope with her emotional demands or to make her happy. The relative gave him a photo of his mother, the first he had ever seen.

It took a long time before Mr. Cohn could see in this story any relevance to his present situation. Much later in our contact he said, "I have learned only now how it all hangs together"—"it" being his relationships in his present and parental families and the way the latter had affected his whole life and the image he had of himself. At about that time he also discovered that he had chosen a wife who somehow resembled his mother in appearance and in whom he admired the same qualities of integrity and intelligence which his father was said to have admired in his mother. His wife, like his mother, was a very emotional woman, and he felt threatened by her demands for a quality of love he was unable to give and for a sexual intensity which was alien to his own needs. He was content with infrequent, perfunctory sexual intercourse—all else was beyond him.

At moments of high emotion he felt completely helpless. Once, after a bad fight with Anne, his wife threat-ened to commit suicide, to gas herself. He sat as if par-alyzed in the room next to the kitchen into which she had locked herself, making no attempt to calm her down or to dissuade her. "I felt hopeless—there was nothing I could do about it." He must have had these very same feelings when his mother disappeared from his life through suicide.

He told me that he had never been interested in girls, and had had no sexual relationship until he met his wife, who was introduced to him by her father, a business acquaintance. She too had been abandoned by her mother, who had left the family for another man and now lived in Australia. Her father had remarried and Mrs. Cohn had a strained, uneasy relationship with her stepmother. She felt abandoned, not good enough to maintain her mother's love, very unsure of herself, and only too vulnerable to her husband's undermining. In our sessions he recalled with some surprise and some shame how from the moment of Anne's birth he had criticized his wife for her handling of this, their first child. He supervised her feeding and care of the baby, and found something wrong in whatever she did. His deep mistrust and resentment of "mothers" were pro-jected onto his wife, and he seemed to identify with Anne as the one who needed care and protection.

Incidentally, Mrs. Cohn's real mother was presented to the Cohn children (her grandchildren) as an Aus-tralian aunt, and the stepmother as the real Granny. Very recently, Anne had discovered this deceit, and her parents were quite uncomprehending and very upset by her fury.

Not only was Mrs. Cohn vulnerable to her husband's undermining, but he was equally sensitive to his wife's criticism of him, never felt valued by her, and carefully hid from her all aspects of his life and personality that

were painful to him, that aroused feelings. Since the end
of the war he had traveled on February tenth every year
to his birthplace to say prayers at his mother's grave—
but to his family this was always presented as a business
trip. These annual acts of duty, consciously chosen encounters with the reality of his mother's death, do not
seem to have pierced the thick armor with which he
protected his emotions.

In all our discussions, his father's death and the fact
that his sister and half-siblings by his father's second
marriage vanished in gas chambers were never mentioned. Only after years of contact with Mr. Cohn did I
learn that his father had died of a heart attack just before
deportation and was in fact buried next to his mother. In
talking about his annual visits to his mother's grave he
had never referred to his father. It seems that he could
not forgive him for not having loved his mother enough
to keep her alive and for the fundamental cheat of her
children, denying them a living memory of her and the
mourning of her loss. The resulting resistance to forming any identification with his father had made it difficult for him later to assume the role of a father, a husband, and the head of a household. In the role of a
breadwinner and businessman, however, he surpassed
his father, which gave him great satisfaction.

His early experiences made him mistrust the world,
men and women, especially where emotions were involved. In his business relationships he felt at ease and
in control of himself and others, but this self-assurance
left as soon as he was outside business premises or concerns, and did not help him to gain any self-confidence,
or to see any value in himself as a private individual or
as a member of his family.

All the deaths in his family had happened behind his
back, so to speak. He knew nothing about the when,
where, or how of any of them. He had been able neither

to participate as a mourner nor to share the loss with anyone. The violence connected with these deaths made him consciously want "nothing but peace," yet he could not refrain from getting irrationally involved in, and stirring up, the violent fights between his wife and daughter. His repressed grief, the cheat and mistrust, the unspoken doubts, the hate and horror, and the complete emotional isolation (in his childhood as well as in his marriage) were transformed into a denial of all feelings, a conscious rejection of all emotions. It was as if he had to kill himself as a feeling individual to atone for the guilt of being the only survivor of his paternal family.

When I first met Mr. Cohn he thought of himself as useless—except as a breadwinner—and as a nearly affect-less and affectionless character. That was how he was made, and there was nothing he could do about it. Yet from very early on in our contact, his behavior betrayed him. He loved coming to his weekly sessions, would press my doorbell impatiently, run into the room like a schoolboy in a hurry to come home to Mum, drop into his chair, and sigh with relief: "At last I can relax." I often wondered what he was reliving in his arrival. Did he run home to his stepmother in this way? There was one feature of our sessions, however, which I always recognized as this man's response to his unacknowl-edged bereavement and which only changed quite re-cently: he could never look at me when he left. It was as if consciously performing the act of leaving anybody who mattered was unpracticed and caused too anxious feelings—perhaps like rushing down the stairs when he could not face a real farewell from his grandmother, who might have told him the truth about his mother.

Mr. Cohn's schoolboyish arrivals were not the only contradiction he brought into our therapeutic sessions. He talked with ease and lively interest about anything that came into his mind. Many of the things he talked

about, in both his present and past, were extremely painful, but he never showed any pain. This was particularly
striking when he talked about his sad infancy, bewildered childhood, and apathetic youth. Yet in spite of this
avoidance of expressing feelings of pain and his apparent
refusal to work through a belated mourning process, Mr.
Cohn and the image he had of himself began to change.
Slowly, gingerly, and with many withdrawals, he allowed himself to experience and express some feelings.

Repeatedly in this book I have stressed the connection
between sex and death. In Mr. Cohn, too, I was aware of
the link between his defenses against facing both his
sexual emotions and the pain of bereavement. As he began to be freer in all aspects of his life and attempted to
explore the causes for his sexual diffidence, his growing
interest in sexuality was stimulated by his daughter, who
loved to discuss her sexual exploits with him, perhaps in
the hope of shocking—or challenging—him, and he
loved to discuss them with me. In these discussions there
was the same schoolboy air, which was familiar to me
from his way of arriving for his sessions. Did he have to
act out, live, these schoolboy aspects, which as a repressed, anxious, passive real schoolboy he had never
been able to do, as part of a growing up, freeing process?

There was a new feeling of being valued for himself,
no longer only for the money he earned and with which,
by the way, he had not been at all generous. This new
feeling of being valued was expressed, for example, in his
wish to celebrate his birthday, which in the past he had
always taken great trouble to ignore, even arranging his
business trips so that he would be away. He became able
to give his family and himself some pleasure, to arrange
outings, vacations. He was able to withdraw a little from
work and increase his leisure hours. He was no longer
half-dead, he was beginning to come to life.

The home situation also began to change—with many

setbacks and repeated crises. Anne and her mother began to relate more positively to each other. And when Anne, who until then had had great difficulty forming stable relationships, found a man to love and marry and moved out of the home, the fights ceased and a much desired peace took over.

While Mr. Cohn expressed great satisfaction about this, he seemed to miss something. Life felt flat at home —with Anne, all the excitement, the fights, his only opportunity to speak his mind had gone. When we explored why he felt that the fights between mother and daughter had been his only opportunity to speak his mind, he said that Anne was like his sister, and he had been told that his sister was much like his mother, so that by standing up for Anne, he was in a way standing up for his sister and mother. In his parental home, he had not done so; he had let his sister express all the anger and resentment about the way they had both been cheated and he had let her be punished for it—while he himself had gained acceptance, and withdrew into "peace." To achieve this, he had also never made any effort to remain in touch with the memory of his mother, and had actively avoided the opportunities his grandparents offered him. I wondered whether in the fights between mother and daughter, in which they were driving each other mad, Mr. Cohn had also tried to be in touch with whatever had driven his mother mad—in relation to his father or himself, his own naughty boy self. His participation in the conflict between Anne and his wife, his drive to speak his mind, not again to remain aloof from the conflict, was some attempt to pay restitution to his sister and mother. He seemed to feel that he had not completed this process, so that the peace he now might be able to enjoy but did not quite manage to recalled the false peace of his childhood and his guilty feelings about it.

Mr. Cohn and I had been meeting for over five years,

during the last year in monthly or even longer intervals. However long the break, he would always arrive in the same schoolboy manner and immediately start to share his news with me. During the period of meetings at long intervals, the change in him became still more apparent, most clearly when on one occasion this man, for whom "disaster had always lurked around the corner," exclaimed, "I really am a lucky guy."

When I began writing this book I asked for his permission to include his story and suggested that we discuss the draft together. He willingly agreed but arrived looking white and tense. I was once again reminded of his flight from his grandmother, when he felt, "Now comes the truth, I can't bear it." I had a writing pad in my hand and took notes, which I do not usually do. As we went over details of his childhood story and the annual visits to his mother's grave, I asked, as I had done several times before, what he felt on these occasions. In the past, he had always answered evasively, "I said the prescribed prayers" or, "I tried to think of my mother." This time he was silent for quite a while and then started to cry. It was later on this occasion that he told me that his father was buried next to his mother. We had a very depressed session—and he left me as a man in grief.

Thinking about this meeting I felt that my writing pad and my taking notes had made the loss of his parents more real to Mr. Cohn than all his visits to their graves. Also he may have felt that now he could share his loss with me in a different way, that it had value and meaning for me also.

Since this very moving meeting, I have seen Mr. Cohn four or five times. He looks younger, freer, his movements are more purposeful and yet more relaxed. Things at home are steadily improving. His relationship with me has changed. He comes less like a schoolboy running to Mum, more like an adult visiting a trusted friend by whom he feels valued and to whom he has something to give.

MRS. DEAN

Mrs. Dean had asked for help for her son Simon, then aged fifteen, who did not seem to function as he should, and was lazy, irresponsible, and provocative both in his boarding school and at home. A younger son, Ralph, appeared to be doing well, but was nevertheless included in his mother's self-accusation that she was bad for her children.

The psychotherapist with whom she discussed her anxieties about Simon felt that the main problem was in Mrs. Dean's relationship with her sons. Along with her tremendous love for them, he sensed an inability to express it, or to allow her children to express their love for her. The therapist was immediately struck by Mrs. Dean's rich personality, her inherent creativity and love, and by the contrast between the sort of person he perceived her to be and the sort of person she saw herself as being. He agreed to work with Simon but felt that Mrs. Dean too should be offered an opportunity to explore the roots of her guilt, her sense of failure, and her fears of destructiveness. She seemed relieved to be given that chance.

Mrs. Dean's husband had died suddenly when Simon was ten and Ralph nine. Since then she had not been able to talk to the children about their father, found it a strain to have them around, and although she lived only for them and cared for them conscientiously in every respect, was unable to show them any feeling. She said that she was terrified to get close to them because she might harm them. When we tried to understand what this meant, she said that she was afraid "to open the flood-

gates of feeling as they all might be swept away." She
had frequent nightmares of being drowned, trapped in
disasters.

Mrs. Dean came from a wealthy, ambitious, status-
minded family whom she despised for their false values.
Consciously they expressed these in their snobbishness
and interest in money, a good address, and careers. It was
a large family with five girls and only one boy, who
naturally was very precious, especially to the mother.
Part of Mrs. Dean's feeling of self-contempt must have
arisen from her mother, who, herself outstandingly
pretty, very feminine, and apparently submissive to the
father, did not really like girls. She did not seem to be
interested in their appearance, never encouraged any
feminine activities, and they could not attempt to identify with her. It seemed impossible ever to please her,
indeed difficult to know what might please her, for she
expressed such contradicting wishes in relation to her
daughters. All her concern, love, and approval went to
her son. This was one reason why Mrs. Dean could not
get along with her mother and aimed for and valued a
special relationship with her father. Her father was
twenty-one years older than her mother and a very exciting person for his children, though also very confusing.
One never knew what to expect of him. He could be
charming, loving, and full of fun, and at other times he
could be unpredictably angry, frightening, and punishing. In spite of her fears of him, Mrs. Dean felt very close
to him and liked to think that she was his favorite, and,
although it never came into the open, there was a feeling
of rivalry between her and her mother in relation to him.

When Mrs. Dean was twelve, her father had a brain
tumor. He survived after a successful operation but as a
completely changed person. He became passive and
withdrawn and the mother seemed only too ready to
abandon her femininity and take over the affairs of the
family and the business. She emerged as a most capable,

active, and successful manager, rather ruthlessly pursu-
ing her family's interests to the astonishment and admiration of their bank manager. Roles within the family
changed fundamentally, in fact, they became the opposite of what they had been before.

This tremendous change coincided not only with Mrs.
Dean's first menstruation, her first awareness that she
was a woman, but also with the beginning of the war.
The family remained in London. Her mother became a
street warden, and all the children were expected to do
their bit, often being exposed to dangerous and frightening situations; only the father was hiding under his blan-
kets when the bombs fell. The girls, who were all in their
teens, were warned by their mother not to get involved
with men—"All men are nasty"—and were much impressed by the dangers of sex. This got all mixed up in
Mrs. Dean's mind with the new topsy-turvy roles at
home, with her confusing feelings about growing into a
woman, and with all the violence around her. Anyhow,
there was no time to have fun or to think about one's
appearance or to have boyfriends, and what boys were
around all seemed to get killed.

Toward the end of the war, at age eighteen, she started
to work at one of the big daily papers, and there she met
her future husband, who was on the editorial staff. He
was thirteen years older than she, from an Irish working-
class background, tall and strong, charming and brilliant. She fell passionately in love with him, and was
determined to marry him and to fight her parents' oppo-
sition. Faced with her fierce determination, a feature of
her personality of which they had not before been aware,
they finally gave their consent. She was the first of the
family to marry and in spite of the parents' disapproval,
her mother insisted on a big affair, a real society wedding, which the young couple felt to be quite inappropriate. For the sake of peace they gave in and hated it.

Mrs. Dean felt that with this marriage she became a new person. Her husband gave her everything she always wanted and was never permitted to have. He created her intellectually and emotionally, and she felt that she owed him everything. It was he who made her think and helped her to get on in her profession (journalism), he who got her in touch with her feelings, which were of quite unexpected strength and power. Without him she was nothing, useless, worthless.

When Mrs. Dean became pregnant, the couple bought a cottage in the country, planning to move there after the baby's birth. A few days before this event, Mrs. Dean's father died, and although he had been ill for some time, she tortured herself with the feeling that his death and the birth of a first grandchild were somehow connected. Because she was so near giving birth, Mrs. Dean let herself be dissuaded from seeing her dead father or going to his funeral, so that "his death never came real to me."

After the birth of a baby boy, Simon, the young family moved to their isolated country cottage. It was in the middle of a very cold winter, and the cottage had not been inhabited for years. Mrs. Dean knew none of her neighbors, nobody. She had never handled a baby before, and was terrified of not knowing how to cope with Simon. Her husband worked long and irregular hours, as newspapermen do—and there was the long journey in addition. Thus, she was left alone a great deal, and must have been very angry with her husband for having put her in this position. But she was not aware of these feelings. Instead, she felt that her husband hated her, wanted to get rid of her, kill her. She was sure that the nightcap which he brought her every night was poisoned, but she drank it willingly, feeling that this was only what she deserved, and that her husband was justified in wanting to get rid of her. But when she could not let him come near her physically, make love to her, it was not because she feared being killed but because "his face looked too much like Father's."

Mrs. Dean's guilt about replacing the no longer exciting father with another exciting and forbidden figure, whom she could only get through passionate rebellion, was reactivated when her father died just as she was about to give birth to her first child, his first grandchild, a son. Now her renewed guilt feelings were linked with murderous feelings, such as "one life for another"; thoughts about giving life and taking it, sex and death, husband and father, were all mixed up in her mind.

The two major stresses that she had recently experienced—the death of her father and the birth of her first child—had been too much for her, especially since they occurred in the most stressful external situation. She was alone in strange surroundings with her newborn baby, without any experience in infant care, in a cold, uncomfortable house, and with a husband who was seldom there. Even though she understood and apparently accepted the reasons for his absence, it felt to her like desertion.

These stresses in her inner and outer worlds affected her with particular force because they were a repetition of a previous frightening situation at a time when she was equally vulnerable: the time of her first menstruation. It was then that her loved, exciting, but frightening father changed, became a stranger, her mother became all-powerful, and the roles in the family were completely reversed. And all this had also coincided with the beginning of the war, death, and violence.

Then, as now, she had kept her fears and terrifying fantasies to herself, alarmingly successful in hiding them from anybody who might have helped her. She did not dare to expose her terrible thoughts about death and murder but felt that she had to be punished, exterminated, for them. It was her husband who would mete out justice and kill her, as she deserved. That she now saw her father's features in her husband's face shows the link between these two painful periods in her life: the forbidden and hidden sexual feelings for her father had been stirred up by his death and the birth of a son.

Mixed up with all this was her quite realistic—but unacknowledged—anger with her husband, who had allowed her to be in such a difficult position, alone with the baby and her fears. He left her, rejected her, just when she needed him most, as her father had done. This more realistic anger was transformed into murderous fantasies toward her husband, which she then projected onto him as if it were he who wanted to kill her.

In spite of all her despair after her father's death she felt that the reality of his loss had never been real to her. There was no real mourning, no pain or grief, only fear and confusion and the terrifying fantasies. She was so skillful in hiding them that neither her husband nor the local doctor appears to have noticed what surely must have been a post-partum depression.

Only when she found herself pregnant again (Simon was six months old) did she let her doctor see something of her terrors, not because she expected help for herself but because she was afraid her nervous state might be harmful to the baby. Once she had shared this with her doctor she felt better.

A few weeks before she was supposed to give birth, it was discovered that Mrs. Dean was Rh-negative, and she was immediately admitted to the hospital. The baby, again a boy, whom they called Ralph, was very delicate. Yet according to the hospital staff, he was their first Rh-negative boy who might survive, and he and his mother were given all conceivable care and consideration. They presented a special case, doctors from hospitals nearby came to see them—she and her baby had become V.I.Ps.

To be "special," cared for, and cherished was a new experience for Mrs. Dean and one that made her feel good. That her baby's survival depended on her own intensive care gave her a new sense of value, and there was no repetition of the post-partum disturbances. In fact, she felt better than ever, except for her guilt about Simon, whose early life had been laden with so many difficulties, first through her unbalanced mind, then through the long separation before and after Ralph's birth, and now through her preoccupation with this second baby who needed so much and such special care. During all this time Simon was pushed around between various members of her family and she was anxiously aware of how much he must have suffered. She was determined to make up for this, and as soon as she was well she devoted herself entirely to her children. This, she thought, was also what her husband expected of her.

Mr. Dean, like his wife, came from a large family, but his mother, unlike hers was "the ideal woman," wife and mother. She had no greater joy than cooking huge meals for her big family, providing a home, which all cherished, caring, and loving, having apparently oceans of love to give. Mr. Dean worshipped his mother and his young wife was only too willing to share his admiration. She felt that he wanted her to be like his mother, which she also would have liked. Since the birth of Ralph, when she was tenderly cared for and made to feel good and important, she felt forgiven for all her bad thoughts and recognized in her love and creativity. She wanted to maintain this sense of value even if it meant giving up her own identity and attempting to become something else, an ideal mother, like the admired mother-in-law. It was very painful for her to acknowledge that she could not achieve this, for the image she was trying to build up could not be hers: it was false and could not be integrated within her own personality. Although she did her duty while the children were small, she often felt bored and inferior and, worst of all, neglected and unvalued by her husband. For just at the time when she had tried so hard to please him and fit in with what he seemed to expect of her, her husband appeared to lose his regard, his love, for her. He stayed away from home longer and longer hours and there were rumors that he was having an affair with one of his young colleagues, a bright young thing much like Mrs. Dean was before she had babies. She was utterly confused, there were fights and scenes and much nastiness, which ended when Mrs. Dean decided to hire someone to take care of her children, and to go back to work and again be her husband's colleague.

By that time, her fury with him had given way to an attempt to understand what had happened. He had never really asked her to make children and home her full-time job or to try to be like his mother. In fact, he had chosen to marry her because she was so different. It was her own interpretation of his unspoken wishes that had made for all the anguish and "nastiness," and he had been quite right to punish her for it. Her full-time mothering and housekeeping had been phony, a sham, and would never make her into the sort of woman she could and wanted to be.

Later, when she talked to me about this period, she said that she had never completed the vital process which had then been set in motion: to find out what sort of woman she was. No two women could be more different than her mother and her mother-in-law. It was impossible for her to identify with either, she had to find her own feminine identity. When she felt so betrayed, so let down by her husband, she had compared him in her mind with her father, seeing him as equally unreliable and unpredictable. Why was it that in critical situations her husband and her father so often got mixed up in her mind? Had she interpreted her husband's wish for her to be like his mother because she needed him to be like her father?

These painful explorations happened years later, after Mr. Dean's death, and long after the crisis that had motivated them was a thing of the past. It had been followed by a period of affirmation and love, in which they worked closely together, were both very successful in their careers, and could share much of this, as well as their joy in their sons. Their cottage in a lovely countryside was a haven of peace to return to after long hours of work, and to be welcomed there by their flourishing children made for great happiness. The only flaw in this happy period was that Mrs. Dean had had much undiagnosed pain since Ralph's birth, and often had severe hemorrhages. Suddenly one day she had to be rushed into the hospital for an emergency operation on her appendix and ovaries. This new crisis renewed all her feelings of guilt and impending punishment. Once again her murderous fantasies made her expect a death penalty. This time she saw the surgeon as the executioner. She was quite sure that she would die, and carefully discussed with her husband arrangements for him and the children after her death.

She did survive, however, and as on previous occasions when she had been the center of care and concern and felt loved and good, life was again worth living and her inherent resilience made for a quick recovery. The operation also removed the anxieties about further pregnancies which were very real for this Roman Catholic couple. Now that their sexual relationship was no longer inhibited by guilt and fears, they were closer and happier than ever before in their married life.

The boys were now at boarding school and because both their parents worked, they often had to stay there for part of their vacations. But the periods the family spent together were all the more precious and full of fun and happiness. Much of the time was spent on the river, her husband's passion and one shared by both boys.

This period of happiness and ease did not last long. About two years after Mrs. Dean's operation, without any previous warning, her husband got ill. There was an uncertain diagnosis, a suspicion of a rapidly progressing cancer. Within a few days Mrs. Dean was told that there was no hope for a cure, that he was dying. She could not tell him, could hardly grasp it herself. He died within a week, but the boys were not informed until his actual death. It was all so fast, there was just no time.

Mrs. Dean was stunned, overcome by shock. She could not grasp that this was real, that she had lost her husband forever. She felt empty and utterly bereft. It was as if all the goodness her husband had put into her had gone with him.

When she had to accept the finality of the loss, she again was overwhelmed by guilt. It was she who ought to have died; he had died for her. It was as if she had killed him. She also felt guilty for not having told him of his impending death and having thus deprived him of any preparation for it; and for not having loved him enough, not given him enough strength, which his mother might have done. In her despair, all the destructive fantasies which had driven her to the brink of insanity after her father's death recurred. It was not safe for anyone she loved to be close to her. This time it was the lives of the children which were endangered. The only way to keep them safe, and to express her love for them, was to keep them away from her.

She wanted to be alone with her grief and drown herself in her sorrow, but this was not allowed. Everybody around her—her family, doctor, priest—expected her to pull herself together, not to make an exhibition of herself, not to upset her children; not to endanger her job by moping; not to worry others with her depression.

Her mother was the most hurtful of all. She more or less said, "It serves you right . . . Why did you marry against our wishes? . . . And a man so much older . . . It was only to be expected of him to abandon you so young . . . Now you will see what it is like to be a widow . . . ."

Mrs. Dean, who at the time of her most acute grief was so much in need of support and comfort, was devastated by her mother's attitude and unable to feel anything but hate and disgust for her. She did not want to see her, or anyone else, wanted to bury herself in her grief and her guilt. She did not want her children to come to the funeral or to see them for some time. Not only could she not bear their presence but she felt so hateful, so destructive, she would only harm them if they came near her. The death of her husband, the most fundamental of her losses, seemed to have confirmed her fantasies about dying, losing, damaging, killing. In order to preserve those she loved, she must keep them away from her, even if it killed her emotionally.

Her husband's death was all the more traumatic for Mrs. Dean because she had been facing crisis situations at such short intervals. Although all these painful incidents had occurred outside herself, she experienced each as if she had caused it, as if it had been brought about through her destructiveness. Each external crisis caused an internal one, yet we have seen how again and again Mrs. Dean's inherent strength and resilience made for quick recovery. This time again, in spite of all her grief and depression, she was soon back at her job, which was now more important than ever—she had to be fit and work for her children's sake.

When I met Mrs. Dean five years after her husband's death, she was still in a state of utter self-deprecation and had no wish to live. Yet in spite of her great distress, she had not broken down after her bereavement, had not gotten ill or missed any work. She had to go on living

because she had to work while the children were dependent on her. That was her lifeline. She was terrified to fail
in her job, in which she felt like a fraud (she had frequent
nightmares about this). As a person she did not count.
She paid no attention to her appearance and had no
social life at all. "Who wants to be with a widow?"

The theater had been a great source of pleasure for
Mrs. Dean and her husband, but although she was often
offered free tickets in her job, she could not go: "I can't
ask anybody to come with me, and I can't bear to go
alone." When after discussing it with me she went alone
for a special occasion, she fainted in the theater.

In spite of Mrs. Dean's self-depreciation and self-
destructiveness, I was moved and impressed from the
beginning of our contact by this fundamentally strong,
intelligent, imaginative, and loving woman. She in turn
responded to my concern and wish to understand her
with an immediate flicker of hope. She wanted to explore
with me what she was really like, what sort of a woman
she was. If only she could like herself better, she might
also become more acceptable to others. If only she could
feel better about her family, they might also begin to feel
better about her. Which of her feelings were really her
own and which belonged to others? Had she, during her
period of despair, projected her own rejecting feelings
onto the people around her, just as she had projected her
murderous fantasies onto her husband after her father's
death and Simon's birth? These were tortuous questions,
which in one form or another Mrs. Dean asked again and
again. She was not ready yet to perceive that what she
felt to be her badness, hate, and destructiveness was the
other side of her exceptionally strong feelings of love and
care.

During these months, in which Mrs. Dean spoke with
the utmost pain, with "screams for help" about fears of
her badness, she started severe hemorrhaging "as if an

old wound has opened" and had to have a hysterectomy. The rest and the concern shown to her by her family, friends, and colleagues seemed to help her with her self-assigned task of taking a new look at herself. Once again it was a great comfort to give in to an illness, to be pampered and cared for. She could accept care, V.I.P. treatment, and allow herself to regress only when forced by illness—yet she needed this regression to gain strength to move on in her task, to take responsibility not only for the life of others but for her own. This "new life," of which her work was only one part, enabled her to find some value in herself. She now could acknowledge the appreciation given to her in her work, and was responding with feeling to her children, who in turn became more accessible. She began to enjoy their company, and was no longer afraid to damage them.

Her image of her family and her husband began to change. The dominant, aggressive mother was now, five years after Mrs. Dean's bereavement, a helpless invalid, unable to move or speak—able to express her feelings only with silent tears or a beautiful smile. Mrs. Dean was now often deeply moved by her mother, and discovered new aspects of her personality. She felt guilty about her previous hate, and could allow her mother to see her love.

Other members of her family also were no longer seen as a threat, but as people with problems of their own, who needed her. Now that she could give them something, the fact that since her husband's death she had had to accept their financial help for the children's schooling was no longer such a burden.

And her husband no longer had to remain so idealized; nor did her father. They both became human beings with many strengths and weaknesses, who had loved her and had hurt her, and whom she had deeply loved and deeply hated. As she began to see them more realistically and acknowledged some of her resentment toward them, she also became able to see herself more realistically and could take some of the goodness back into herself, could link up some of her destructive fears with her great potential for loving. It was only at this point in therapy that she was able to tell me about the "nasty" periods in her marriage. Her most important "nasty" memory was the time when she felt forced into being like her husband's mother, and had submitted to what she felt he had expected of her. Equally painful, or more so, were the memories of those times in her marriage when she had made her husband be like her father, and thus had forced a role on him which was in conflict with his identity.

Much later, when Mrs. Dean's life had changed fundamentally and we met only very occasionally, she told me that she was now able to have close friendships with men but that she would never consider marriage again, because she could not tolerate either being dominated by the other's possessiveness and expectations or being the dominating one. She felt that in her own and in her parents' marriage, one partner had always been the victim of the other. She could not comprehend a marriage in which both husband and wife could maintain their autonomy.

This is one indication that in spite of her now being a highly successful and much valued woman, she has not overcome her distrust of her own autonomy, still doubts her strength to hold her own. She also still does not have much of a social life, but this is no longer important, for her present position enables her to travel all over the world and meet many interesting people. In her job she is now a V.I.P. in her own right in spite of being "only a widow." Her sons, too, are proud of her, value her— and this in turn helps her to let them be what they need to be, even though this is sometimes not what she would wish for them. She is glad about her many travels not only because she enjoys them but also because it separates her and the boys. She is well aware how painfully her own life was affected by her unresolved fantasies in relation to her father—and of the danger that this may be repeated with her sons, who had to grow up with only one parent. She now makes links for them with their father wherever she can, with his interests, his hobbies, "just as an offer." For their twenty-first birthdays she gave Simon a tiny river-island which his father had cherished for fishing, and bought Ralph a carefully selected site in his father's favorite Irish village.

Although we can see clearly that Mrs. Dean's responses to her bereavement had their roots in her childhood, during which her inner world was built, we can also see how at the moment of her greatest need the outer world, the people around her, failed her completely. They not only gave her no support in her grief but colluded with her worst fears by actively stimulating her anxieties. Yet these people loved her in their own way, and were not especially malicious. Their attitude expressed their culture and social class, their own denial of death and mourning. However much they might have wanted to help her, their own defenses against the pain of bereavement and death made this impossible.

Mrs. Dean's story has been difficult for me to write— not only because of the many contradictions of her fascinating, creative personality, but because of her exceptional need to be helped to feel safe with the strength of her emotional powers. We have seen how throughout her life each crisis threw her into a whirl of destructive fantasies but also how she then created situations in which she could be given special care and concern, and feel loved and loving. In her therapy she relived the crisis situations and the terror of her destructiveness, which she needed to have accepted by her therapist as part of her loving, caring personality so that she could experience her fears as one aspect of her creative imagination. Once this process of self-integration was achieved, Mrs. Dean was free to express in her personal and professional life a message which proclaims that her previous compulsive "living with death and dying" was no longer a threatening part of her life.

POSTSCRIPT

At the end of the therapeutic contact in the four cases discussed above we could observe considerable changes in the life situations of all the people. Let us have another look at them: they were different in age, social and religious background, training and occupation, and above all in their individual characteristics. They had very important features in common, however: they had all felt insecure in their childhood attachments and were ambivalent toward their first love objects, their mothers. And at some point in their lives all had experienced a bereavement they had been unable to mourn. They all had asked for help in a crisis situation because of their inability to express feelings.

We should ask ourselves: Are the similarities, the common features which emerged during the therapeutic process, in these otherwise so different individuals interconnected, and can they be linked with the fact that all of them appear to have made good use of the therapeutic intervention?

Repeatedly in this book we have seen how the loss through death of an important person strikes at the deepest roots of human existence, recalls the experience of previous attachments and losses, and reactivates the pain of earlier bereavements, physical as well as psychological in nature. The emotionally deprived and threatened child may have learned to avoid the fear of abandonment and isolation by denying feelings and pain, and may thus have laid the foundation for defenses against feeling the agony of the final bereavement through death. If life does not help him to resolve the anxieties which underlie these defenses, he will go on repressing, denying feelings —feelings of love as well as hate, those of joy as well as sorrow—and develop the image of an unfeeling, unemotional person.

Through the therapeutic relationship the people in this chapter became able to get in touch with their feelings, recaptured their capacity for new attachments, and experienced themselves as loving and hating human beings, who could be understood and valued. This process is implicit in all therapeutic intervention. The special feature in these four cases was that the blockage of feeling, the obstacle to emotional communication, was repressed mourning on the occasion of bereavement through death. With the regained capacity for attachment in the therapeutic relationship, in which loss could be faced and accepted, the patients became free enough to live their lives with diminished guilt and increasing self-confidence. Communication in their important relationships could then be established and the problem for which they had sought help lost its pressure.

The changes which occurred in these families were part of the normal life cycle, and were likely to have occurred without therapeutic intervention. We are entitled to ask, however, whether these people, who had all been so confused and inhibited, so unable to express their feelings, would have been able to participate freely and feelingly in their new life situations and to respond realistically and hopefully to the new challenges if the obstacle to their expression of feeling, their grief inhibition, had remained untouched.

Let us then consider in what way the lives of the four families have changed. The Allens, in their early thirties, have become proud parents of a baby daughter. This event fills them with hope that their still unresolved conflicts have lost their threatening power, and they now feel that they can live with them.

The sons of the Bonds have left home to start families of their own. Their parents feel enriched by these young families, and are now content to build a life for "just the two of us." It remains unclear whether their sexual difficulty has been overcome, but it certainly has lost its destructive power.

Anne Cohn has outgrown her adolescent rebellion and confusion, and her parents have been able to support her in her independent choice of life. They themselves no longer need to fight the battles of their childhood in their marriage, nor is Mr. Cohn constantly anticipating "disaster around the corner," now that he has understood the cause for this threat to his existence. Both he and his wife are still gingerly testing out how far they can expose their feelings.

Mrs. Dean's sons have grown up and can share with their mother, in mutual interdependence and in a feeling relationship, their interest in the world and in their absorbing careers. Yet there remain areas in which communication is impossible, and Mrs. Dean still avoids a new committed relationship through remarriage, and still builds safeguards against overcloseness with her sons.

We can see that the life situations of all these people have changed fundamentally. While there are only limited changes in their personalities, the total climate of feeling is sufficiently different to give them a chance for further growth and development. The vicious circle of mutual mistrust and destructiveness has been replaced by a more benevolent one of mutual support.

The four cases discussed in this chapter are examples of failures to mourn. In each of them, unresolved grief led to a defense against emotional commitment, a denial of feeling, and an impoverishment of the personality. It placed the people concerned in danger of mental and physical illness. Such severely denied mourning requires therapeutic help.

In both marriage and bereavement problems, the urgent need is to relive experiences of earlier attachments and losses in order to be free for new, realistic relationships. The aim of therapy is to assist in this process. In marital therapy the work can be done with the two partners, whose interrelationship may need to be modified in order to achieve the mutual attachment which allows autonomy and growth. In bereavement there is only the surviving partner, who has to understand and modify the ongoing interaction between himself and the internalized deceased. He is faced with the difficult double task of accepting the reality of the loss and yet holding inside himself the memory of the lost partner, who remains part of his regained autonomy. Only by achieving this can he regrow the ability for new attachment and become free enough for a new life.

It would be fatal, however, to give the impression that bereavement as such, with all its agonies and confusions, all its pain and bewilderment, needs therapeutic intervention. What it needs is the recognition that grief is the normal response to the loss of a loved person, and that it is of fundamental importance to work through the mourning process and for it to be completed without harmful interference or repression.

8.

Widows in Our Time:
Social and Personal Implications

In previous chapters we have attempted to understand responses to bereavement primarily in connection with the lives of the bereaved and their earlier attachments and losses—responses arising out of their inner worlds. In this chapter I shall change somewhat the focus of the exploration, and try to see how aspects of the external situation reflect the survivor's conscious and unconscious attitudes toward the lost partner.

Everything that goes on in the outer world of the bereaved—the circumstances of a husband's death, the relationships in the family at that time, the legacies, material and spiritual, which he left behind, the situation in which the widow finds herself—will reflect her inner world. This conclusion is not revolutionary, indeed, no other is possible. Yet, again and again, it is not taken into consideration, and the help, advice, and support offered to the widow are based primarily on the situation as it appears from outside.

Although sons and daughters play a part in the stories that follow, the chief characters are widows—partly because there are such vast numbers of them that even a non-sociological study such as mine must include a special attempt to understand their situation in our time and place; and partly because it is these women whose lives are most likely to change fundamentally after their partners' deaths.

What does it mean to be a widow in our time and place? A time in which equality of the sexes, women's liberation, and dual-career marriages are major themes for discussion in the media, universities, factories, government, and homes? Death takes no notice of these discussions. So far as death is concerned there is no equality of the sexes. Men die at a considerably younger age than women. Women are adding not years but decades to the statistics of average age at death. And many more men than women remarry. The statistics on page 177 show the great discrepancy in mortality rates for men and women, and in remarriage rates of widows and widowers. Widows certainly do not have the rarity value of their male counterparts, which makes for very different attitudes toward widows and widowers in our society. Many widows feel that they are being rejected or avoided, while widowers are made to feel precious, like eligible bachelors. None of the "touch of death" attitudes with which widows are often tainted seem to affect widowers—here too there is inequality.

Needless to say, all this is overgeneralized: attitudes toward widows will vary with their personalities and ages, and the rejection may be modified for those with jobs or professions. Since the number of such women is steadily growing in our society, more rational attitudes toward widows are likely to appear. But as we have seen in previous chapters, contact with death and bereavement stirs up all sorts of irrational fantasies and feelings, and these unconsciously motivated attitudes will continue to affect widows until their roots are more clearly understood.

Death and Remarriage Rates in United Kingdom 1971[1]

DEATH RATES

age	females	males
all ages	316,541	328,537
45–54	15,358	24,242
55–64	35,621	63,657
65–74	73,502	102,139
75–84	107,057	81,183

REMARRIAGE RATES OF WIDOWED (per 1,000 population)

age	females	males
25–29	128	237
30–34	99	194
35–44	53	125
45–54	27	84
55 plus	3	22

In looking over these stories, I have become aware how few of them are about working-class families. This is so not only because of my own middle-class background but because the clients of the Institute of Marital Studies, where I worked, were mainly middle-class people. I was happy, therefore, when a taxi driver, who has driven me for years, told me the story of his mother, Mrs. Leather, who was born in 1873, widowed in 1901, and died in 1944.

When her husband died of a brain tumor, Mrs. Leather was twenty-eight and had five children, four

[1]From population census for 1971 of the Registrar General's office.

boys and a girl, between the ages of one and twelve. Her husband had owned and worked in a small boot repair shop. After his death she tried to carry on with this but failed, and was swindled out of what little money there was. There were no relatives to help and no pensions of any sort. The family lived in a poor neighborhood near a big street market and Mrs. Leather knew many of the stall holders. The Leathers had been a popular couple in the neighborhood. He was good at magic tricks and his pretty young wife could sing and dance. Together they had given pleasure and entertainment, and earned pocket money at fairgrounds and clubs.

The obvious solution for Mrs. Leather, as for many widows with young children in the time before washing machines, was to take in washing, and the obvious place to find her customers was the street market. She and the children collected and delivered the laundry there. Mrs. Leather was a conscientious, hard-working woman determined to please her customers. They, in turn, let slip into the laundry bags odd bits of food and other goods from the stalls.

The family did not manage too badly. The children were fed and on the whole better clad than the majority of children in their poor neighborhood school, for Mrs. Leather had high standards. Her son knew little about his parents' background except that his mother was orphaned at the age of five and was brought up in the family of a married aunt, hard-working, clean-living people. That was where she learned to cope in adversity and cope she did. During the First World War she worked in a hostel for factory workers, and after the war at a West End hotel, where she was in charge of the linen closets. My informant, her youngest son, by then eighteen, worked there with her doing odd jobs, and she still liked to keep an eye on him. Her only daughter married young and emigrated with her husband to Australia, so that when the Second World War started there were only the sons to worry about. They were all married, had children, were respectable citizens. It was most upsetting when the youngest son's wife left him early during the war, and the natural place for his young children, a boy and a girl, was his mother's home. They loved her and she loved them and their father knew that they were well cared for. He says that he would never have dared to bring home another woman while his mother was alive. "At that time they were 'one-man women.' My mother would never have looked at another man after my father died, when she was twenty-eight."

By the time the flying bombs made London a dangerous place to live, Mrs. Leather was over seventy. When her eldest son, who lived in the country with his family, was wounded and discharged from the army, he offered to take his brother's children. This seemed a natural solution to which everybody agreed in spite of the pain of parting from their grandmother. She never said what it meant to her, but it must have been a great deal because a few months later she had what was called a nervous breakdown and was admitted to the hospital. Her sons were given leave and found with horror their mother's apartment full of mice and rats. For many weeks she had not eaten her rations, but had hoarded them in the cupboards where they went bad. She was very confused when they visited her in the hospital and insisted that God had forbidden her to eat. After a life of caring for others, Mrs. Leather saw no purpose in caring for herself now that she had no one else to care for. She died a few weeks later, in 1944.

Today not all widows adhere to the "one-man woman" ideal, nor do their lives necessarily need to be dull and monotonous if they remain alone. There are clubs, evening classes, groups for the over 55s. In England widows can now go to their local pubs without

feeling embarrassed, although that would have been un-
heard of in Mrs. Leather's time. Television helps people
to feel less lonely and telephones, too, protect against
isolation to some extent.

The care of children and grandchildren offers the most
natural source of emotional comfort for the loss of a
partner. In spite of often being exhausting, it gives the
widow a purpose in life, makes her feel needed and
wanted, and helps to minimize loneliness, the greatest
curse of widowhood. That is why childless widows often
find other people's children to look after, and young
relatives or neighbors may become the center of their
lives. Whether or not, these relationships can truly help
to make the widow feel better depends ultimately on her
own inner security, her feelings of goodness about herself. Children, friends, and neighbors can help to affirm
this sense, but they cannot create it if it is not there.

The widow who has not felt secure and loved has
difficulty giving or accepting love and affection from
others, including members of her own family. She may
have felt unsure of her husband's love and envious of his
affectionate relationship with their children; a daughter,
especially perhaps an only daughter, may have been
deeply resented as a rival. Such feelings are unacceptable
and are kept in the dark, away from consciousness. As
long as the husband is alive, they are kept under control
but after his death, when defenses crumble and unconscious drives take over, feelings of anger, hate, and resentment may get on top of the love and concern, and
may affect the widow's responses to her bereavement in
her attitude toward her children and her husband's
legacy.

Conflict between the generations is as old as
humanity. Dramas about jealousy and envy, love and
hate, battles of dominance and submission between the

young and old have always been major themes in myth, legend, folklore, and literature. Since psychoanalytic theories have probed all areas of life, there have been attempts to understand the cause of these conflicts and to learn to cope better with them. At the same time, however, the new status of youth, with all its privileges, the adoration of youthfulness, and corresponding fears of getting old and being left out have greatly increased the strain of generational conflict. Older people's attempts to bridge the generation gap by pretending to be young have not solved the old problems and have created new ones. A perhaps not too serious one was brought home to me by a six-year-old who was playing, deeply absorbed, with a sort of dummy which she lovingly called "Granny." As she has four living grandmothers (both sets of grandparents were divorced and remarried), I asked why she had created still another one. The child replied sadly, "I haven't got a real granny."

As grandmothers nowadays want to look and behave like their daughters or even granddaughters, and grandfathers have love affairs with their grandchildren's girlfriends, the confusion between the generations and the conflicts arising from it have become very troublesome. A young wife's close involvement with her youthful father may be threatening to her husband. Equally, a wife may be anxious not only about her husband's attachment to his mother, but also about her own mother's rivalry for his attention.

I remember vividly a most dramatic therapeutic session with a married couple, in which the wife insisted that her husband had only married her because of his interest in her mother. The husband's attempts to repudiate this and to show affection to his wife were met with furious accusations that his loving behavior was only put on for my benefit. This young wife had been an only child and had felt excluded from her parents' close relationship; when she married after her father's death the young couple shared her mother's house, and she again had felt threatened in a threesome. The threesome in the therapeutic situation had painfully reactivated these earlier anxieties.

External factors, such as sharing a house or a job, may not only create realistic conflicts, but uncannily reinforce the irrational internal ones. This was so in the case of Mrs. Draper, whose husband owned a furniture shop. Their son-in-law, their only daughter's husband, was his partner. He was an efficient young man but found it difficult to stand up to his father-in-law, and this lack of cooperation was detrimental to the business. There were considerable debts and many worries, for which Mrs. Draper blamed her husband. After his death, however, she blamed herself, feeling that her nagging may have contributed to the heart trouble which killed him. To make up for having been so hard on her husband while he was alive, she entered the business immediately after his death and made it her full-time concern. There was no time for mourning. Her son-in-law was now her partner and they worked closely together, appreciating each other's contributions. They put life and soul into the shop, were full of initiative, had new ideas, and within a year the business began to flourish.

A year later, Mrs. Draper asked for therapeutic help because of bouts of depression. She had become increasingly unable to enjoy the success of the business, feeling uneasy about succeeding where her husband had failed. She also began to be worried about the close relationship with her son-in-law—the sort of relationship she had always longed to have with her husband but never had. She was anxious whether her daughter was feeling excluded and what her husband would feel if he were alive. She was full of guilt and needed reassurance that she was not again being destructive when her conscious wish had been to pay restitution for not having loved her husband enough. Her guilt and depression could be seen as aspects of a delayed mourning process and she needed her therapist's support to work through this.

I would like to look now at widows who have a profession of their own and worked throughout their marriages, whose identities apparently did not depend on their husbands, and who were financially independent of them. It would seem that in this situation, at least on the social and economic level, only minor social adjustments would be necessary. I will let the journalist Mary Stott speak for this group of women:

> Self-pity was easy to identify as the supreme enemy— easier for me, I dare say, than for many, because as a woman's page editor I knew more than most about the problems of widows. "Why did it have to happen like this to me?" could not be allowed, for I knew very well that there were three million widows in this country alone and that for many of them it must have been very much worse than for me. No doubt my obsession with their plight, their lack of money, lack of job, of experience in standing on their own feet, was part of my defence mechanism. Putting things into words was my habit of life, the need to identify with the Three Million, to try to help the still secure to prepare themselves just a little for the state of widowhood, was a compulsion. *In grief we do as we must.*
> ... Even now I find it difficult to imagine myself into the life of the happily solitary people who feel no need to talk about what they have read, seen, heard, thought, to any other person. It wasn't, with me, that there was really no-one to talk to—there were colleagues, friends, neighbours, and in the early days I understood very well the need to make it easy for them

to talk to *me*, to protect them against the embarrassment that they might be "intruding on my grief," or that I might burst into tears. . . .

It was a little later that it came to me that there was no-one I could talk to as of right. When you are suddenly bereft of your "speech-friend" (as William Morris called it) you fear that by engaging in conversation with anyone else you are asking a favour. Social assurance is more precarious than we think, for it rests on the assumption that by and large it is mutually agreeable.

But even Mary Stott, who had managed her bereavement as she had managed her dual-career marriage, needed her regression: "The day after K.'s death I wandered about, clutching for what reason is now beyond me, a shaggy white toy poodle belonging to my granddaughter, vaguely stroking it and holding it close."[2] Maybe allowing herself this regression was an important factor in enabling her to enter and complete successful mourning.

Whereas earlier we discussed widows who, during their marriages, were primarily wives and mothers and became career women after their husbands' deaths, I know of some professional women whose identities apparently did not depend on their husbands, who had always defined themselves in terms of their careers, yet who seem to have lost interest in these careers when they lost their husbands. To understand this, we have to examine in greater detail their original identification with their fathers, which first determined the choice of their self-image.

This small group of women, all in their late forties, came to my notice two or three years after their hus-

2. *Forgetting's No Excuse* (London: Faber and Faber, 1973), pp. 184–85.

bands' deaths because they were still grief-stricken and very depressed. Their depression and emotional paralysis were quite alien to their previous personalities and frightened them. They considered this "moping" shameful, a "waste of time," and were upset about their inability to give it up. At times they were angry with their husbands for deserting them and resentful at the consequent deprivation. In outbursts of bitterness and indignation these widows expressed the feeling that they had wasted their lives being the people their fathers and husbands had wanted them to be—that now these men had abandoned them, leaving them with no true self, no secure identity of their own.

The similarities in the family backgrounds of these career women were striking: they all had had very successful, intellectual fathers to whom they felt close, and whom they wanted to please by becoming successful, intellectual women. They all hated their mothers, whom they saw as stupid, aggressive, and above all intrusive, the opposite of the loving, gentle, highly intelligent, and interesting fathers. Each of these women had one brother whom they described as "good-for-nothing," ruined, and spoiled by his mother's preference for him, while they themselves were undoubtedly their fathers' favorites, intent on usurping the brothers' place.

All the women had married much older, gentle, maternal, not very masculine men, who were uncertain about their sexual potency but brilliant and successful in their careers. Their wives saw them as possessing the same "saintly" qualities that they had so cherished in their fathers. The only complaint these women expressed about their husbands was that they felt rejected in their needs to mother them, which they tried to do surreptitiously in all sorts of bizarre ways: one women always laid out her husband's clothes for him, dressed him for special functions, even brushed his hair. (This same woman insisted on laying out her husband's body after his death.)

The most outstanding feature in all these women was the hatred of their mothers—which must have made their own attempts at mothering their husbands as well as their children ambivalent and false.

These women had continued their careers after marriage with the same intensity as before, with frequent absences from home and extreme involvement in their work. They insisted that their husbands had supported them in this and that there was no rivalry about work and achievement. At the same time they sometimes conveyed the feeling that their husbands' successes owed much to their support—much as, perhaps, the husbands' sexual potency had depended on their stimulation and help.

The loss of their husbands increased their guilt and undermined their defenses to such a degree that these women, who normally seemed to manage so well, were not only unable to manage their grief and mourning but dramatically changed their way of life. They gave up or considerably cut down their work, which was previously so important to them, and attempted all sorts of reparations in relation to their children or people in need (one became excessively religious, and joined a closed order). The need for career and intellectual successes seemed no longer to exist now that there were no fathers or husbands to identify or compete with.

I want to stress that my interpretation of the stories inevitably involves oversimplifications, and also that my small sample cannot be taken to be representative of professional or career women in general. Nevertheless, to be able to understand them better, I would now like to look in more detail at one of them, Mrs. Bright, who asked for therapeutic help two years after her husband's death because she was still unable to control her grief in spite of desperate attempts to do so. She found it an intolerable strain to maintain her work and the demands of day-to-day life. Whenever she let herself be persuaded to be with friends, she would break down. She felt that they did not understand or help her in her pain. She was bitterly ashamed of her tears, which she felt were "like wetting my knickers."

This paralyzing grief was in extreme contrast to Mrs. Bright's previous life, in which she and her husband had maintained firm control of any emotional display. Finally she succumbed to her doctor's suggestion to seek therapeutic help, a difficult decision for this intelligent, active woman who had built up for herself a very successful career as a public relations official. Since her husband's death, however, she had lost interest in her job and found it hard not to neglect it.

Her husband also had been a successful professional. He was sixty when he died, she fifty. They had four children between nine and twenty years old, two boys and two girls. Although the couple had wanted a fairly large family, Mrs. Bright had interrupted her work for only the permitted four months' period of paid leave for the birth of each child. Thereafter the children were largely in the hands of au pair girls, as they were when their mother's work took her abroad.

Throughout their childhood the three older children presented considerable problems, especially the sons. After their father's death they showed great hostility toward their mother, increasing her despair and sense of abandonment. The children's rejection also added to her guilt, which centered on her inability to mention their father or to do anything to "keep him alive" for them.

In spite of these pressing immediate anxieties, Mrs. Bright told her therapist during their first sessions that her despair and depression were caused by unresolved guilt and mourning in relation to her parents, which her husband's death had reactivated. She only wanted to talk about her childhood and her early relationships. It took many weeks before she was able to talk about her present situation and her husband.

She grew up in Malta where her father was in the diplomatic corps. They were wealthy, and had a large house and several servants. She was the only daughter, with an older brother whom she envied and disliked and described as coarse and stupid. Her mother, she said, was a silly, twittery woman with a delicate constitution, with whom it was impossible to hold a real conversation. The only thing she could do well was exquisite, useless embroidery. She was possessive and intrusive, and throughout adolescence her daughter had to fight to maintain autonomy. Only after some months of therapy did Mrs. Bright change this picture of her mother.

Her father she saw as charming, interesting, and highly intelligent. She spent much time with him, for he preferred her company to that of her brother. When she was thirteen her father died, quite suddenly. She was told of his death by the servants, which she considered an insult, and she responded with frozen disbelief. When she finally had to accept it, she could not understand how the world went on without him, that the gardener continued to mow the lawn and the servants went on polishing the floors. She could not tolerate the thought that life should continue as it had before her father's death, but when it evolved that it could not do so, this was still worse. The house in which they lived had to be given up, the servants had to be dismissed. Her brother at that time no longer lived at home, so just she and her mother moved into a small apartment. Her mother had chosen it on the assumption that the two would share a bedroom. This suggestion was met with furious rejection and a threat to run away unless the plans were altered. The girl could not bear the close proximity to her mother, her intrusiveness, her possessiveness. She dreaded meal times, when she felt repelled by her mother's finicky eating habits. Almost everything about her mother disgusted her. She built a protective wall around herself in order not to be overwhelmed by her growing hatred. She felt that her mother's love masked suppressed hatred toward her, and anything might happen between them, so that the wall was a two-way protection.

Mrs. Bright had never valued being a girl and had had few girlfriends or girlish interests. She had always envied her brother for being a boy. Now she felt that if being a woman meant being like her mother, then she certainly did not want to be one. The result of her identification with her father was a denial of her femininity and a lifelong battle against her mother.

She did not menstruate until she was sixteen, just after she met her first boyfriend, Kenneth, the man she later married. She devoted herself to her education, studying alone as much as possible and concentrating particularly on the subjects her father had valued, even when these were hard for her. She passed all her exams brilliantly.

Kenneth was ten years older than she, delicate in health, tall, very intelligent and gentle. His friends called him "a gentle giant." He reminded her in many ways of her father. When they met he was still studying and had accepted a three-year fellowship in the United States. They kept in close touch while he was away, and when he returned they decided to get married. She was still under age and needed consent from her mother, who was much opposed to the marriage: her daughter was so young and Kenneth so delicate. But his charm and beautiful manners won her over. They got married before he had his degree, and she had to take a job to help to support them. Once he had qualified she returned to her own studies and earned degree upon degree.

Kenneth was an only child. He and his young wife viewed his mother as selfish and unpleasant—even more so than his mother-in-law—and largely responsible for her own unhappiness. Her husband had treated her badly, was often rude and unfaithful to her, but although this happened under Kenneth's eyes, he did not recognize it.

Even when Kenneth was established in a good, well-paying job Mrs. Bright continued to work full-time, and often had to travel abroad. Both partners supported intellectually the idea of dual-career marriages, were delighted about each other's successes, and took great interest in each other's work. Yet, although Mrs. Bright did not acknowledge it, there appears to have been a strong element of competition. During the first few years of their marriage, she earned considerably more money than her husband. It was very important to Mrs. Bright to stress that later in their marriage she never tried to earn as much as he did, since she felt that this might become potentially disruptive to her marriage. She also denied her competitive drives in all other areas, although when at last she began to talk in her sessions about her husband she often mentioned her anxiety that she wanted things he had had, for example, the same sort of car. She was a tall, well-built woman, usually dressed in expensive pants-suits, and she spoke of her admiration for her husband's taste in clothes and his perfect suits.

At this stage in her therapy Mrs. Bright had to maintain that the relationship with her husband had been perfect. According to her they had never argued and were highly critical of other married couples who did. There had never been a cross word, they had only helped and supported each other, walked through life hand in hand, and were blissfully happy. She did not talk about their sexual relationship.

One of the uniting bonds between the couple was their

shared hatred of mothers. They had both felt very guilty about this, and this guilt and hatred dominated their lives. It led to a mutual rejection of mothering, so that neither could allow the other to be caring. Mrs. Bright's only complaints about her husband were his neglect of his delicate body, which needed special care, and his rejection of her attempts to give him this care. Her own inhibitions about mothering and caring may well have colluded with his rejection.

We know already that Mrs. Bright was most ambivalent about leading a woman's life. She hated cooking and housework. With each baby she stayed at home for only three or four months, while she breast-fed, which was not satisfying to her nor did it seem to make the baby content. Each time, after her return to work, her mother came to look after the baby. Mrs. Bright hated this situation, which after all she herself had produced, and found it so difficult to be welcoming to her mother that only Kenneth's conciliatory behavior enabled her to stay on. What his attitude toward the children had been was unclear to Mrs. Bright, but he does not seem to have compensated them for his wife's lack of mothering through his own maternal care, for the children seem to have been very deprived—except for the youngest, Vivian. She was conceived as a sign of reconciliation after Mrs. Bright's infatuation with another man and later, especially after her father's death, took over the unique role in this family of the cherished, affectionate, and dependent child. Vivian shared her mother's bed after her father's death and continued to do so until, through therapy, Mrs. Bright was able to tolerate her own dependent needs, and no longer needed Vivian to express them for her.

The rather platonic affair which preceded Vivian's conception was the second during Mrs. Bright's marriage; the first was five years earlier. In both cases the "lovers" were very different from her husband. They were "flesh and blood men," perhaps like her brother, who did not share Kenneth's gentleness and inhibitions, nor his anxieties about potency. As they had nothing of the other-worldly, almost saintly quality which she described in her husband and father, these men could be expected to accept those less nice qualities in herself which she thought would cause pain to her husband and disrupt their relationship.

On both these occasions she had wanted to confess to Kenneth and talk to him about her feelings for the men, but he did not want to know, just as he had refused to see his father's unfaithfulness to his mother. He only wanted to know good things about his wife—perhaps he was afraid that this would lead to a break of their marriage. During their courtship, while he was studying in America and was separated from her for three years, she once kissed another student and confessed this in a letter to him. He had responded with cold contempt, calling the innocent kiss of the girl, whose mind was so ambitiously bent on her studies, promiscuous, and had threatened to break the engagement. This story, one of the rare ones with the slightest hint of criticism of Kenneth, makes it clear how much he had colluded with—or even provoked—Mrs. Bright's splitting: the ideal father and the repellent mother could never meet, could never be united; the clean, good, hard-working girl must not get in touch with anything that might be greedy, bad, sexual.

A year before Kenneth died, Mrs. Bright's mother, who by then was living in the United States, had become very ill. Mrs. Bright gave up her work for several months, and stayed with her mother until her death. She looked after her with great care, and spent hours preparing delicacies for this dying woman who could no longer enjoy them. If we remember how much Mrs. Bright had always disliked cooking, and how disgusted she had been in the past by her mother's eating habits, we can sense her guilt, her frantic need to repair, her attempts to rewrite her life story.

When she talked to her therapist about her mother's death she sometimes cried, but there was also a sense of relief—as if she felt that she had managed some restitution. When she talked about her husband's death there was only grief, no relief. She felt guilty and destructive. The following facts emerged: soon after Mrs. Bright's mother died her husband's mother got very ill. She too lived in America, and Kenneth had also insisted on traveling there to be with her in her last days. When he returned, it became clear that his own health had deteriorated. His doctors told him that he had a heart condition which made it necessary for him to lead a very quiet life, the life of an invalid, unless he underwent an operation. Kenneth was undecided, but Mrs. Bright thought that he would be very unhappy as a permanent invalid, and did not try to stop him from having the dangerous operation.

After his death she blamed herself, feeling that it was her passive acceptance which made Kenneth decide for surgery, and which resulted in a series of operations and terrible suffering for him.

In the periods between operations, when Kenneth felt better, he had become immersed in the life of the hospital and she felt excluded, as if she had lost him already. Either way the hospital visits were agony for her. But she could never let herself break down in front of him or share with him the terrible experience they were both undergoing.

In the end, after yet another drastic treatment, Kenneth suffered so much that his wife no longer wished for his survival. During the last weeks she did not leave his bedside and watched his suffering and dying in anguish. After his death, she was desolate and inconsolable. She could not talk with her children about their father, could not mention his name, could not bear to have any photographs of him around, or anything that reminded her of him. As soon as possible she moved to another house, leaving everything behind including the furniture. She did not want to be reminded of anything that belonged to her past, yet could not get away from it in her grief. She found herself frequently passing the deserted house or following a car which looked like the one her husband had owned. Her own career lost all meaning for her.

Mrs. Bright, who had so reluctantly asked for therapy, was beginning to make good use of it. The turning-point came when she was able to tell her therapist about her infatuations for the men to whom she had shown features of her personality which she herself despised and which she could never show to Kenneth. By talking about this, she exposed them also to her therapist, whose acceptance and understanding was a first step toward reconciling the split inside herself.

The aspects of Mrs. Bright's personality which she had repressed from earliest childhood now appeared in her dreams in rather bizarre forms. This woman, who had had rigid toilet-training and later internalized this disapproval of everything dirty, now had frequent nightmares about "piles of shit"—not her own but other people's—which she was compelled to clear away only to find them eternally returning. In her dreams these piles of shit were sometimes associated with Kenneth, whom she had never allowed to have any contact with dirt. Not only had she carefully hidden from him her own dirty side, including anything to do with menstruation or the births of her children, but she preferred him not to come into the kitchen or help with the washing-up. She did not like him to help with the babies, change diapers, or even be present during this process. Her fantasies about the dirty, bad aspects of her controlled, polite, and civilized husband seemed to be so overwhelming that she had to keep him removed from any contact with dirt.

The unconscious arrangement between the couple was that men were good and saintly (the husband, her father, and even his father in the face of all evidence to the contrary) and women were stupid and repulsive. Mrs. Bright did not want to accept such a role herself and felt that her marriage could be kept perfect by denying or depreciating the feminine aspects of her personality. She counteracted them with her intellectual efforts and successes which were valued by her husband, just as they had been valued before by her father. In other words, femininity was excluded from their "ideal" marriage, and all badness was split off and projected onto the two mothers. When Mr. Bright died, within months of the death of both mothers, his widow was left with all the "badness," to which was now added her feeling of guilt that she had contributed to his death and that she had been full of hate toward her mother.

This crisis of despair brought her finally into therapy, in which her fear of being criticized became a major theme. Because for Mrs. Bright there was nothing between total goodness and total badness, any criticism implied that she was completely wrong and bad. Slowly she became able to modify the images of the all-bad mother and the idealized all-good husband and father. With this, she also became more able to acknowledge her own conflicting drives, her own goodness and badness, love and hate, and at the same time, to make links with her own femininity. The greatest change could be seen in her attitude toward her children. Instead of the previous obsession always to be giving to them, in an attempt to atone for the past, she could be more relaxed, more attuned to the children's individual needs. Similarly she developed a greater flexibility in relation to her work, which she began to enjoy without feeling dependent on it or overwhelmed by its demands.

At this point in her therapy, Mrs. Bright reported a dream, with great excitement and satisfaction. She had jumped over a big wall, on the other side of which she discovered a lovely white girl and a crowd of black boys, who danced around her and made love to her in turn. The girl seemed to enjoy it, but Mrs. Bright, in her dream, was worried about what would happen if the girl should have a baby. When she asked this question, the boys chanted in chorus: "We'll all father it," and the girl smiled contentedly. Mrs. Bright, too, was beginning to feel that this was quite a good arrangement. This dream, in which she identified both with the sexual woman and with the baby, gives some indication of the move toward change in Mrs. Bright, toward self-acceptance as a woman who could better understand herself.

In the past her children had responded to their mother's own rejection of her feminine and maternal attitudes with anger, hostility, and irrational demands for "things." Now they responded to any move toward change in their mother by a more loving acceptance. A mutually more satisfying relationship began to be established. Simultaneously Mrs. Bright modified the picture which she had of her own mother. She began to see her as having been a capable woman who had given valuable voluntary service to her community and who, like herself, had suffered from an unhappy childhood and early widowhood.

While it is too early to risk a prognosis for Mrs. Bright's recovery, we can already see that the crisis of bereavement which led her into therapy could be used as a turning-point toward self-integration. She had always felt guilty about her relationship with her parents, and her feelings of guilt became overwhelming when her husband died, for which she blamed herself. Her children's rejection of her at this point seemed to confirm that she was bad, and threw her into despair. Her request for therapeutic help expressed her hope that she might survive and change. She is still working on this process, in which a very different image from that of the career woman who had no faith or enjoyment in her femininity is beginning to emerge. While after her husband's death there was a danger that she would abandon her job altogether, she can now continue to work in a less obsessive way and have time and energy for her children.

Mrs. Bright's experience helps us to understand other career women with similar histories, women who also dramatically lost interest in their careers when they lost their husbands, and who had equal difficulties in successfully completing their mourning process.

Queen Victoria, the most famous perpetual mourner, showed many of these traits. She, like Mrs. Bright, was obsessed with an intense hatred of her intrusive mother, with whom she had to share a bedroom until she became Queen of England. Her first royal act was to demand a bedroom of her own. She too idealized her gentle husband and had a most ambivalent relationship with her oldest son. After her husband's death she had the greatest difficulty in returning to her royal career, and might never have done so if her ministers had allowed her to give it up. Although Queen Victoria remained a deeply mourning widow until her own death, she too was infatuated with "flesh-and-blood" men. At one stage it was an Indian footman, but her greatest involvement seems to have been with her servant John Brown, the only person who could cheer her up. The saying at the time was: "All that is not Brown is black."

Now I would like to leave these career widows and look at two women who had no careers of their own but did appear to have clearly defined "feminine" identities. These women were severely damaged after their husbands' deaths. In spite of all the differences between these two sorts of widows, there is a fundamental similarity I would like to explore.

Joy and Sibyl had been outstandingly attractive as girls, were adored by their fathers, were very popular all round, and had lots of boyfriends. In their late twenties they married men twelve and fifteen years older than themselves, who had both been married before. They were very special men, interesting, creative, highly intelligent, geniuses of love and friendship, and were surrounded by a circle of admiring friends in spite of their critical and inherently pessimistic attitudes toward life. These men were in many ways the extreme opposite of their wives, who were both indefatigable optimists, gay, "rays of sunshine," "children of nature," who loved long walks, out-of-door activities, gardening; they enjoyed and provided good food and were gifted homemakers in spite of their extreme and amusing clumsiness. In neither house was it rare to find the hostess in the kitchen scraping up from the floor the special meal which had just slipped from her fingers. Neither of them had children or a liking or gift for being with them. They were, in a way, child-wives, and their marriages were successful continuations of their previous father/daughter relationships. Yet both had made serious efforts to understand their husbands' work and interests and share in conversations with their intellectual friends. They themselves had never tried to acquire professional skills or to have any committed work of their own.

Both these marriages exuded a sense of beauty and goodness, and created homes which became a source of delight for their friends. The wives adored their husbands, calling them most inappropriately by baby-endearment names; the husbands cherished their wives and despite frequent teasings and admonishments were deeply attached to and dependent on them as the optimistic, life-affirming counterparts to their own intellectual existence.

Both husbands had had several heart attacks, which they themselves ignored as much as possible and which their wives refused to recognize as serious warnings. In fact, it was the wives who insisted on living as before, with walks in all weathers and strenuous outings and travels.

What had to happen did. Both husbands died suddenly of heart attacks. I was present at the death of one and closely involved with the other. Although my intention was to recount these stories because of the widows' responses to their losses, I would like to give a small space in this book to a memorial of Joy's husband Ben, and his unforgettable and extraordinary death.

It was the night of Boxing Day, 1968, the night of man's first attempt to circle the moon. We had a beautiful evening together, Joy, Ben, a male friend of theirs, and I. Joy had surpassed herself as a cook and hostess, and Ben, who had recently celebrated his eightieth birthday, was at his sparkling best, full of wit and wisdom. We talked a great deal about the current event, the circling of the moon, and its effect on the shape of the world. Ben was apprehensive. He was a great lover of stillness and conservatism in spite of his tumultuous and often rebellious life and his manifold and contradictory leanings. At one time he had wanted to join a circus troupe, and indeed had the makings of an acrobat. At another time he entered a monastery, but after a year the wise abbot sent him out for a taste of the world before taking orders and, needless to say, he never returned. But his deepest commitment, fundamentally and ultimately, was to the arts, and he could use words, images, and dreams to make them alive for others.

At one point during this enjoyable evening we talked about death. I think it was initiated by me with the question which bothered me already then: Why is it that some people who seem so securely rooted in themselves and in the world are so frightened of dying, and others, weak and helpless in life, show such unexpected strength and dignity when facing death? Ben would not have this: "It can't be like this . . . You have got something wrong . . . The attitude toward life and death must always be the same." "As far as I am concerned," he added, "all I wish for is to remain conscious, be in control of myself, into death."

Time passed rapidly. Soon it was past midnight, and we had forgotten to listen to the exciting news of whether or not the astronauts had circled the moon and resumed contact with earth. When I expressed regret, Ben offered a substitute, a poem to the moon, which he had written that day for his granddaughter. He got up, a small and slender figure, and leaning against a bookcase read us his poem. The essence was his sorrow that now that we knew the other side of the moon, the moon of Matthias Claudius, a late eighteenth-century German poet, could no longer exist. Matthias Claudius was Ben's special love and concern, and the special love of Matthias Claudius was the moon, which he celebrated in many beautiful poems.

> *The Moon has risen high,*
> *the golden stars in the sky*
> *are shining bright and clear.*[2]

The last lines of Ben's poem expressed sadness that his own life, which had been dedicated to poetry and the arts, would now be taken over by the computer. He read

2. *Ernst und Kursweil*, (Munich: Siebenstern Taschenbuch Verlag, 1969), p. 91.

these lines with mounting emotion, then took a quiet step forward, laid himself gently, face downward, onto a nearby divan, and without any sound or movement was dead.

This step from highest consciousness into death was the perfect fulfillment of Ben's wishes. Wonderful as it was, it was difficult to comprehend. That his wife could not do so, was quite unable to take in what had happened or to assimilate the shock, was very natural. Before and during the funeral she remained stunned and very calm, but within a couple of months it became clear that she had undergone fundamental changes.

Now I would like to link Joy's story again with Sibyl's, whose husband died at about the same time, also suddenly of a heart attack. She too after a period of incomprehension responded with unexpected and fundamental changes in her personality and appearance.

While their husbands were alive, Joy and Sibyl seemed to be very sure of their feminine identities, had distinct characteristics, likes and dislikes, interests and talents. Neither they themselves nor the people around them would have doubted their autonomy. Yet within months of their bereavement both women lost all those features which had made them "adorable" and special—as if they were no longer worth having. Both became very depressed, which in itself was so alien to their previous nature that it fundamentally changed the image they used to present.

Even now, five years after their husbands' deaths, both women's lives are aimless and empty. They have not been able to find a new meaning, a new identity, either in the role of a mother or grandmother to somebody's children or in a job, which might have given them some degree of self-affirmation. Both stayed on in the houses in which they had lived with their husbands and in which they had been outstanding hostesses, but this role too they have completely given up. Their appearances altered almost beyond recognition. Sibyl became a compulsive eater and nearly doubled her weight. Joy's body got out of control in other ways: she had frequent falls, sudden movement-blocks, and the great wanderer now can barely walk. A crippling illness, whose onset can be traced back to the time of Ben's first heart attacks, rapidly accelerated after his death. Her loss and grief may have provided the conditions which allowed the physical disorder to appear.

The question I constantly ask myself is whether these dramatic alterations in Joy and Sybil represent fundamental changes or whether they are logical continuations. Both these women's identities were expressed in roles they played for others, through which they gave joy and pleasure and received love and admiration. In their childhoods as well as in their marriages, these women were charming and lovely for others; now without a significant other, there is no one to call forth the charm.

That the career widows changed the images they had given before their bereavement as dramatically as these child-wives, though in a different way, that they too lost their identities with the loss of their husbands, indicates some similarities between these apparently very different women.

It must be remembered that none of these widows had in any way identified with their mothers. The career women had built their self-images on their identity with their fathers in complete rejection of their mothers, which must have made their feminine self a very precarious one. The child-wives were their fathers' love objects, which meant always getting the better of their mothers. Their femininity was not really owned by them but was called forth by men.

All these women seem to have had a sort of negative

self-awareness, that is, one that can be achieved only in a very close relationship in which their identity is continually confirmed. This confirmation was provided by their partners—their identity was an echo and when the echo stopped, identity and self-awareness were lost.

From my limited sample, it is impossible to assess how frequent such fundamental changes are in widows who before their bereavement gave the impression of being very sure of themselves and having distinct personalities. The women who come to my notice because they need help to cope with the adjustment to widowhood are likely to be those who were never sure of their true selves, whose identities always depended on others. The crisis of bereavement highlights their inner situation.

A little girl is brought up with the idea that the greatest achievement for her will be to marry, be a beautiful bride, and become a wife and mother. Getting married, therefore, is an occasion for rejoicing and is seen as the achievement of a new status and new identity. On the other hand, it is also the moment when a girl gives up her name for that of her husband, moves to whatever place of residence is appropriate for him, and submits to the innumerable laws and regulations that do not consider her as a person in her own right but as the wife of her husband. While this situation offers many compensations and is freely and joyfully chosen by the majority of women in our society, it may also weaken their sense of autonomy.

This double meaning of marriage has become particularly striking in our time, when increasing divorce and separation undermines the security of the identity a woman gains through marriage. At the same time, many women now have more opportunities to gain a new identity through their work or profession. This dual situation can also be observed in bereavement. There are widows who blossom out after their husband's deaths and find new meanings for their lives. It is these women who hate the term "widow" for its connotations of pity. But there are others who lose their identities with those of their husbands. It is perhaps due to the existence of these two alternative responses to widowhood that so little support is offered to widows who need it in our society, unlike societies in which the majority of widows unquestioningly accept and rely on being taken care of materially and emotionally.

What about widowers? Although I have not been able to observe personally the phenomenon of loss of personality in widowers, surely there must be men whose identities are defined by the important women in their lives and maintained in close relationship with them. Are these men also unable to hold onto their autonomy after the loss of their wives? Or do society and job provide for men the needed support for their distinct personalities? While little girls are brought up to look forward to fulfilling themselves by becoming wives and mothers, boys are brought up to look for their identity in their work, be it as an astronaut, football player, or writer. It is more likely, therefore, that the "bereavement" following retirement, which entails the loss of their job and their role in society, constitutes a greater threat to a man's autonomy than the loss of his wife.

There are many fewer widowers than widows, and a much higher percentage of them remarry. Of those who do not there is a relatively high mortality rate. In their study of 4,486 widowers over the age of fifty-four, Michael Young and his colleagues discovered that during the first six months of bereavement the death rate of these men was almost 40 percent higher than that of married men of the same age. Three-quarters of this increase was attributable to heart disease, and after the first six months the rate dropped rapidly back to around normal.[3] Did these widowers, did Mr. Sachs whose story follows, die of broken hearts?

Mr. Sachs was a well-known producer in Austria, highly successful and clearly at the beginning of an outstanding career. He was an impressive person in every way, had married an attractive woman, and had two beautiful children—in fact, he seemed favored by fate and had everything a man could wish for.

At the age of forty-five, Mr. Sachs, a gentile, fell passionately in love with a Jewish woman who was half his age. He asked his wife for a divorce and married the woman. Soon afterwards Hitler overran Austria and Mr. Sachs immediately lost his job at a State Theater and every chance to pursue his career. His life was in danger, but he still had the option of parting from his Jewish wife. He rejected this solution and to the distress of his family and friends, emigrated with her to England.

Partly because of language problems, he found it difficult to re-establish himself. To earn a living he had to accept any offer of work, however inferior to what he had done before. The couple had been used to every luxury, to the spoiling given to a very successful artist. Now they were just struggling foreigners in an alien world, in very restricted and restricting circumstances. But they loved each other, and made the best of their changed life, until Mrs. Sachs became ill with an incurable cancer and died within nine months. She was thirty-eight at the time of her death, her husband sixty. He was desolate and desperate in his loss and loneliness. By that time he had friends and admirers who tried to comfort him but could not reach him. All he felt was the emptiness, the uselessness of his life.

Although he rejected the sympathy of his friends, he

3. Michael Young et al., *Mortality Rate of Widowers* (London: Lancet, August 1963).

very painfully experienced what he described as an "unpenetrable silence. No voice can reach me." He would complain pathetically that the telephone had not rung once during a whole weekend, and would confess that he sometimes lifted the receiver simply to hear a sound. Those of his friends who understood something about bereavement processes felt that Mr. Sachs' refusal of any comfort or sympathy was a bad omen for his chance of working through his grief toward survival. He got more and more depressed and died within six months of no real illness. Of a broken heart? Or of the deep resentment that his so much younger wife, for whom he had sacrificed everything, had left him, deserted him? Would he have survived if he had still been able to do the work which had been his vocation, had formed his distinct personality and determined his role in society?

What, I wonder, are the differences between widows and widowers in the special bereavement situation—the death of a partner in a dual-career marriage, an institution which has been much idealized in recent years? Career wives have very real problems to face. However much their husbands support the philosophy of the dual-career marriage, whenever there is a breakdown in household routine, an illness of a child, or a strain in family relationships, it is the wife who feels guilty. Yet only if these external pressures collude with her internal personality problems will the widow devalue her achievement and become unable to continue her career after her husband's death. Husbands, who have not been burdened with the external pressures and need not feel that they are doing something wrong and unnatural by having a career, are less likely to change their attitude toward their work after the loss of their partner. It will probably become more important for them than ever before, as it does for the majority of career widows.

In partnership marriages, those in which husband and

wife share the same work, the psychological situation is unique. Couples who can sustain this situation successfully have very special qualities. Pierre and Marie Curie, who jointly discovered radioactivity, are a classic example of such a partnership, and Marie Curie's response to the loss of her husband, whom she succeeded as Professor of Physics at the Sorbonne, is among the most moving testimonies of love and widowhood. Although she was perhaps the more brilliant of the two scientists, all her work after his death was felt to be and presented as a tribute to him. Perhaps the fact of his cruel and violent death—his head was trampled by horses—had something to do with his young widow's need to keep his mind alive in herself in abnegation of her own.

Mrs. Rodgers, the widow of a contemporary scientist, who had also worked in closest creative partnership with her husband, has found a somewhat different solution for the difficult task of promoting the legacy of the partnership and yet continuing to grow and fulfill her own autonomy. After her husband's death she went through a phase of violent grief and despair, but she knew that she had to continue the joint work and now carry alone the responsibility for what had until then been a shared commitment. In addition, she had to take over some of the jobs, roles, and functions which in the past her husband had performed alone. In both situations, with him inside her, she could add his contributions to her own, and by further developing the joint work and strengthening what had been her own, she has emerged as a more creative and stronger personality in her own right.

9

Sons and Daughters of All Ages

Although in previous chapters I have mentioned the responses of children to the death of a father or mother, it has been in connection with the surviving parent's responses to the bereavement, which will inevitably affect the responses of their sons and daughters, a fact we must keep in mind when we now look more closely and directly at these.

I would like to repeat at this point that my material is not based on systematic research, but is derived from stories that have come my way. It is therefore in part anecdotal and always incidental, especially in this chapter. I have never worked directly with children, and have, for example, no material on the death of a sibling. I have also refrained, except for the case of Mr. and Mrs. Bond (Chapter 7), from considering bereavement through the loss of a child, perhaps the most painful loss of all in our small families.

I do have some uneasiness here, as in the chapter about widows, about the fact that my stories concern almost exclusively middle-class people. I have wondered whether these people, several of whom have been or still are in psychotherapy, are producing "Freudian material" because they feel that it is expected. But social work colleagues who work with people not used to verbalizing complicated emotional concepts have helped to dispel my doubts. Their experiences with very different clients were similar to my own. I feel that I can conclude, therefore, that my stories are not esoteric fantasies of middle-class people who are familar with psychological concepts but deep-rooted, age-old phenomena arising from unconscious processes, which can be found in the Bible, mythology, and legends.

The widows whose stories I have told spoke little about the more obvious deprivations and frustrations which the loss of their partners must have caused them. There was, for example, hardly any mention of the sexual frustrations which could be expected at the often sudden loss of a husband. The feelings most often conveyed to me, which appear to have caused the widows greatest anxiety, were those which expressed their need "to let go," to be furious or to regress. Regression into infantile behavior as the first response to loss—a need most adults, especially those with children to care for or a job to maintain, cannot acknowledge, is strongly discouraged in our culture. Weeping in public, or even in private, something that only children do, may be just tolerated from adults at a deathbed, a funeral, or immediately after bereavement. From some of my stories, however, the need for childish behavior emerged in more bizarre forms: the woman who gratefully let herself be fed and bathed by her mother-in-law; the one who wrapped herself in a soaking hot bathtowel at her moment of greatest despair; the man who had to be restrained from attacking the officials who buried his son; and even Mary Stott, who alongside her concern for the "Three Million Widows" needed the comfort of hugging a soft toy. Such temporary regressions at the loss of a partner are not only not pathological but should be acknowledged as benign and seen as an aid to coping with severe stress.

In looking at the responses of sons and daughters to the loss of a parent, however, I could observe none of this need for regression, rather the opposite: there was a need for self-assertion, for taking the dead parent's place both in relation to the surviving parent in the family and in relation to the lost parent's position, his work, his creativity. Therefore, it seems that the loss of a spouse, a sexual partner, rouses the need to regress, while the loss of a parent rouses the need to progress, to mature, to be potent.

It may well be that a widow's fury and her anxiety "to let go" are an expression of her sexual frustration. The widow's inhibition about talking about sex seems to indicate that sexual feelings roused by fantasies about the dead man who was a sexual partner while alive are more frightening and forbidden than those stimulated by the death of a parent, in relation to whom sexuality was always confined to the realm of fantasy. Many of the adult sons and daughters who talked to me about the loss of a parent stressed the immediate and direct effect on their sexuality, in exciting, stimulating, or inhibiting symptoms. Some of this can be understood as the conscious or unconscious wish of a son or daughter to take the dead parent's place with the surviving parent, which may be felt by children of all ages. The little boy, who had always wanted to have his father's place in the mother's bed, clearly expressed his changed attitude toward this hitherto hopeless wish in his first remark after his father's death: "Now I am going to sleep with Mum."

If the lost parent is of the same sex, the fantasy of the son or daughter seems to be one of succession. The little girl who had always wanted to be in Mum's place will now readily move in to fill it in all sorts of ways, especially if her sad and bereaved father colludes with her need by turning to her for comfort. He will then play into her fantasies as well as depriving her of mourning her mother. We have seen this in Chapter 1 in the case of Robin and his little daughter, and will meet it again in the story of Mrs. Cooper.

An adult son who had never been able to stand up for himself while his father was alive may feel supported in his masculinity by his internalized dead father. I knew a very ineffective, passive young man who after his father's death showed surprising strength and initiative. Suddenly he was the man of the house and what he said was law. His previous passivity seems to have been largely due to repressed and defeated rivalry with his powerful father, with whom he only dared to identify after his death.

The adult daughter who had despised her mother and built her life in identification with her father was hoping in this way to be first in his heart. After her mother's death, she tried to fulfill her childhood dreams more directly by giving up what life she had of her own and living with and for her father. She was devastated when a few years later her father, perhaps worried about too close a tie with her, chose a new wife. Only then did she herself decide to marry.

For married sons and daughters the response to a parent's death will depend largely on how far they have resolved in their marriage conflicting feelings and childhood fantasies about the parent. In some of the cases that follow we will be able to see how such fantasies are reactivated after the parent's death.

When her father died, Tamara had been married for ten years and had two children, a boy six and a girl three. She herself had been an only child, born when her

mother was approaching forty and her father was thirty-
five. The mother, who had been a professional, gave up
her career when Tamara was born, not only because she
now had a baby to look after but because her husband
became increasingly dependent on her support as he
climbed up the academic ladder and had more and more
demands made on him. He was helpless in all practical
things, and in very delicate health. She had to do everything for him: be his housekeeper, his nurse, his secre-
tary, his chauffeur, and at the same time be the wife of
a man of growing fame. She did it all, and if there was
any resentment, it never showed. But to be a mother to
her daughter did not come easily to her, especially because in this area her husband was a great rival. Whatever cuddling, spoiling, nursing, comforting the little
girl got, she got from her father. He loved being maternal with her, while with his wife he was always the
helpless, delicate baby. In his career, which his wife had
originally shared with him, and in which, being five
years older, she was actually his senior, he was an outstanding success. This produced a most confusing situation for the wife. She had married this junior colleague
and supported him in his studies. Now that he had
fulfilled her high expectations for him, he had become
increasingly dependent on her mothering and care, had
stopped being a husband in the accepted sense, and was
taking over the mothering of their daughter. On all levels, as his wife, a former colleague, and their daughter's
mother, she became uncertain of her role, and often felt
undermined and humiliated, feelings which found their
expression in her tense and ungiving relationship to her
daughter.

The inevitable result of this situation was a close, loving tie between father and daughter. Tamara identified
with her father, and later studied and wrote on subjects
which were their shared interests. Her mother's increas-

ing jealousy, which Tamara often provoked, did not help to improve their relationship.

When Tamara was twenty she married a man with a very different, more artistic background than her father, but with his gentle and maternal features. The father showed no open disapproval of her choice but withdrew from his daughter the moment it was made. He did not explain the reason and she could not ask. There was a complete breakdown in communications, an insurmountable estrangement, which eased the relationship between Tamara's parents but was extremely painful for her. Nevertheless, she was happy in her marriage and became a good mother to her children, in whose care her gentle husband shared, since she felt that "full-time mothering is not for me." In her career she maintained the identification with her father, and went on working and writing in the areas that had interested both of them. The split between these adult aspects of Tamara's life and her unresolved childhood ambivalence was expressed in her appearance and manner, which alternated between those of a serious scholar, a responsible mother and wife, and an often childish, immature student-daughter.

When Tamara was thirty her father became seriously ill with a poor prognosis. As soon as she heard of the nature of his illness all conflicts were forgotten. She gave him her undiminished love and concern, and he responded without reservations. His determination to fight for his life in spite of repeated operations and painful treatments was consistent with this delicate man's lifelong struggle to overcome obstacles, and was now reinforced by his wife's threats that she would not survive without him and his colleagues' pleading that they still needed him. Tamara, too, could not bear the thought of her father's approaching death, but for her the two years he managed to continue to live held special compensations. In the shared knowledge of the approaching final separation, the old closeness between father and daughter was resumed with a new intensity. They had long, confidential talks, and worked together on a book of Tamara's which was of special interest to her father and strengthened their bond. As might have been expected, the old rivalry between mother and daughter flared up again, each wanting to be the one who was most important to the patient, the one in whom he confided, the one who had his love. They shared his last hours, each convinced that his last words, his last glance was for her.

When Tamara left the hospital after her father's death, bereaved, grief-stricken, and burdened by her near-murderous fantasies toward her mother, who, she felt, was standing between her and her dead father, as she had always stood between her and the living father, her first impulse was the wish for another baby. She could communicate this need to replace the lost life by a new one to her husband, and he was able to understand it with her. He helped her, however, to accept a breathing space in which she—supported by him—might become able to integrate irrational with more rational feelings. After a few weeks, Tamara's wish for a baby had subsided. The definite grief for the loss of an Oedipal father, by whom she had wanted to have babies, could be replaced at least in part by a strengthening of identification with the intellectual, creative, achieving father now that she had internalized him. With him inside her, she wrote her most important book on a theme which had also interested her father. She set up a new study for herself, adding his books to hers and buying herself a desk like his.

But this development was preceded by the difficult period immediately after her father's death, when inevitably her mother was acknowledged as the chief mourner, the widow of a famous man. It was she who was consulted about everything concerning his funeral and memorial service and all the many arrangements connected with his professional legacy. Tamara's intense grief, guilt about the years of estrangement, and deep sense of loss were not helped by the feeling that her mother kept her in the background, especially since she felt that her mother was not really fit to take these responsibilities and had gone to pieces since her father's death.

While she herself was not able to give comfort and affection to her bereaved mother, who now lived alone in a big house, with some delight she allowed her six-year-old son to do it for her. He decided that Granny could not be left alone, and went to stay with her for a few days.

It delighted Tamara that her little son, whose aggressive masculinity she had previously found a problem, could now show concern and affection to her mother, and thus relieve her guilt about her own inability to do so. That the little boy's attitude indicated such definite traits of gentleness and concern, traits which had always been so important to Tamara in her father and her husband, made her feel that perhaps her son would continue the line of maternal men whom she needed as a complement to herself. Her little daughter, in whom she fostered both feminine appearance and feminist independence, was to be the true heir of herself. Through her children, Tamara was trying to resolve her own bisexual conflict, which had been reactivated by the death of her father. The renewed competition with her mother as to who was the best loved and most important revived old jealousies and guilt about the wish to have the father to herself in rejection of the mother. Although Tamara had married a man who valued his own bisexual drives and those of his wife, she herself needed constant confirmation that she was cherished as a woman, and also that her professional successes were expressions of her own personality and not achieved by identification with her father.

In trying to understand Tamara we must keep in mind that she is a representative of a new sociological dilemma which has several aspects. In our small Western family there is often no son who can be seen as his father's intellectual heir. The daughter steps into this place, especially if she is an only child. A growing number of professional women choose careers in identification with their fathers, yet also marry at an increasingly younger age and want to follow the pattern of early motherhood. This inevitably creates a problem between the masculine career needs and the feminine mothering needs, and reactivates the dilemma of bisexuality.

That we have encountered similar problems in many of the stories in this book may well indicate that in the face of death and bereavement the conflicts of bisexuality, like other conflicts with their roots in infancy, are reactivated. We have seen that Marion, who had always blamed Tony's uncertain masculinity for her own lack of femininity, could not accept her resentment against him when his life was in danger. She died rather than wish him dead. Mrs. Green's autonomy had been so undermined by her bisexual conflict that she could not survive the loss of her husband. We have more fully discussed this theme in relation to the widows who rejected their mothers, became career women in identification with their fathers, and lost interest in their careers after the death of their husbands. All these women who were so uncertain about their femininity were thrown into a crisis of despair threatening their existence when they had to face the loss of an important man, their father or husband. Can they have felt that they had caused the man's death by robbing him of his masculinity?

Tamara appears to have good chances of using her crisis as a turning-point toward growth. She belongs to a younger generation, in which bisexual attitudes have become more acceptable, especially in middle-class families. She also has the support of her husband in finding a solution to their joint problem. It would seem that in her life situation she may become able to contain both the intellectual masculine aspects of her personality and the feminine, maternal ones, as her husband already does. Her marriage is of fundamental importance in enabling her to resolve successfully the loss of her father and the bisexual conflict his death increased.

Clearly the interaction in the marriage will always have a crucial effect on the way a married son or daughter responds to the loss of a parent. Alternatively, the bereavement may strongly affect the marriage, as we shall see later, in the case of Mr. and Mrs. Cooper.

Felicity's father died a few weeks after her mother. Although her parents' marriage had been a good and united one, their eldest daughter, who was now forty, had been aware throughout her adult life that she was too close to her dominant and attractive father to become an independent person. The fact that she looked exactly like him endorsed her anxiety about her identity. She had fought in every way against the strong tie with him, and had moved as far as possible away from him, spiritually and physically. Thirteen years before her father's death she had accepted a job in Africa in the hope of achieving freedom.

Felicity was an extremely attractive woman, intelligent, capable, and very much in control of her life, so long as no strong emotions were involved. Men were attractive to and attracted by her, and she had had some meaningful relationships, including sex, which were gratifying and enjoyable as long as they remained uncommitted. The thought or mention of marriage, changing her name, and setting up a joint home was unacceptable to her. She was aware that the obstacle was her involvement with her father, and whenever she thought about having a baby, it was her father's baby she wanted.

She gained this self-awareness in a psychotherapeutic relationship, which she started when she returned home after ten years in Africa and realized that the long separation had altered nothing. Neither then nor ever before had the special relationship she had with her father been verbalized between them—but it was clear that the external separation had failed and that the necessary separation would have to be achieved internally.

When her father contracted an incurable illness a year before his death, Felicity used her therapy to prepare herself for her loss. After his death, which followed so closely that of her mother, she coped well with all that double bereavement involved, including selling the house which had been her home. Only when she found in her father's wallet, as his only personal possession, the letter she had written to him thirteen years earlier, before her departure abroad, did she stop functioning. It looked as if it had been read a thousand times and made her realize that the struggle not to submit to incestuous fantasies had been a mutual one. She had been loved by her father, as she had loved him, and this knowledge was good and painful at the same time.

She started to have severe abdominal pains for which no physical cause could be found. These were followed by an overwhelming depression and distinct menopausal symptoms, which improved only when she learned to understand and accept that the pain, the symptoms, and the depression were responses to the loss of her father, who had now deprived her forever of the baby she had dreamt of.

The connection between the death of a father and a daughter's wish for, or guilt about, having a baby recurs again and again in my stories. It seems to be linked with a reawakening of the daughter's Oedipal fantasies about "having a baby by Daddy," as well as with the age-old idea of "one life for another," which we still find in primitive cultures and in children. Recently at a wedding reception, the eleven-year-old brother of the bride anxiously whispered into my ear, "I only hope Dinah is not going to have a baby." When I inquired whether he would not enjoy being an uncle, he said, "Oh yes, but then Granny must die."

How a father's death may become a threat to a marriage we can see in the case of Mr. and Mrs. Cooper who first came to see me when they had been married for two years. They both were architecture students, and the immediate cause for seeking help was Mrs. Cooper's depression and her inability to concentrate on her studies.

Her husband came with her to the session "to support her," but it quickly emerged that they were both worried about problems which threatened their marriage, and that he was seeking help for his share in them. He blamed himself for being unemotional, unable to show affection, and for angrily withdrawing from his wife when he found her unreasonable, "which she so often is." Perhaps he was selfish—both complained about this in the other one: "We had the telephone cut off because we have not been able to pay the bill—but he has to have an expensive sports car"; "Her wardrobe bursts with clothes, but she has to go and buy new ones." Both were very unhappy.

The Coopers were a delightful-looking young couple; he dark, tall, masculine; she blue-eyed, slender, with long fair hair, and very attractive. Their affectionate concern for each other, their supporting, loving nonverbal interchanges, conveyed a deep bond and took the sting out of their mutual accusations.

Mrs. Cooper felt very unsure of herself and unlovable,

and stressed from the beginning of our meeting that her unhappy childhood was the cause for all this. For her first five years she had been the cherished only child of very loving parents, her father's darling, with all the jealousies this entailed in a household in which her young parents uninhibitedly expressed their own great affection for each other. While she was still at the mercy of her Oedipal conflict, her mother became pregnant and preoccupied with the coming baby, which increased the little girl's anger with her and longing for her father. Then the baby turned out to be a boy, a special gift from heaven, and the little girl was supposed to love this hated rival. Soon afterwards the mother became ill (a brain tumor); this meant a new separation, her mother's death, her father's misery, and her own guilt.

The baby was immediately given a home with the mother's parents, for whom he not only replaced the lost daughter but became the son they had always wanted and never had. He was loved and cherished, and stayed with them in perfect security until his father remarried. But Mrs. Cooper had no secure home for the five years after her mother's death. She made the rounds with various relatives, intensely jealous of the little brother, who was the "best loved," and became naughtier and naughtier and less and less manageable. When she was very unhappy and cried for her mother, her aunts would shower her with toys and presents, and then punish her when she rejected these gifts with furious temper tantrums. Nobody could understand her misery and guilt, which, of course, she did not understand herself, for if they had, they would have offered her love instead of toys. She remembered later how much it hurt her when her relatives complained that she made them all suffer because she was different from them and did not try to fit in.

Her only comfort was her father, who spent as much

time with her as possible and always took her on vacations with him. Even while small she was allowed to stay
up for dinner at the hotels, dressed in beautiful clothes
which her father had specially chosen for these occasions. He himself was so handsome and looked so young
that everybody thought he was her older brother.

All this was shattered when she was eleven years old.
Her father remarried and was able to provide a home for
his son and daughter. Mrs. Cooper was a bridesmaid at
the wedding, and very excited. She thought that everything was going to be so much nicer. She would have a
mother and a home of her own, and her father would
always be there. The stepmother was kind and loving to
the children, and they got along quite well together, but
her father was no longer the same. He did not seem to
have time for her, became withdrawn—perhaps, she argued later, because he was anxious about divided loyalties between his wife and his now adolescent daughter.
She felt that she had lost him, felt once again rejected,
replaced by her stepmother, of whom she became intensely jealous. At the same time she felt guilty for being
so ungrateful to the kind and helpful stepmother—it was
a repetition of her childhood situation, for again she was
putting herself in the wrong, refusing kindnesses offered
to her.

Although Mr. Cooper had assisted his wife in telling
her story by occasionally reminding her of something
she had not mentioned or clarifying something she had
said, he could not see that the present difficulties were at
all connected with *his* childhood, which, he said, was a
very happy one. "Except," intervened his wife, "that you
were adopted." This happened when he was three
months old. He knew nothing about his natural parents
except that they were students and that he was a New
Year's Eve accident. His adoptive parents had lost their
own baby and although they cared well for him, he felt

that he must have been a disappointment, for he could never replace the child who had died. Surely they would not have sent their own child to a boarding school when he was six. From then on, he saw little of them, for he made friends with a boy, also an only child, whose parents had a farm in Cornwall, and who always invited him for vacations, as company for their son. Materially his parents were generous—he was given all he needed, they supported his academic interests, enabled him to study, and were proud of his achievements. But they never discussed anything with him that concerned their own affairs, and although they sometimes hinted that they were quite well-off and he would never want for anything, he was always uncertain whether or not he would be their heir. This added to his feeling of unease with them. He was never really relaxed, was afraid to make any demands on them, and resented having demands made on him.

When he got engaged his parents made his fiancée welcome, and although there was never any warmth between them (which he said was probably his fault) he had nothing to complain about. The wife's father had made more difficulty about welcoming a son-in-law. It seemed to Mrs. Cooper that the moment she found a lover and future husband, her father's old attachment to her flared up again, and he gave his blessing reluctantly.

It was striking how similar this couple's emotional experiences were. Both had felt abandoned by their natural mothers and cheated by the available parent figures, whose promises of love were never quite fulfilled. Both had always felt "second best," never "the best loved" (Mr. Cooper had repeated this experience as a schoolboy even during his vacations), and both felt intensely guilty and ungrateful that they could not value what was offered to them, which was never what they really wanted, never first best. Their (unconscious) attraction to each other was probably based on this feeling that neither had a parent with a claim to be the best loved, so that nobody stood in the way of their becoming each other's best-loved and fulfilling their deepest need at last. Hence their despair when all sorts of muddled and preoccupying feelings in relation to their parents seem to come between them and threaten their love.

At the time I met this couple, in response to an emergency call, I had no vacancy for regular meetings. As they themselves were in the throes of examinations, and our first session appeared to have coped with the immediate emergency (the wife had threatened to give up her studies because she could not work), we decided to have ten joint sessions, one a month. After the first of these, there was a crisis, with panic telephone calls and a request for another "emergency meeting," which I resisted. They had read a book to which I had contributed, and from which they saw that my usual practice was to see couples weekly for an unlimited period. They were furious that once again they were offered a "second best." In all the many other situations in which they had felt let down by their parents, they had never risked showing their feelings of resentment, so that I was very glad that they were able to express their anger with me.

After this temptestuous start—and probably because of it—our work together went better than I would have ever dared to hope from therapy at monthly intervals. They were both insightful and very intelligent, worked hard during the sessions with me and together during the intervening monthly intervals. They made it very clear that they needed to feel that they were my best-loved children, and not only made me feel but actually said in so many words that I was their joint best-loved Mum, the only one whom they had ever completely trusted. During the time of our contact they both earned professional qualifications and bought a house. They also had long talks with both sets of parents, which made for better communications and helped considerably toward mutual understanding. They felt safe and good in their marriage, and we stopped meeting.

Three years later I got a frantic telephone call. Mrs. Cooper was in the depth of depression. Could I see them immediately? Again they came together, the husband to help to bring me up-to-date. Both insisted that since we had stopped meeting all had gone very well. They had both been successful in their work, delighted with their house, and overjoyed to have a baby boy who was now nine months old. Three months after the baby's birth Mrs. Cooper's father had died quite suddenly of a heart attack, and since then she had again been severely depressed, and angry and aggressive toward her husband, who had tried to use all his insight and compassion not to respond with irritation and rejection. He found it particularly difficult that his wife would not let him comfort her, rejected him sexually, and could not bear to let him get close physically because, she insisted, "Then you look like my father."

Although they were both frightened and bewildered, they conveyed an unshakable feeling of belongingness, and Mrs. Cooper was obviously very grateful for her husband's support in her despair and plea for help. This time I felt that she needed and wanted help for herself rather than for the marriage, and we agreed to have a few individual meetings.

At first these were filled with angry feelings toward the stepmother, who was grief-stricken and behaved as if she were the only mourner, as if Mrs. Cooper's and her brother's losses were insignificant compared to her own. She would not let them have any share in the bereavement, nor in anything that had belonged to the father, even refusing to give the brother a wallet which he had given his father and which the father had particularly cherished. She constantly talked about money, although the father's will was quite clear and left everything to his wife. Worst of all, the stepmother now demanded the support, compassion, and affection due to a mother, which made Mrs. Cooper feel hateful. We spent the first individual session talking about her reactivated feelings about giving, taking, and being cheated, and her anguish about not being recognized as the chief mourner, being rejected in this role, and again being second best. She was then able to look at her guilt at not being able to feel for or with her stepmother, although she recognized how lonely the stepmother was, how bereaved she was feeling, and how hard she had tried to be a good mother to Mrs. Cooper and her brother. She could not forgive the stepmother, however, for always pretending to be their real mother when she was not, and for making claims on them which might be appropriate for real children but which they could not accept without being untrue to themselves.

At the next session, she recalled her anguish when her father had remarried and rejected her. The picture she now drew of her relationship with her father was different from that of our past contact. He emerged as much more seductive, and she as very determined to be the little mistress. She described how she knew hardly anything about her mother, for her father would never talk about her. She had pestered relatives for information and had learned that her mother had been an actress, very beautiful, full of fun and vitality, a sweet, kind, honest person, and that her father had been passionately in love with her. He himself was very different, quiet, a bookworm, and must have missed his stimulating wife terribly. The family confirmed that he was desperate after her death, and it seemed that he had tried to get some comfort from his little daughter, who replaced the mother in his affections. He took great pride in her appearance, loved to brush her long fair hair, bought her beautiful clothes, and enjoyed showing her off. He always gave her a present not only on her own birthday but also on her mother's.

Her stepmother told her later how relieved the family had been when her father remarried, for they had been quite worried about this close relationship. Mrs. Cooper herself was aware that her father had not wanted her to grow up, and had tried to keep her a schoolgirl. She spoke with a mixture of satisfaction and annoyance about her father's persistent attempts to put off her getting married. Yet she felt that only after her marriage did her father become a happier, more relaxed man, much more at peace with himself. She had always felt that he was not really happy with her stepmother. After her own marriage he had found a woman friend, a neighbor, who was a philosopher and with whom he could share his intellectual interests. Mrs. Cooper seemed to find it easier to accept this philosopher friend, who was so different from her mother and herself, as a comfort for her father than the stepmother, who had been his sexual partner. In her sessions, Mrs. Cooper said of her father: "I idealized him, and still do—all the things about him are precious. It would be a challenge to achieve some of the things which he has achieved—not least the feeling that he has made peace with himself, and come to terms with so much."

The last time Mrs. Cooper was alone with her father, he gave her with great secrecy a box with photos of her mother and himself, many of them snapshots of a happy, handsome young pair. This was soon after her little boy's birth, which had given him tremendous pleasure— and she had felt that the box was a present to her for having made him a grandfather. Later she felt that her father must have had a premonition of his death when he gave her this precious box, and she is deeply unhappy that she missed this opportunity to talk to him about her mother and their life together. Now that her father is dead, she feels that she has finally lost her mother. "While Father was alive, Mother was alive in him, and not completely lost to me." Only now did she feel truly orphaned, and it was this feeling which had made her so resentful of the stepmother's "false claims" to be her mother.

In our sessions, Mrs. Cooper's mourning shifted from grief about the loss of her father to mourning for her mother. "I can now remember more clearly how when my mother died I so much wanted to be like her in every way. I suppose that was so that I could keep her alive within me, and I know that for my father's sake I also wanted to be like her ... I wanted to know all about her, what she looked like and what had been important to her in life. I wanted to understand her personality, and was always pleased if anybody remarked that I was like her in any way."

This grieving for her mother which was now possible seemed to be a great relief to Mrs. Cooper. Soon she began to make plans for the future and talked with increasing pleasure about her lovely little boy and his father's "crazy delight in him." "I know that thinking about my lost parents will always be painful, but now I can look back on these feelings as belonging to the past —knowing that my life belongs to the future and to Peter [Mr. Cooper]."

As I write this, Mrs. Cooper is much less depressed, but she will still need considerable help really to bury her dead parents and to be free enough to choose her husband once again as the man she truly wants and not as a "second best." As he himself has become surer of himself, of his own worth, his own autonomy, he may be able to help his wife in this difficult task.

The opportunity to work with this couple before and after the death of Mrs. Cooper's father has helped me to see more clearly the similarities and differences in marital and bereavement therapies. Fundamentally the same conflicts underlay both crisis episodes. In our first contact, Mr. Cooper colluded in his wife's incestuous fantasies, her envies and jealousies, her doubts about herself. His own doubts about himself, his confusion about dependency, giving and taking, and his own guilt and ambivalences about his parents were increasing those of his wife. Our work together at that time was clearly focused on the couple's collusive interaction.

Mrs. Cooper's father's death so soon after she had given birth to her son reactivated all her unresolved conflicts, especially her incestuous fantasies and the guilt about her unmourned mother. The idealization of both her parents, who had had everything that was worth living for, made her own life seem without value. The therapeutic effectiveness of my sessions with her was helped by the fact that her husband no longer colluded with her anxieties. He was able to let her have and work through her separate grief and depression, and made her feel supported by his affection and understanding. This helped her to work through the grief for her father and reach the long delayed and repressed mourning for her mother. Once this was achieved, she became free from the preoccupation with the past and began to look to the future. The last news I had from her was that she was going to take a few months' leave, to make up to her son and to her husband for all the time she had felt so removed from them. And also because she wanted her son to feel secure with her before they had a second baby, which they planned.

So far I have spoken mainly about adult daughters—what about adult sons? Mr. Todd, whose father was a member of an old, well-known family, had always blamed his mother, who came from a somewhat lower social class, for making it impossible for the children to continue the family's role in society. More personally, he felt that his father had never really valued him, either for his intellect or as a man. After his father's sudden death he was deeply distressed and powerfully seized by contradicting impulses. At this moment he needed a demonstration from his father's wider family that he belonged, that he and his siblings were accepted. When after the funeral family and friends stayed together in the house for two full weeks, a united group of mourners, this was extremely important to him as "an experience quite beyond bereavement."

Side by side with his need to be acknowledged as a respected member of a highly respectable family, he was at the mercy of overwhelming homosexual and heterosexual impulses, which were new and unexpected. At first he had the compulsion to touch anonymous penises in public lavatories. He felt that he was linking himself with his father's potency in the anonymous men who seemed to stand for his father. Until then he had been very inhibited and unsure of his masculine sexuality, but now he had equally compulsive urges to have sexual intercourse with girls, especially those in whom his father had been interested, and in places closely connected in his mind with his father, such as his library and his bedroom.

Three months after his father's death Mr. Todd married one of the girls who had been a member of the mourning group, a girl from a working-class background. Because of his great need to secure his father's potency for himself, he exaggerated in this as in all other aspects of his life what he saw as an expression of his father's personality. It was important to him to give his wife a wedding ring which had belonged to his father's mother.

Sigmund Freud, in his "Notes Upon a Case of Obses-

sional Neurosis," demonstrated the link between a father's death and a son's sexuality most clearly in quoting
his patient the Rat Man as saying after a successful copu-
lation, "This is a glorious feeling! One might do anything for this—murder one's father for instance."[1]

How the death of a mother can affect her son's inhibited drive toward growth, achievement, potency, and
ultimately his marriage may be illustrated in the following story.

Walter, the son of my friend whose tragic death
through electrocution I mentioned in the first chapter,
was shocked and devastated. He had always worshipped
his mother, a well-known actress, although he had
shared her life only up to the age of four, when his
parents' marriage broke up. After that he had had a very
deprived, insecure childhood and youth, and barely any
education. Although none of his anger and resentment
against this "adored mother" was ever allowed to come
into his consciousness, it was expressed in his refusal to
learn or make use of what opportunities he had, and in
accepting jobs (such as that of a taxi driver) that were
humiliating to a public figure. Throughout her lifetime,
Walter stayed in inferior jobs and showed no ambition.
Although disapproving and highly critical of her son, his
mother was affectionate and quite seductive toward him
in their more intimate moments. Yet in public she disowned him, especially after his first marriage to a girl
whom she found completely unacceptable. Largely
through her agency the marriage broke up.

He remarried, this time a friend of his mother's, a very
nice, warmhearted woman who loved him deeply, ac-

---

1. *The Complete Psychological Works of Sigmund Freud*, trans. and ed. James
Strachey (London: Hogarth Press, 1953–66, distributed in the United States by
the Macmillan Co.), vol. X, p. 264.

cepted him as he was, and provided him with a comfortable home in which his mother was a welcome guest. The couple seemed to be very happy, but at the time of his mother's death, when Walter was in his forties, he told me that any man who had had a mother like his would never be able to truly love another woman. A year later, while he and his wife were spending a holiday with me, he casually confessed while washing dishes to very disturbing dreams, in which his mother came to see him and he rejected her, saying, "That is not fair, Mummy, now that you have gone away you must stay away." In connection with these dreams he was able to tell me of the ties he had always felt to his mother, which "held me down like heavy weights and I am only just beginning to feel a bit freer." Soon afterwards he got a better job and developed new interests. He seemed freer to use his potential, less weighted down by guilt about his incestuous fantasies and his unconscious need to punish his mother, which was so much a part of them.

Several years after his mother's death Walter, still apparently happily married, fell in love with a woman who, though different in appearance, has many of his mother's characteristics. She certainly does not accept him as he is, as his wife did. She makes great demands on him, is very critical, and in many ways treats him like a helpful, attractive inferior—as his mother had done. She, too, has ambitions for him and spurs him on—but in contrast to his mother, she supports him in them and makes it possible for him to come nearer to fulfilling them. Walter has asked his second wife for a divorce, although she is still his best friend and he still feels that he can relax with her and laugh with her in a way he cannot with anybody else. But he has chosen the woman whom he can identify with his mother, and with whom he can repair some of the mutual hurts and rejections which burdened his relationship with her. He says that through this new love he feels closer to his mother than he ever had while she was alive.

We know of Marcel Proust that following his beloved mother's death he had to find something to take her place, and for the first time in his life set himself seriously to work. The product of Proust's bereavement and of his subsequent labors was *Remembrance of Things Past*, which transformed him into a major novelist. For Proust loss became the significant element which led him to his preoccupation with lost time and people. In seeking to retrieve them, he became an international literary figure.

Side by side with the grief at their bereavement, we have seen in all these adult sons and daughters an upsurge of growth, a freeing of their own potential. It is also evident that these people, who in their external lives were independent of the lost parent, were struck to the deepest roots of their being by their loss.

What effect does the death of a parent have on an adolescent, who in the normal course of development will sway between his needs to regress and progress, who will behave one minute like an adult and the next like a baby, and who is likely to be confused in his identification between mother and father, male and female? The death of a parent will inevitably disrupt the working through of this bewildering state, and unless the adolescent is helped by a supportive environment, he may suffer badly.

Oscar was fifteen when his father died after a long illness. His family, which consisted of a helpless mother, a rather bossy older sister, and a younger brother, came originally from another country so that there were no relatives about, no adult male to support him, nor was he offered community support in the family's liberal Jewish background, in which in the case of death the male, especially the son, is expected to do all that has to be done. Oscar, who had always been kind and sensible, coped unquestioningly and calmly.

After the father's funeral, the family went to the seaside for a short vacation. One sunny afternoon when Oscar and his sister, who had always been tremendous friends, were sharing a shady spot on the hot, sunny beach, he suddenly attacked her in mad fury, hitting her hard with his fists. The apparent cause of his fury just then was that she was occupying more than her share of the shade; in other situations she often might have been too much in the limelight. This attack was so unexpected, so out of keeping with the boy's personality, however, that the sister was frightened and bewildered. Her anxiety increased when immediately after the attack Oscar disappeared without having spoken a word and could not be found for the rest of the day. When he returned, he was white and silent, and the incident was never mentioned. A few weeks later it emerged that Oscar had developed kidney trouble.

We now know that the loss of a parent is particularly traumatic during early adolescence. For Oscar, the strain of losing his father, having to be so controlled and instantly adult, and not being allowed his own mourning obviously was too great. He could not express his resentment against his vulnerable, helpless mother or against the younger brother who had to be protected. He could only hit out, or at, the bossy sister. But since she was also his friend and support, hitting her increased his conflict rather than bringing him relief.

The following two accounts of loss of parents in adolescence became known to me only when the bereaved boys were married adults. In their different ways, both these men were still trying to resolve problems which had remained unresolved since the time of their bereavement.

Mr. Hall and his young wife consulted me about a marital problem. The husband was bewildered by his wife's unreasonable and eccentric demands; the wife, an Alice-in-Wonderland creature who wrote poems and lived in dreams, complained of her husband's lack of initiative and assertiveness: "He never puts his foot down, he lets me get away with murder." Mrs. Hall's father had left her when she was three, and she met him only for treats and outings. Her mother, anxious to be first in her affections, spoiled her. Neither parent provided the security of loving control.

Mr. Hall's father, a mathematics teacher, could cope with his eccentric wife, a poetess, only by withdrawing behind his facts and figures, and the more he did this, the more emotional she became. When Mr. Hall, their youngest son (there was a much older brother), was fifteen, his mother was in and out of mental hospitals, and one day when she was still under the influence of drugs and he was alone with her in the house, she accidentally set herself on fire while cooking a meal. He failed to save her and she died a few days later in agony. As if this were not bad enough, the older brother now blamed the boy for never having understood his mother, never having loved her enough. When Mr. Hall was twenty he married as near a replica of his mother as he could find, intent on repairing with his wife what he had done to his mother. He was always gentle and understanding, never got angry, "never put his foot down." In fact, he did not relate to his wife as a person with her own needs and her own identity, but related to the image of his disturbed mother, whose needs he had failed to recognize in the past. In paying restitution to his dead mother, he failed to be in touch with his living wife.

Mr. Gough is a deeply committed Swiss naturopath who, when I asked what had influenced him in that direction, replied, "My parents' death made me interested in survival."

Mr. Gough's mother died when he was fourteen and, to his great relief, away at boarding school. He did not go to her funeral. His father died two years later, during his vacation, when he was at home. His death was a relief to Mr. Gough because he did not want to follow his father in the business, which he knew to be his wish. He had been fond of him but had not respected him, and had been much closer to his mother, who got ill with cancer just about the time that he first went to boarding school. He assumes that he was sent there to be out of the way. He did not think so at the time but now feels that he has never forgiven her for leaving him by dying. His father had been so miserable without her that he did not want to live and, therefore, the son could not be sad about his death.

He is aware that he did not mourn for either parent, that he defended himself against the pain of loss by finding good reasons to be relieved. His one important memory in connection with the two bereavements is what he recalls having heard the minister say at his father's grave: "There is no death, life is going on in other forms." This, he feels, first sparked off his interest in the philosophy of survival.

Mr. Gough had one sister, four years older, who got married a year after their mother's death (her father was then living alone) and divorced her husband soon after her father died. She started studying medicine but did not complete her studies and is now also a nature-cure practitioner. This shared vocation has become a great bond between brother and sister, who previously had only a very distant relationship.

After his parents' death, Mr. Gough got interested in spiritualism: "I wanted to know that they were all right." From there he began to be fascinated by various esoteric philosophies which, together with his sister's influence, led to his present profession as a naturopath.

He married at the age of twenty-three, much earlier than he had planned, because his wife looked like his sister. As they seemed to be unable to have children, they adopted two. Mr. Gough said that he considered it more important to give deprived children a home than "to project oneself into children of one's own." "I do not believe in blood ties," he added.

After ten years of marriage, the couple went through a serious crisis. The young wife complained about her husband's lack of emotional commitment and of interest in her and the family. They asked for therapeutic help, which enabled them to overcome the crisis and through which Mr. Gough realized that he had not developed emotionally since his mother's death, and that his sexuality and his relationships with women had remained very inhibited.

Almost immediately after the reconciliation the wife became pregnant. She had a baby daughter whom she breast-fed for fourteen months and could not let out of her sight. Mr. Gough registers with surprise the great changes in his wife through pregnancy and motherhood but insists that his own feelings for this youngest child are in no way different from his feelings for the adopted children. "If anything, I feel closer to them now because I leave the baby to my wife and withdraw from this special relationship."

Recently Mr. Gough's sister suggested that his family join her in her nature-cure establishment, and that he work in partnership with her. He would be tempted to do so but his wife refuses. She is afraid that the sister may become a threat to their marriage.

I was fascinated by Mr. Gough's story and the theme of fear of incestuous relationships which runs all through it. These fears are likely to be based on fantasies of the fourteen-year-old boy whose mother died before he could cope with them, leaving him with intense feelings of guilt about what he had done to cause her death. He is terrified of the pain emotional commitment may cause him. We do not know what in his early life conditioned him for this terror. His interest in survival may recall a struggle to survive at a very early age, perhaps to survive as an autonomous being in an overclose relationship with his mother or in rivalry with his father. His denial of the importance of blood ties is likely to be linked with his incestuous fantasies about his mother and sister. Yet, against his conscious wishes, he married a girl who looked like his sister. The timing of the sister's marriage and divorce may well indicate that she too has been fleeing from her family because of similar fears in relation to her father and brother. Now brother and sister feel protected by their mutual interest in nature-cure and survival, but Mrs. Gough still senses a danger.

Mr. Gough is already setting the scene for withdrawal from his little daughter, and may well try to avoid getting close to her. He has become aware of his denials and repressions however—the crisis which threatened his marriage has mobilized a drive toward change. He has done some belated mourning for his parents, and has understood that the previously repressed grief blocked his development, and that emotionally he has remained the fourteen-year-old boy who could not face the pain of his mother's death.

While Mr. Gough was unable to help or comfort his living parents, he had to reassure himself that the dead parents were all right. I wonder whether the minister's reassuring words —"There is no death"— which he remembers from his father's funeral two years later were, in fact, ever spoken? This was the beginning of his concern for survival, and his present vocation to help sick people, with whom he has no personal relationship, to understand this. In his devoted care for his patients he attempts to repair all that he has been unable to give to those who make a claim on his feelings. He has become a highly skilled and much appreciated helper and healer but he still has difficulty entering into a dialogue of affection and care with his family. In particular, he is still resistant to acknowledging the importance of the relationships he would be most frightened to lose.

In talking to Mr. Gough, a man who always smiles, I felt that he was living in a reality of his own, one in which there is no pain and no death, and which has become his defense against a reality of attachment and loss.

In the preceding accounts of the responses of adolescents and adults to the death of a parent, we have seen how powerfully their reactions were affected by fantasies, guilt, and fears. How much more true this must be for the small child, whose hold on reality is tenuous at the best of times and whose very life depends on his parents. Any change in his life situation is a threat to his security and brings about fears and attempts at withdrawal into fantasy from the frightening reality. This flight from reality, and the behavior which often goes with it, is hard for parents to understand. The anger and fury the small child is almost bound to feel against the "deserting"—dying or dead—parent as well as the surviving one, who appears to be so changed, may add to the parent's own anxieties and set up a vicious circle, in which each increases the despair of the other.

In our time, when the fundamental importance of the earliest years for a child's further development is so strongly stressed, parents are burdened with guilt and a sense of failure if they feel that they have not been able to provide their child with the security which makes for healthy growth during the severest crisis of loss, the death of a parent. It is particularly painful for only children because siblings often can help each other at a time when the bereaved parent has to try to cope with his own grief and depression, anger and guilt. In this situation the surviving parent may best help his child indirectly by trusting in others who are not quite so much affected by the loss, perhaps a grandparent or a schoolteacher.

We shall see how important such help became for Tim, who suffered severe and repeated loss, and how later when his father remarried, his stepmother, supported by his father's confidence in her, became a healer.

Tim was seven when his mother died. This was not his first experience of painful separation. When he was eighteen months old and on vacation with his parents in a strange house, this much loved only child upset a pan of boiling fat over himself. The result was agonizing pain and a long stay in the hospital, where for some time he was more or less crucified, his arms and legs tied to the cot. The hospital discouraged visiting, and Tim's parents had to fight for every hour with him. That they were strangers in the place, with no home or friends, added to the misery of the long, anxious separation. The scars, very real physical ones for Tim and emotional ones for all of them, were still unhealed when only a year later Tim's mother showed signs of illness. Periods in the hospital began, separation following separation. Once cancer was diagnosed, the atmosphere at home was one of intense anxiety, with increasing sorrow and stress for almost five years. His father was so distraught with grief and sorrow, made worse by all sorts of practical problems, that twice during these years this exceptionally good driver had car accidents, and an old T.B. condition flared up.

Tim's father had lost his own father as a little boy, and at that time his mother had colluded with him in denying grief and mourning. Now, in this new crisis of his wife's terminal illness and death, the unresolved pain of the earlier loss was stirred up, and the only way to cope with the despair seemed once again to be denial. This time the vicious circle of denial and repression of pain, a defense established in three generations, included Tim. When he first showed signs of disturbance, by soiling during a visit to his mother in the hospital, his parents interpreted it as a recall of his own painful hospital experiences. But they soon became aware and upset that Tim's soiling was an expression of his furious anger with his mother, whom he wanted to punish for what he felt to be her desertion.

When his mother died, Tim showed little overt concern. His external life was not immediately changed, for his father's widowed mother had looked after her son and grandson throughout all these years, and Tim appeared to accept her readily as a mother substitute—too readily to allow his feelings of loss to become accessible. Only when his guinea pig died a few months after his mother's death did Tim begin to show severe and persistent regressive symptoms, the most worrying being protracted sleeplessness. His father then arranged for treatment at a child guidance clinic, to which Tim responded well. His symptoms soon subsided and when his therapist had to leave England, he seemed well enough for his treatment to be terminated. During this time Tim's teachers showed patient understanding and support, and contributed much to the effectiveness of the therapy. Yet neither they nor anybody else was aware of the strong defenses of denial in this little boy, who escaped into "health" as quickly as possible rather than face his pain.

When Tim was nine, his father remarried a much younger, insightful, and warmhearted woman, and in spite of Tim's angry question: "Why do you want another woman here?" he seemed to relate well to his new mother. Yet three times within a year he had symptoms of motor discharge in slight fits, which could be recognized as an acting out of his aggression.

A year later the family moved. Soon after, during one of his father's frequent absences, when his stepmother was helping him with his bath, Tim let go in a fit of fury. For the first time, in response to the stepmother's understanding and compassion, he could express directly his anger, pain, and resentment at being so different from other children (not having his own mother and having the scalding scars), and at all the changes, confusions, and upsets. After this episode he settled down in his new surroundings, did well at school, and made friends.

When Tim was nearly thirteen, his best friend's father died, and from that day, Tim did not want to know him, making it clear that he could not face his friend's sadness. Soon afterwards, on returning from summer vacation, Tim learned that his headmaster, with whom he had not been on good terms, had suddenly died. His immediate response was relief, almost triumph, yet he began to show symptoms of depression and withdrawal and was unable to work at school for a considerable time.

Tim's grandmother, who had played such an important part in his childhood, now decided to remarry a neighbor, who had become bereaved about the same time as she. The two elderly people had been a great support to each other, and for Tim this man long had been a grandfather-substitute. The old couple moved into the country, and their new home promised to become a great enrichment for Tim's life. After only a few months of happiness, however, the step-grandfather suddenly died of a heart attack. Tim responded immediately with great distress and concern for his grandmother. Then, within a year, his stepmother's father, who had become a great friend of Tim's, contracted an incapacitating illness and quickly deteriorated. Tim could show his sorrow and anguish, and when the man died a few years later, he was able to express his loss and sorrow. By sharing the grief of his two grandmothers, he was then also able to work through his long-delayed mourning for his own mother.

Despite all emotional stress, Tim successfully finished his last years at school and later did well at a university. He married a co-student and the two young people live a full and adventurous life.

At the recent death of the mother of the schoolfriend whose father's death had caused Tim to renounce the friendship, Tim was a great support to the bereaved family, not only by showing warm sympathy but also by offering active and imaginative help with all the necessary arrangements.

It seems that Tim has worked through his childhood traumas and anxieties, centering on his fears of what his aggression may have done to his mother.

We now have to ask the question: Could Tim have been helped with less danger to his existence, in spite of his insistent denial mechanism, and by whom?

In "The Complexity of Mental Pain Seen in a Six-year old Child Following Sudden Bereavement," Martha Harris describes the muddled pain of James, who fears that his aggression has killed his father. She quotes him as saying, "I wish he hadn't shouted at me. . . . I shouted back at him." When asked by Mrs. Harris if he thought that his shouting could have made Daddy ill, he looked at her very intensely and said, "When you are little you are very strong and when you are old, even if you can shout loud, you get weaker and weaker and then you die." Mrs. Harris explained to James the implication of this: although James *knows* that he is little, he *feels* that when he is angry he gets big and powerful, and able to make a big man like Daddy disappear.[2]

2. *Journal of Child Psycho-Therapy* 3, no. 3 (Dec. 1973): 35–45.

James was a very intelligent and fundamentally secure child. He had a slightly older brother with whom he could share his first experience of painful loss. Within three months of his father's death, in six therapeutic sessions, James could be helped to look at his fears of his own destructiveness and at his conflicts, which he called his "muddles." Marjorie Mitchell points out that

> it has become a truism to state that the secure child will be able to deal with death more satisfactorily than an insecure one, but what still needs to be pointed out is that the more dynamic, the more creative, the more intelligent the child is, the deeper will be its feelings and the stronger its relationships. . . . These children will suffer terribly if bereaved, but unlike the psychologically insecure child they will be able to express their sufferings in some form and objectify them.[3]

We have seen how for Tim, who had to cope with long and repeated stress and loss, therapeutic help set in motion a healing process. This became a basis for healthy development on which his family and his teachers could then build, each in their own way. But therapeutic intervention is not always available or even necessary for all children who lose a parent through death. The surviving parent himself may be under too much strain to be sufficiently in touch with his child's need. Can teachers, who have an ongoing contact with their pupils and are often the first to notice symptoms of disturbance, take on the helping job? To do so, they themselves may need some help (for example, at teachers' training colleges) in understanding and becoming more sensitive not only to a child's special needs at a time of bereavement, but also

3. Marjorie Editha Mitchell, *The Child's Attitude to Death* (New York: Schocken Books, 1967), p. 113.

to their own defenses against feelings which may be aroused in themselves. Only if this becomes possible can they make a child feel safe with his feelings of loss, hurt, anger, and above all his fears of his own destructiveness. It is not easy to comprehend a child's often irrational anxiety and hostility, and to meet it with tolerance and compassion.

Perhaps the teacher's most important job is not to wait for bereavement to occur but to talk to children about death whenever the opportunity arises, and thus counteract the taboo which leads to built-in repression of curiosity and all sorts of irrational fears and nightmares.

To be able to meet such a task in a relaxed way, the teacher needs sanction and support. When I recently learned that at one of the new universities a student's thesis on "How to Talk to Children About Death," submitted during a year's special course on education, was turned down as "not educational," my heart sank. It was lifted up again, however, by the attitude of two individual teachers in the following stories of Sue and Paul.

Miss Roberts had in her class a sad, withdrawn five-year-old named Sue, whose father was killed in a mountaineering accident when she was two. His body was not found and her mother never stopped waiting for his return. During Sue's first school year, Miss Roberts was taken ill and had to stay home for three weeks. When she returned, Sue was furious with her and took the first opportunity to kick her hard against her shinbones, which really hurt. Miss Roberts tried to understand why Sue had to do this, but the bewildered child could only say, "I thought you was dead." It was only after this incident that Miss Roberts learned about Sue's early bereavement, which had happened before the family moved from the West Indies to England. From then on, this teacher used every opportunity to talk to her class about death. She was surprised how many opportunities offered themselves, from the dead mouse found outside the classroom to the little boy who every time he heard a fire engine or ambulance passing (he used to confuse the two) put his hands over his ears in order not to hear the sound. It emerged that his mother was expecting a baby and would have to go to the hospital. He had heard that people die in the hospital, and his grandfather had died in one.

During the ensuing discussions Sue sat silent and anxious and, for the first few weeks, didn't participate. Then came a holiday break. When school reopened Sue was there an hour early and, having anxiously waited for her teacher, rushed toward her when she arrived, embraced her, and cried out in delight, "I thought you was dead" —the same words she had used some weeks before, but what a different feeling. During this term she began to participate whenever the class talked about death and seemed eager to help other children if they seemed to be worried. She is now a more outgoing and much happier child, although she still waits anxiously for her teacher after each vacation.

We must remember that Sue met her helpful teacher three years after her father's death, three years with long periods of anxious waiting by the whole family and eventually a move to a strange land. Paul, who is seven years old and attends a school-*cum*-hospital for mentally retarded children as a day-boy, was given help with his anxiety and confusion within a week after his father's death. One of his teachers, Mrs. Beck, a grandmother of eight, is a potter who uses clay in her work with the children to help them to express themselves. Like almost all the children, Paul loves her. I will let her tell his story:

"When I first met Paul, his mental age was about three, he could hardly speak, was enuretic and withdrawn. I liked to work with him, as with most of the children, individually and he always eagerly awaited my arrival. One morning, about ten months ago, he seemed more pale and tense than usual, but greeted me eagerly. He showed me a wristwatch with which he was obviously pleased and which was rather big for him. When we settled down to work with clay, with many sighs, he formed what evidently was a coffin. I asked whether this was what he had wanted to make, and then, with great intensity, he made a heavy lid and banged it with a hammer with all the strength he could muster, onto the coffin. When I asked why he wanted to close this box so tightly, Paul started to howl and throw himself about as if in great pain, clutching his tummy. I tried all I could think of to comfort him—without success—and then decided to take him to the woman in charge. She was unimpressed, insisting that Paul often had tummy-aches, and that there was nothing to worry about. I could not get the poor suffering child out of my mind, however, and before starting work with the children the next morning, I went to see the nurse to ask how Paul was. She again insisted that there was nothing the matter with him, but I refused to accept this. Did she know Paul's family? Was it possible that something had happened at home which might have upset him? At last the nurse remembered that Paul's father had died the previous week.

"When Paul came to greet me that morning and again showed me his big wristwatch, I admired it, adding that he was so proud of this watch because it was his daddy's. He responded with a smile and we settled down to work with clay. Again Paul made a coffin and then looked at me. I said that by making this box, he wanted to tell me something about his daddy. He seemed relieved that I understood him and made a lid, this time laying it gently onto the coffin. For a whole week Paul repeated what now seemed to be almost a ritual. He greeted me every day, pointing to the watch, and each time I said something about the pride and care he took in daddy's watch. Then he would settle down to make the coffin, looking at me expectantly, and I would make a comment connecting the coffin with his father. Every day the lid, which Paul produced after a comment of mine, became lighter and lighter, and was put on more and more gently and with greater and greater care. I began to wonder how long this would go on.

"On the seventh day Paul made the coffin as usual and a very thin lid. Then he took a sharp tool and made big holes in the lid. When I said, "That's right. Now your daddy can breathe," he smiled with great relief. The next day, after the watch ritual, Paul started again to make a coffin. Then, looking impishly at me, he transformed it into a basket and made clay fruit to fill it. My usual routine at that time was to take the children's clay works home, fire them in my own kiln, and let the children paint them the next day. I had not done this with Paul's coffins, but when he confidently handed me the basket of fruit, I knew that his concern had returned to life and color. And indeed, when I gave Paul the now baked basket the next morning, he was delighted and eagerly chose all the brightest colored paints, looking for my approval as he painted each piece of fruit. All this happened ten months ago, and the change in Paul since then has been most striking. He speaks much better, is no longer enuretic, is trusting and outgoing, eager to please at school, and busily collecting badges for good performance. His mental age in these ten months has grown by at least two years."

For the story of Paul, as for the stories of Tim and Mr. Cohen, the following quotation from Robert Furman seems most relevant:

Why is it important that a child master his emotional response to the loss of a loved one? First of all, not to assist a child in perceiving and understanding his responses to the most important event of his life would be to participate in denying him something of his basic birthright as a human being. In addition, psycho-analytic studies have shown that when a person is unable to complete a mourning task in childhood he either has to surrender his emotions in order that they do not suddenly overwhelm him or else he may be haunted constantly throughout his life with a sadness for which he can never find an appropriate explanation.[4]

4. Robert A. Furman, "The Child's Reaction to Death in the Family" in Bernard Schoenberg et al., eds., *Loss and Grief: Psychological Management in Medical Practice* (New York: Columbia University Press, 1970), p. 76.

IO.

How to Help the Bereaved

Shakespeare has Hamlet's mother say, "Thou know'st 'tis common; all that live must die." It is equally common, therefore, that bereavement through death has to be faced as a fact of life. Yet however honestly it is faced, bereavement brings about a crisis of loss, probably the most severe crisis in human existence. In this situation of inevitability and crisis, what help does the bereaved need and what help can be offered?

We have seen from the accounts of bereaved children how vitally important the attitude of those around them, their teachers, their relations, is for their recovery from the crisis of loss. Although the adult mourner is not so totally dependent on his "outer world" and is more able to understand the reality of his bereavement, many of the people to whom I spoke told me how lost and bewildered they felt, how frightened about the "grave departures from their usual attitude toward life," and that they did not know where to turn for help. Some were afraid of going mad or of getting themselves into irrevocable situations, such as hastily giving up their homes. Many developed symptoms of physical illness, but even if they did not go to a doctor or some other helper the symptoms were a disguised request for help of some sort.

In physical as well as mental health, it has become at least theoretically accepted that prevention is better than cure. We cannot prevent bereavement, in fact, one of the most important preventive measures would be to acknowledge the inevitability of death and bereavement, not as a horrible threat looming over us, but as an important part of our lives, for which we can prepare ourselves. In our culture there are now attempts at preparation for most situations we all have to meet: for marriage, for parenthood, ever earlier nursery education in preparation for school, all sorts of preparation for jobs and professions, preparation to cope with retirement and with hospital stays—and probably many more. But there appears to be nothing to prepare people for the most fundamental and universal task, which might have to be met at any age: death and bereavement.

Thinking and talking about death need not be morbid; they may be quite the opposite. Ignorance and fear of death overshadow life, while knowing about and accepting death erases this shadow and makes life freer of fears and anxieties. The fuller and richer people's experience of life, the less death seems to matter to them—as if love of life casts out fear of death. A child therapist once said to me, "Children of parents who are not afraid of death are not afraid of life." In that sense, education for death is education for life, and should be an underlying feature in all education in schools, universities, and through the media.

Yet while one part of me firmly believes that education for death is a major task in our time and culture, I also know that our attitude toward death and bereavement is not easily affected by rational learning; it has its roots in the unconscious and often is expressed with a degree of irrationality which appears to be out of keeping with the personality of the mourner. A friend of mine lost her mother, who was nearly ninety. This once intelligent and gracious woman had badly deteriorated in the previous two years, and it became impossible to look after her in her own home. Just when her daughters were struggling with the painful decision to find institutional care for her, she became ill, went into the hospital, and died peacfully within a couple of weeks. My friend, a very competent, sensible woman, freely admitted her relief that her mother had been spared suffering and upheaval, and acknowledged that a great burden had been taken off her. Nevertheless, she showed all the symptoms of distress, confusion, and disturbance with which we are familiar in bereavement situations. And in *A Very Easy Death* Simone de Beauvoir describes the sudden outburst of tears that almost degenerated into hysteria when she heard of the terminal illness of her seventy-eight-year-old mother. "I had understood all my sorrows up until that night: even when they flowed over my head I recognised myself in them. This time my despair escaped from my control: someone other than myself was weeping in me."[1]

In previous chapters I have attempted to understand such "irrational" responses in terms of early childhood reactions to loss and abandonment which are revived whenever loss is experienced in later life. The insights of depth psychology have helped us to make the link between emotional processes in infancy and later life situations in which we feel helpless and dependent, such as illness, old age, and dying. In spite of the apparent dichotomy of birth and death, both they and sex are closely connected in our fantasies and in the reality of nature.

There has been a remarkable shift in taboos in the last two centuries. In the nineteenth century, when every

1. London: Weidenfeld and Nicolson, 1966, p. 31.

family expected to lose some of its children, when many mothers died in childbirth, and people died at an earlier age, death in all its aspects was often exhibited in a spectacular way, while sex and birth were unmentionable. While the literature of the nineteenth century was a literature of death, the literature of our time is about sex. Sex is now hectically displayed and limelighted and death has become unmentionable. A newspaper editor recently commented to one of his contributors, "Don't mention death, it loses readers."

> *Birth, and copulation, and death.*
> *That's all the facts when you come to brass tacks:*
> *Birth, and copulation, and death.*
>
> —*T.S. Eliot,*[2]

If we can truly (not only intellectually) accept the connections between these fundamentals of life, our attitude toward them all may become more realistic, better balanced, and we may then be able to retrieve death and bereavement from the dark corners in which we try to keep them hidden.

Since the majority of patients now die in the hospital, death is kept away from the home. Children are protected from knowing about it, and relatives are prevented from being in close touch with a dying patient, who is generally too sedated to die consciously. Sedation may, of course, be necessary to ease pain and discomfort but we should realize the vital importance of using it with utmost discretion, in order not to deprive the dying patient and his relatives of the most fundamental experience of "awakenings" on the threshold of death and the message they convey.

Again and again bereaved people have complained with sorrow and bitterness that they were not allowed

2. "Sweeney Agonistes," in *Collected Poems 1909–1962* (London: Faber and Faber, 1963), p. 131.

to be present at the moment of death, that they were ushered out at the last minute "for their own good." They felt cheated, wondering whether there might not have been a last contact, a word, a glance—but even without that, they felt that the finality of their loss might have become more real if they had been allowed to stay. One of the major tasks of mourning, accepting the reality of loss, might have been made easier.

When talking to the relatives, it often became clear, however, that they had willingly colluded with the hospital staff because of their own fears of what the encounter with death would mean to them, especially without the privacy so essential for this encounter. There are situations, of course, such as death through an accident and certain illnesses, where the deceased is so changed and distorted that it may be better for those who loved the living person not to see him. But these are exceptions, and almost all the relatives to whom I spoke who were present at the moment of death or able to see their dead mentioned the relief, the feeling of peace this gave them. One young man of eighteen who was with his grandmother when she died said, "I ought to have had this experience long ago, then I would not have been so frightened of death." One widow said that seeing her dead husband was an unforgettable experience. "He looked so young, so beautiful, so relaxed—I felt with deep gratitude: this is the body of my lover." This widow became a counselor for the bereaved, partly because she wanted to share her experience with others.

In our culture, the attempts not to know about death, not to be reminded of it, are predominant. The house of a deceased person no longer is marked in any way, no drawn blinds, no indication of recent death. The bereaved rarely wear mourning clothes or any other outward sign. No respect is paid, no notice is taken of funeral processions. Funerals and cremations are "got over" as hurriedly as possible. I recently attended one that lasted altogether seven minutes.

There seems to be a general conspiracy that death has not occurred. This glossing over allows for no psychological transition, no *"rites de passage"* to help the bereaved to adjust from relating to the living to relating to the dead person or to the change in his own status from a wife (husband) to a widow (widower). It does not create a climate in which grief and mourning are accepted, supported, and valued. Yet human beings need to mourn in response to loss, and if they are denied this, they will suffer, psychologically, physically, or both. The first therapeutic task in our society, therefore, is to give sanction to mourning.

Loss through death is not only an individual concern, it also affects the community in which the loss occurred, and the bereaved needs the understanding and support of this community. In the past, community support found expression in rituals. These *"rites de passage"* gave sanction to mourning, helping the bereaved to make adjustments to the world in which he had to live without the lost person. The world around him, be it his family, neighborhood, parish, work group, also had to make adjustments to life without the deceased and with the bereaved in a new status. If there is some interaction in this groping toward reorientation between the community and the mourner, the mourner feels less isolated. This has been one of the functions of rituals.

Some religious communities in our society still observe mourning rituals: Quaker meetings, the Irish wake, the Jewish shared mourning, come to my mind. In the latter, relatives, friends, and members of the Jewish congregation gather in the mourner's house for a full week and take care of everything that has to be done, setting him free to grieve. Such care and sympathy provide comfort for the mourner at the moment of greatest distress. How much this helps him to find a way back to life I do not know.

Many societies offer social solutions as substitutes for rituals, which seem to be designed primarily to define a place for the widow. In a Portuguese fishing village in which many husbands die young at sea, there is a particularly large group of widows whose work and identity before their bereavement was based on their function as wives of fishermen. When the man dies the widow immediately joins what looks like a widows' club. They all wear the same clothes, and on Sundays they go together to visit their husbands' graves, each with a bunch of flowers in her arms and a bucket of sand on her head. They find some security in their joint fate and in the obligations and privileges appropriate to their status.

The Beguines in Belgium, though more sophisticated, perform a similar task for themselves by doing good deeds collectively.

In China today the government provides individual workshops for widows. They make, among other things, the blue clothing which is the standard feature of Chinese dress. In this way the widow feels useful and caring, earns her living, and establishes a new type of contact with the community at large and with her individual customers.

The East African ritual of the second burial seems to be designed to care for both the living and the dead. This funeral takes place one year after the death. During the year the dead person is kept alive in the minds of the family with grief and mourning and endless talks about him, and any child born during this time is named after him. Meanwhile the whole family is also preparing for the second funeral, to which relatives, friends, and clan members come from all over the country. If the dead person is a man, his son prepares an effigy of him. On the day of the anniversary of death the grave is slightly reopened and with much lamenting and grieving, the effigy is put on top of the body but facing in the opposite direction. This means that the dead man has now left the living world and joined his ancestors, and the surviving are free to live their own lives. His widows (there may be as many as four), who throughout the year have worn mourning cords around their waists, remarry, and their new husbands cut the cord at the grave. The atmosphere changes from mourning to rejoicing. Through this ritual, the step from death to life and sex and birth is sanctioned, and the bereaved can take it without guilt. Since the wife has no ancestors in her own right, being connected to the past through her husband, it is vitally important that she remarry before she dies. If the dead person is a woman, she receives a second burial but no effigy, and her husband does not have to remarry.

Rituals express the collective unconscious of the culture, for which they perform a religious, social, or therapeutic function. For our Western society, with its emphasis on the importance of close personal relationships, different—more personal—forms of *"rites de passage"* are necessary. In their absence, an increasing number of counseling services, set up by both voluntary and statutory organizations, are offering help to the individual bereaved or to small groups of mourners.

I am not concerned here with discussing the work of these services but rather with exploring more generally the needs of the bereaved and the ways in which they might be met, bearing in mind that the majority of mourners may not actually make use of therapeutic services. Nevertheless, it may help them to know that they can do so, just as physical symptoms sometimes disappear as soon as the patient knows that he can go to see a doctor.

The experience of counselors for the bereaved confirms that help is most needed and most effective in the period immediately after the funeral. It is when the first numbness and the distractions preceding the funeral are over that the pain of loss is most severe. At that time, too, adjustments to a changed life have to be made, and the bereaved needs somebody to hold his hand, just as the baby who experiences loss needs to be firmly and lovingly held.

As I myself have never done counseling work with newly bereaved people, I owe some of the following observations to discussions with social workers who have.

The immediate task may consist mainly of letting the bereaved talk, letting him tell all the details of the last weeks and days again and again, and just listening in the knowledge of how important this is. The need to talk, to complain, "to mope," to "get it off my chest," and to be listened to is great.

In a climate of trust the bereaved may be able to express his feelings of guilt about having failed or harmed the deceased, or not having loved him enough. He may be frightened by his occasional feelings of hatred, perhaps a wish for the patient to die quickly, to "get it over with," so that he would no longer have to watch and participate in the suffering. There may also be guilt about the fury against the dead person who has left him with all the pain of loss. To have these feelings accepted and understood as a normal part of bereavement is true therapeutic help which a counselor or good friend can give.

The need for a person who is simply around and quietly gets on with the various tasks which otherwise the bereaved would have to do—thus setting him free to grieve—may be equally great. In his grief, he may be as self-centered as an infant, and totally unaware of the needs of the other person, who after some time may be desperately in need of a cup of coffee or completely exhausted. It is not easy to be a helper in bereavement. Our usual way of behaving may not be relevant for the bereaved. True help consists in recognizing the fact that the bereaved has a difficult task to perform, one that should not be avoided and cannot be rushed. He not only has to accept the ultimate loss of the loved person, he also has to assimilate the experience of having been in touch with death. John Donne's words will always be true: "Any man's death diminishes me because I am involved in mankind."

Colin Murray Parkes has said, "There is an optimal 'level of grieving' which varies from one person to another. Some will cry and sob, others will betray their feelings in other ways. The important thing is for feelings to emerge into consciousness. How they appear on the surface may be of secondary importance." While the mourner is in great need of sympathy, pity is the last thing he wants. Pity puts him at a distance from and into an inferior position to the would-be comforter. "Pity makes one into an object; somehow being pitied the bereaved person becomes pitiful."[3]

Any sensitive friend can provide comfort for a mourner by regular contact at times of special vulnerability. A telephone call at the moment of waking may take the sting out of the early morning depression that another day of loneliness and misery has to be faced. If this call can be counted on every day at the same time it may be of great therapeutic value.

Saturday afternoons, which may have been a married couple's regular time for a joint outing, may be another vulnerable time. A friend of mine who had adjusted exceptionally well to her widowed life told me that even years after her husband's death she avoided being alone at home on a Saturday afternoon, in order not to watch

3. Colin Murray Parkes, *Bereavement* (London: Tavistock Publications, 1972), pp. 162, 163.

compulsively and with envy her married neighbors going out together. And Mary Stott writes: "My own best help came from a friend who turned up almost every Saturday evening to play two piano duets, bringing the pudding for our supper in the boot of his car."[4]

The regularity of such arrangements is what is most helpful, because it is the routine of married life, often little things taken for granted, which has been lost and is so sadly missed.

All such help derived from affectionate understanding of the needs of the bereaved, whether given by counselors, neighbors, or friends, can be termed therapy in bereavement situations in which there is no evidence of complications. If there are signs that all is not going well, if the bereaved is suffering from lasting physical symptoms, excessive guilt or anger, persistent depression, or uncontrollable grief, then more direct therapy may be indicated.

Absence of grief in bereavement is one such sign. Yet those who cannot mourn are also likely to deny any need for help. "Therapy is only for mad people," said one such widower. This man, in his forties and in good physical health, had tenderly and devotedly nursed his dying wife. Immediately after her death, he plunged into work, moved, and got busy with arrangements for himself and his children, intent on keeping a stiff upper lip and denying any needs of his own. He became angry and upset with his children, who showed clear signs of disturbance after their mother's death. He not only was unable to help them but alienated them and kept away from them as much as possible. Six months after his wife's death, this man contracted a terminal illness and died.

It may not be the bereaved himself but rather the

4. *Forgetting's No Excuse* (London: Faber and Faber, 1973), p. 185.

people around him who first sense that all is not well. An example of this was a recently widowed woman of seventy-two who since her husband's death had caused much trouble in her local clinic by turning up at all hours and shouting abuse at the doctors who, she claimed, had killed her husband and were now killing her. The puzzled doctors felt that this woman needed frequent home visits and asked a social worker to call on her. On his first visit, after knocking at the door, the social worker heard energetic movements in the apartment, but when the woman opened the door and recognized the caller, she collapsed into his arms. She seemed to have to impress on him her need for support. Her first verbal communications were complaints about being let down by everyone since the death of her "angel-husband." She produced photos of him and also of her only daughter, who had married a Swiss and lived abroad. She, too, was described as an angel. Everyone else was nasty: her friends exploited her, her neighbors annoyed her, nobody cared about her or was prepared to help her. What help she needed she could not say but it was clear that she expected the social worker to provide it. On each of his subsequent visits she collapsed into his arms when he arrived, but as soon as he had guided her to a chair, she got up, went into the kitchen to make tea for him, and showed that she was perfectly capable of looking after herself. On the one and only occasion when, early in their contact, the social worker brought one of his students with him, the widow showed her disapproval of this interference in their relationship by dropping the tea-tray and then collapsing on the floor. She needed one person to herself.

Soon the stories about the angel-husband began to change. It emerged that for many years and up to his death he had been having an affair with another woman and had on several occasions deserted his wife. When he died suddenly she must have felt that her hatred and resentment about his desertions had killed him, and transferred this self-accusation onto the doctors and all the others who had "killed" him and would now "kill" her. It also emerged that the 'angel-daughter" showed no interest in her mother. She had gone abroad when she was still very young, there was little contact, and she had not even come home for her father's funeral. Obviously no one could stand this woman's demands and confused communications—her anger had driven everyone away. The social worker was well aware that he must not repeat this pattern. He had to watch his own reactions in order to stick by her in spite of all her frenzies and provocations. Only then could he hope to help her to show her pain and anger more directly and not to act it out so madly. He understood that this woman had probably always felt unacceptable and insecure, and since her husband's death, which she saw as his greatest, most punishing act of desertion, her anxieties about her own badness had become overwhelming. Her only chance for recovery was to feel understood and accepted as she was. After she had been able to tell the truth about her husband and to face her hatred of him and her resulting self-hate, she no longer collapsed when the social worker came to visit her, and did not feel so persecuted by all the people around her.

For elderly and dependent mourners neither the short-term bereavement-focused therapy, which I shall describe later, nor more conventional psychotherapy, which aims at increasing insight, is appropriate. Their need is for a long supportive contact on a counseling or social work level. Once a trusting relationship has been securely established, other helpers may be included, and the agency may then become "the good object." This widening of the contact can help to avoid a degree of dependence which throws the mourner back into the

original grief situation at the slightest threat of termina-
tion, or on any occasion when the individual helper is
not available. Careful timing, however, is very important. In the case we have just discussed, the social worker
brought his student along too early, and his client pro-
tested justifiably. She felt that this visit was not planned
for her sake but as a learning experience for the student.

Not many bereaved show their need for acceptance
and love in such a bizarre way. Yet many, perhaps all,
feel at times that they have lost their own loving self with
the loved (but also sometimes hated) person. Extreme
ambivalence, the fear that the hate is greater than the
love, makes it impossible to integrate the lost person and
thus complete the mourning process.

In a previous chapter I quoted from Freud's "Mourning and Melancholia":

> Although grief involves grave departures from the
> normal attitude to life, it never occurs to us to regard
> it as a morbid condition and hand the mourner over
> to medical treatment. We rest assured that after a lapse
> of time it will be overcome, and we look at any inter-
> ference with it as inadvisable or even harmful.[5]

This was written in 1914, before the First World War. In
Freud's Jewish middle-class world mourners were likely
to be less isolated than they are in our time and place;
death and grief were still acknowledged facts of life, and
the mourners' emotional responses to bereavement were
generally accepted. Also since Freud's time the practice of
psychotherapy has become more flexible. Now many
therapists see the human and supportive relationship as the
most important element in the therapeutic situation. This
is especially appropriate and helpful in work focused on
bereavement.

5. *The Complete Psychological Works of Sigmund Freud*, trans. and ed. James
Strachey (London: Hogarth Press, 1953–66), vol. 14.

In spite of all the changes since 1914, it is crucial, as I have stressed repeatedly in previous chapters, that normal mourning should not be regarded or treated as an illness and that therapeutic intervention be considered only in exceptional situations.

Vamik Volkan calls such therapy "re-grief work." Although I am not entirely happy with this term, I believe that his concepts of bereavement therapy are important. He writes:

> The short-term psychotherapy of re-grief work helps a patient suffering from pathological grief to resolve the conflicts of separation—however distant in time this resolution may have spent itself. . . . The author has attempted to show that the clinical entity of pathological grief, with its predictable symptomatology and characteristic findings, lies between uncomplicated grief and those reactions to death which turn into depression or other identifiable neurotic, psychosomatic or psychotic conditions. Only those patients who occupy middle ground are suitable for re-griefing. . . .[6]

Although I have described pathological cases such as John and Mrs. Green, most of my accounts of therapy in bereavement are of people who occupy this middle ground. Let us have a closer look at one of them, Dr. Allen (Chapter 7). I shall repeat here those elements of the case history which are necessary in the context of therapeutic intervention.

After seven years of an apparently happy marriage and only a few weeks after she and her husband had moved into the first home of their own, for which they had saved since they had decided to get married, Dr. Allen walked out without giving any warning to her

6. "Study of Patient's Re-grief Work," *Psychiatric Quarterly* 45 (1971): 255–73.

husband, who naturally was completely bewildered. She immediately asked for psychiatric help at her local hospital, who referred the couple to me for marital therapy. The question in my mind was: How far was this extreme symptom of disturbance, Dr. Allen's walking out, caused by the move into the new house?

The first time I talked with the couple together it emerged that Dr. Allen had been married before and that her husband had died within weeks of their wedding. From the way she mentioned this, and the way her husband tried to ignore it, it seemed that Dr. Allen's present irrational behavior might be connected with this bereavement, and I asked her to come for individual sessions. In these we focused firmly on the loss of her first husband, Frederic, who, when she met him, had been dying in the hospital where she worked. Through her love and devoted care he recovered sufficiently to be discharged from the hospital. Frederic was a widower of her father's age and in Dr. Allen's mind became closely connected with her father, whom, owing to the war, she had met for the first time when she was seven years old. Her mother was her headmistress, and as a little girl she had always had to behave very well. These circumstances concerning her parents made it difficult for Dr. Allen to resolve her ambivalence toward her mother and her fantasies about the exciting male stranger by whom she wanted to be loved. As she grew up, this situation made her feel increasingly guilty.

Through Frederic, whom she had miraculously saved by her devoted care, skill, and love, she felt released from her fears of destroying her parents' marriage. The love for this husband, who was so like a father, was good and life-saving. She desperately wanted to have his son. In the therapy she recalled that during her adolescence she had dreamt of having a son by her father.

When Frederic died, she cried on her father's shoulders, and the two father images merged. Her tabooed love for her father was re-evoked and with it the guilt and fear that that love was destructive. Because of this association, mourning and grief for Frederic had to be repressed.

In her second marriage, to George, who was her age and in every way unlike either her father or Frederic, she tried for seven years to be a good and loving wife, just as she had tried for seven years to be her mother's perfect little daughter. She succeeded in maintaining this until they moved into a house of their own. Only when she was seven, and her father had returned from the war, did she feel that she had a full family. Now, again after seven years, the house implied permanency, a family. Now there should be a child but George was not the father of whom she had dreamt for her son. She repressed the wish for a child as she had repressed her love for her father and her grief for Frederic. All these repressions made her feel trapped—the only way out was to break away and break down.

Although she came to me about her marital problems, she sensed that, as a therapist, I could help her to uncover her repressed grief for her first husband, and all the pain and guilt which centered around the issues of love, death, and birth. My response, different from what she got from friends and relatives after Frederic's death, helped her to abandon herself to intense grief and belated mourning. Once this had been completed, she regained a glimmer of hope that she could come back to life, and with this returned the wish for a child. When she then actually had not the son who in her fantasies was so closely linked with her father and Frederic, but a baby daughter, in whom she could love herself again, she recovered her equilibrium.

Here, as in all the cases of short-term, bereavement-focused therapy described in this book, the most striking

feature was the immediate, strong, and unshakably positive loving transference-relationship with the therapist,
which none of the bereaved's angry or negative feelings
for others, or for their dead, was allowed to affect. The
therapist accepts this, knowing that he has a limited task,
concentrated on the immediate situation, to help the bereaved to bring back to life the loving part of himself
which he thought was dead. By finding a new attachment in which his capacity to love may be recaptured, he
may regain hope in his own goodness. Past relationships
are explored only if they directly affect the response to
the immediate bereavement. Temporarily the therapist
becomes the substitute for the lost person, whether
parent, child, spouse, or lover, and aims to give hope
and comfort. The therapist must remain aware of the
mourner's feelings of guilt and destructiveness and must
let him see that this awareness does not diminish his
compassion and concern for him.

The second important feature in all short-term bereavement work is the firm focus on the crisis of loss. We
are not treating an illness or attempting to affect personality disorders, yet it is imperative to understand what
problems in the mourner's personality and in his pattern
of relationships have been highlighted by the crisis.
These cannot be resolved in short-term therapy, but the
specific problem each person brings into the bereavement crisis has to be grasped by the therapist and the
mourner. Only then can the bereaved hope to distinguish between his immediate and previous—real or fantasied—losses and abandonments, the pain of which has
been stirred up by the present loss and made the response to it so frightening.

The mourner's external life situation will naturally
greatly affect the way in which the therapy can be used.
For example, Dr. Allen had a living husband who
wanted to love her, and through whom she could gain
affirmation of her loving self once she had mourned and

internalized her first husband and was no longer preoccupied by a false image constructed out of guilt, fear,
pain, and denial. When this obstacle of repression was
overcome, she could love and be loved again. Later her
flourishing baby daughter completed the recovery which
short-term therapy had set in motion.

Through bereavement-focused therapy some bereaved
become aware of previously unacknowledged conflicts
and confusions with which they feel unable to cope without further help. Once the acute grief problem has been
resolved, they may, explicitly or implicitly, make a new
contract with the therapist in order to work on the wider
problems. We have discussed this in the case of Mrs.
Bright (Chapter 8).

In all therapy one of the major aims is to help people
toward more satisfactory relationships in the broadest
sense. In bereavement work this task is of paramount
importance. The bereaved often feels that with his lost
object he has lost all that is good in him. In this situation
of self-doubt he is faced with the task of adjusting his
ongoing relationships, and having sufficient trust to risk
new attachments.

To offer help in this difficult task is implied in all types
of work with the bereaved. Often it is expressed in encouragement to join clubs, attend evening classes, "get
out of the shell." A frequent suggestion is to do some
charitable work, for to have nobody to care for is one of
the great deprivations of bereavement. Such advice is
absolutely right and valid in uncomplicated grief situations. Often, however, such suggestions end in disappointment and frustration both for the well-meaning
adviser and for the bereaved who may be too shut up
inside himself to get out of his shell. Because he is struggling to deal with extremely intense feelings of guilt,
anger, and agonizing regret, he may retreat into denial
and unreality.

The difficulty of taking advice in emotional turmoil

was shown by an elderly woman who had recently suffered multiple and very painful losses in situations for
which she justifiably blamed others. She was a deeply
religious person, who throughout her life had successfully coped with many problems, and was now pro-
foundly disturbed by her depression and unabating
grief. In talking to her it became clear that she found it
impossible to tolerate her own hating feelings toward
those whom she blamed for her losses. This woman was
living alone in a huge, isolated house, which not only
created many problems for her but also increased her
depression. She was unable to take steps toward a move,
however, nor could she make use of any advice given to
her. She was convinced that because of her hatred and
subsequent self-hatred, nobody could help her or would
care for her, and that she would only be a burden and
evoke negative feelings wherever she went. Only after
she had understood and accepted her guilt about her
hateful feelings, which she found irreconcilable with her
religion, did she begin to consider plans to move and
become able to perceive that relatives and friends were
affectionately supporting her in them. She had to feel
justified in having hating feelings, and be good enough
in spite of them, before she could ask for and accept help
from others.

The greatest obstacles in the way of making new relationships after bereavement and being able to live mean-
ingfully again are ambivalent feelings about the deceased
and the denial of one's own hating self. By denying his
hate the mourner impairs his love, and with it the capacity to be in loving contact with other people.

In some cases, this aspect of therapeutic work can be
done by a lay person who cares for and understands the
bereaved and offers him the degree and quality of compassion and reliability which will enable him to regain
hope. Only when this has been achieved can he risk a
new attachment. This should not be an attempt to re-

place the lost one, but rather an expression of renewed confidence that life is still worth living and meaningful relationships are still possible.

New life-affirming attachments may take a wide variety of forms, according to the needs of the individual bereaved. It may be a job, an interest, a cause, or a child, perhaps a new grandchild. Or it may be a new committed relationship with a person of the same or the opposite sex with whom the bereaved can share his life, someone who will both give and accept care.

The majority of bereaved people will return to a new life without therapeutic help after they have mourned their dead in a way appropriate for them. A general climate of acceptance of the importance of mourning will support them. If that climate is lacking, the completion of the mourning process may be hindered or delayed, which will increase the mourner's anxieties that his responses are abnormal or childish and must be suppressed.

The task of mourning, and of returning to life with renewed strength, may take a long time—often much longer than the traditional year. It is important for the bereaved and for those around him to know and accept this, but also to know that the phase of mourning will pass.

From the statistics in Chapter 8 it appears that only a small proportion of the bereaved are remarrying. These figures may well be misleading, as they ignore those people who decide, for various practical reasons, to set up homes together without the marriage ceremony.

Marriages after bereavement are not really "remarriages"; they are new marriages. Yet we know that no emotional relationship can be completely new, for experiences from previous relationships, previous attachments and losses, especially those from infancy and childhood, will greatly affect it.

Marriages after the death of a spouse are more likely

to be affected by the previous marriage, however, than by any other previous relationship just because there is inevitably some sameness, some similar pattern of relationship unique to marriage. Can we learn something about this from the case histories with which we are familiar?

The marriage of Marion and Tony (Chapter 4) was a stressful one. After Marion's death, Tony married a woman who was like her in many ways. She was less vulnerable, more stable, and more resilient, however, so that Tony felt less in danger of damaging her. At the same time she appeared to be less threatened by his feminine identification, and was able to let him use it with ease and without guilt. Here it appears that the survivor needed to continue in the second marriage the pattern of interaction which had made for strain in the first. The choice of the second partner, with whom modification of this pattern and restitution for past failure were possible, indicates that Tony had learned something from the pain in his marriage to Marion.

Dr. Allen, on the other hand, who saw her first, short marriage as perfect and her first husband as a father-figure, chose as a second partner a man who was different in every respect from the first and from her father. She could not envisage him as a father, and, therefore, could not have his child until she understood what in her had made for this choice and for the denial of the feelings that had kept the marriage going for seven years.

Mrs. White (Chapter 5), who in her "ideal" marriage had subordinated her own identity to the demands of the family, was in danger of continuing this pattern after her husband's death with her son—and thus robbing him of his identity. When she became aware of what she was doing and why, she chose as a second husband an artist who encouraged her return to the artistic and more individual life which she had given up on her first marriage.

Robin's mother, who had idealized his father and her

marriage, chose as a second husband a completely different kind of man, more like her own father and brothers and altogether more familiar to her. She did not have to keep him on a pedestal and could relax in a less demanding, more comfortable relationship.

From these examples it appears that changed attitudes in new marriages are based on new insights in the bereaved. These insights may be used to modify patterns that caused stress in the first marriage and to try out new patterns where the first marriages were "ideal" at the price of diminished autonomy on the part of one of the partners. In all new marriages there are likely to be modified expectations, making for more realistic attitudes toward both the new and the previous marriage.

The above instances confirm the impression I gained from other second marriages, in which the survivor, having deeply mourned the first partner, surprisingly quickly finds a new and utterly different one. This appears to be particularly pronounced if the lost partner was felt to be superior, intellectually or otherwise. It may not always have been easy to live up to the standards and expectations of this loved and greatly admired person. The new partner is often considerably younger and more lighthearted, and the survivor will find himself in a different role in this relationship.

Divorce, like death, means loss and bereavement. Marriages that have ended in divorce may be regarded as failures, yet unless some new insight has been gained through the pain of this failure, here too the previous unhappy pattern of interaction may be almost compulsively re-enacted in a new marriage. The emotional pattern was probably acquired in the parental families of the people concerned, and unless they can understand and learn to modify it, they will go on repeating it in spite of all practical and intellectual arguments against it.

An attractive, intelligent young woman whose artistic, exciting, and irresponsible father had left her apparently inferior mother while she herself was a small child, married a man much like her father and had a stimulating, but always difficult and insecure marriage. She was shattered when her husband left her, yet soon got involved with a man very like him but even more selfish and unreliable. Her many friends trembled for her and warned her against this relationship, which was likely to become still more disastrous. Although she accepted their rational arguments intellectually, their advice was of no avail. Only when—after a great deal of thought and work—she understood emotionally why she was attracted to these difficult men did she gain sufficient confidence in herself to dare to make more satisfactory relationships.

In marriages that have ended in divorce, the partner may still be loved and the loss deeply mourned. If the mourning for the lost partner can be completed, his loved aspects internalized in a way similar to this process in bereavement, and the spouse freed to make a truly new choice, a new partner may be chosen who is significantly different from the first. The developing pattern of interaction in the new marriage may minimize comparisons with the previous one as well as with the early conflict-laden relationships, and may offer opportunities to develop hitherto neglected aspects of the personality.

One striking feature in my case histories is the repetition of fates and dates. We have seen, for example, that the period of seven years was recurrently connected with important changes in Dr. Allen's life.

Marion and Tony were both eldest children; both lost their fathers when they were ten years old, and Marion died when their eldest child was ten.

In Robin's family there were ten-year-old orphans in three generations; both his father and his grandfather had died when their oldest child was ten, and so did Anne, Robin's wife.

Mrs. Dean's mother's grandfather died when she was twelve. Her own father had a brain tumor which killed him as the person she had known when she was twelve, though he survived physically and died a few days before she had her first child, a son.

Most people know from their own personal experiences about such repetition of dates as well as recurring birth or death anniversary dates in families, and usually they brush them aside as coincidences. Nevertheless, they compelled me to look up the work of Wilhelm Fliess, which in my youth had been much discussed on the Continent. Fliess, an ear, nose, and throat specialist of some renown, had sought to establish by numerous observations "facts" which led him to far-reaching hypotheses about the role of periods and periodicity in human life. In his early years, Sigmund Freud was greatly inspired by Fliess's work and personality, and his letters to him have been published. I quote from Ernst Kris who in the introduction to Freud's letters to his friend, explains Fliess's theory:

> The facts. . . . teach us that, apart from the menstrual process of the twenty-eight day type, yet another group of periodic phenomena exists with a twenty-three day cycle, to which people of all ages and both sexes are subject. . . .

The friendship between the two scientists faded in 1901, when

> Fliess seems to have asked Freud to accept the validity of his attempt to explain the specific nature of neurotic illnesses by periodic variations resulting from the twenty-eight and twenty-three day cycles. Freud obviously replied that such assumption excluded the whole

psychical dynamism which he was struggling to explain, and that in all the evidence at his disposal he
could find nothing to justify it. Fliess thereupon attacked the methods by which Freud's insight into the
dynamics of the mind had been obtained and accused
Freud of projecting his own ideas into the minds of his
patients.[7]

From the way I have described the lives of the people
who are discussed in this book, it will have become clear
that my interest centers on "psychical dynamism" and
the resulting relationships. From this standpoint Fliess's
speculations, and the exclusive way in which he based
everything on biological observations, may appear absurd. Yet I have come across quite spectacular repeti-
tions in which it seemed impossible to detect psychological motivation, and which, to me, have remained
unexplained.

Fliess's theory may help us to understand some of them,
as well as the ever-recurring theme of "one life for another"
which I have frequently noted. While this can suggest the
joyful experience of rebirth, the completion of the life
cycle, and the continuation of the dead, it can also play into
destructive fantasies and create great anxiety, especially if
the birth of the first child, a son, coincides with the death
of a father—as it did for Mrs. Dean and Mrs. Cooper.

Let us end with "Ecce Puer," a poem by James Joyce,
whose father died at the time his only grandson was born:

7. Sigmund Freud, *The Origins of Psycho-Analysis, Letter to Wilhelm Fliess, Drafts and Notes, 1887–1902* (London: Hogarth Press, 1954), pp. 7, 40.

Of the dark past
A child is born
With joy and grief
My heart is torn.

Calm in his cradle
The living lies.
May love and mercy
Unclose his eyes!

Young life is breathed
On the glass;
The world that was not
Comes to pass.

A child is sleeping:
An old man gone.
O, father forsaken,
Forgive your son![8]

8. *Pomes Penyeach* (London: Faber and Faber, 1966), p. 29.

Epilogue

When Socrates left the court after being condemned to death, he said with calm sincerity, "Now it's time we were going, I to die and you to live; but which of us has the happier prospect is unknown to anyone but God."[1]

I set out to write about bereavement and family relationships. Now that I have come to the end of this book I find that it is also about life and death, birth and sex. This connection, which emerged from much of my case material with astonishing clarity and frequency, is by no means new. Writers, artists, thinkers have always known about it, and on some level so have we all. It is explicit in the Christian conception that Satan, on bringing sin into the world, introduced with it sex, death, and painful birth, where before the Fall there had been love, joy, and eternal life.

Many years ago, at a seminar of the philosopher and theologian Paul Tillich, a student asked, "How did the idea of creation emerge?" Tillich replied, "When man had to face death, finitude, he had to invent creation." And went on to say, "Those of you who work with people from primitive cultures, or with children, will be

1. Plato, *The Apology* (Cambridge University Press, 1953), p. 145.

aware of the validity of this thought association."

In the last chapter we saw how clearly this connection is re-enacted in the East African ritual of the second burial, which ends with a marriage ceremony. I have also come across it in Crete, where as part of the Good Friday service brides and young women of marriageable age come to the church for a fertility rite. The Body of Christ is placed on a bier in the middle of the church, and one by one the young women crawl underneath it. When they emerge at the other end, they receive a blessing from the priest. This burial-resurrection symbol illustrates the underlying fertility rites in Good Friday celebrations.

Small children express the association of birth and death often very clearly. Some time ago I stayed with a friend and her four young nephews and nieces, whose father had just died in another part of the country. Because the children could not go to the funeral, the village priest arranged a small service for them. On leaving the church and passing through the graveyard, Simon, aged four, walking between his aunt and me and holding our hands, asked, "And where is my Daddy now?" "Perhaps in Heaven," his aunt said hesitatingly. Simon stopped in front of a big memorial: "But how can they get there? How can they get out of these stones?" Before we could think of an answer, he went on eagerly, "And how did I get into this world?"

A very lively three-year-old, whose Uncle Joe had recently died, asked the widow rather aggressively, "Why did you kill Joe?" He was not satisfied by her reply that Joe had died because he was ill, and went on, still very angry, "Who killed him then?" The aunt was still wondering how to cope with this when he continued, "And do you know how Beatty [his dog] got her puppies? Blacky pushed them into her."

It is fascinating how in these examples the small boys in their death/birth associations remain in the same emotional climate: leaving this earth—coming into this world; killing and raping.

Another child who deeply mourned the death of a beloved cat, Barney, was comforted by the thought that Barney was now in the ground where he could help to grow flowers.

Does it comfort the adult bereaved to know that their dead help to grow something, that something remains as seed in the ground, in the universe, in other people, in the bereaved himself? Do adults—like children—have a heightened awareness of new life, of creation, when they have to face death? Does it comfort the bereaved to know that death and birth are part of the continuing cycle of life—transitory and eternal?

There is no growth without pain and conflict; there is no loss which cannot lead to gain. Although this inter-connection is what life is all about, it is difficult for the newly bereaved to accept. Only slowly may he, who has been in touch with death through the loss of a significant person, regain touch with life. A life which may bring new growth through the acceptance of death and pain and loss, and thus become truly a new life, a rebirth.

2. Francis Bacon, "Of Death," in *Essays and New Atlantis* (London: J. M. Dent).